The Changing Sky

A PRACTICAL GUIDE
TO PREDICTIVE ASTROLOGY

SECOND EDITION

The Changing Sky

A Practical Guide
to Predictive Astrology

Second Edition

Steven Forrest

ACS PUBLICATIONS

Published by ACS Publications
5521 Ruffin Road
San Diego, CA 92123
www.astrocom.com

If you do not fear the human future,
then this book is dedicated to you.

If growth turns the body of a boy into that of a man, the body of a girl into that of a woman, will it not also put wisdom into those mature bodies and teach them to put away childish things? But it will not. It will bring accumulation of experience, but not the digestion of that experience. It will bring accumulation of knowledge, but not development of being...An unconscious and involuntary process cannot possibly bring consciousness and will. Consciousness cannot be developed unconsciously, nor will involuntarily. These qualities, incomparable with the growth of muscle and organ, can only be acquired by another and quite different process, conscious and intentional from its origin.

—RODNEY COLLIN

CONTENTS

ACKNOWLEDGMENTS

The solitary author, I am discovering, is a myth. My affectionate gratitude to the following people. Without them, nothing:

Alison Acker, Antero Alli, Michael Baldwin, Chad Brock, Keith Cleversley, Laura DesJardins, Hadley Fitzgerald, Dick and Bunny Forrest, David Friedman, Karen Galey, Tracy Gaudet, Laura Gerking, Laurel Goldman, Jeffrey Wolf Green, Robert Griffin and Diana Simmons, Melanie Jackson, Bill Janis, Barbara Jensen, Debi Hansen, Rob and Lisa Hand, Sam Heaton, Barbara Higbie, Jeff Jawer, Danny Kee, Callie Khouri, Sinikka Laine and Cyril Beveridge, Alphee and Carole Lavoie, Rob Lehman, Michael Lutin whom I have shamefully omitted on past occasions, Carolyn and Richard Max, Doug Margel, Maggie, Greg and Noubar Nalbandian, Luis Lesur, Jose Antonio Lugo, Jim Mullaney, Marc Penfield, Maritha Pottenger, Betty Pristera, Fran and Gary Rackow, Phillip Sedgwick, Linda Sherwin, Maria K. Simms, Phyllis Smith-Hansen, Paul Hansen, Sting, Trudie Styler, James Weinberg, Joanne Wickenburg and everyone involved with promoting the Kepler College of Astrological Arts and Sciences, Roger Windsor, Cindy Wyatt, Vincent the Cat, Pyanfar the Cat, and finally a warm thanks to everyone participating in my Astrological Apprenticeship Programs.

A special thanks to Jodie Forrest for editing, both literary and existential.

Finally, my gratitude to the many thousands of individuals who have shared their transits and progressions with me over the years. Anything new you might read here is their gift to me, passed on to you.

PREFACE

Years ago, when I began to study astrology, those musty old books held the promise of a remarkable power: I would be able to foresee the future. For an insecure kid, that was the next best thing to having Superman's home phone number. No longer would I find myself at the right place at the wrong time, facing "Freddie's gang" with an ice cream cone in my hand or arriving at the pizza parlor ten minutes after my heart throb Mary had walked out the door. With the future in my pocket and astrology on my side, I would be unstoppable.

Or so I thought.

The trouble was that it didn't work, at least not well enough to be reliable. My predictions were sometimes uncannily accurate. But other times I strolled confidently into that pizza parlor just in time to see Freddie and Mary arrive arm in arm. Something was wrong with my books.

Astrology can be mind-boggling in its accuracy, but it can never consistently predict who is going to walk through the doors of the local pizza place. It doesn't naturally speak the language of outward, concrete events, at least that is not where the symbolism is most eloquent. The future astrology foresees with such startling exactitude doesn't unfold in the world "out there." It unfolds between your ears.

Astrology cannot predict definitively that you're going to wreck your car. It cannot point out in advance with absolute reliability the date of your marriage, your death, or the arrival of your new TV set. That kind of astrological prophecy is bogus and untrustworthy and we will not be concerned with it in *The Changing Sky*. What modern predictive astrology can do is inform you in advance of the natural rhythms of your life—and moods—thereby helping you arrange your outward experiences in the happiest, most harmonious and efficient manner. If it saves you some repair bills and Band-Aids as well, then so much the better.

Predictive astrology takes us one step beyond the birthchart, which is the territory we mapped in my previous book, *The Inner Sky*. There, we were concerned with the dynamics of the individual personality. Now, in *The Changing Sky*, we add another dimension: We consider the forces that move through the birthchart over the course of a lifetime. We will mark the development of those personality dynamics, time their peaks and troughs, and watch them move step by step from mere potentials into actual human reality.

But we reject the notion that these minute-by-minute astrological forces make your decisions for you. They might affect your moods.

They might help define the developmental challenges you are facing. But they don't create events. That's your department.

Although fatalism is admittedly part of astrology's history, it bears the same relationship to modern astrology that using leeches to draw out "bad blood" bears to contemporary medicine. Modern astrologers predict questions, not answers. The old practice of "fortune-telling" is nothing but a skeleton in astrology's closet, a mistake made long ago, now grown musty with cobwebs, but still capable of haunting us. Just recently, in fact, that skeleton gave me quite a fright.

I was a guest on a radio talk show. Moments before we went on the air, the interviewer handed me an article her father had clipped from the local paper. As I scanned the newsprint, my face paled. The story, to put it mildly, was critical of astrology. And in a few minutes I would be expected to refute it.

What scared me was that the story was irrefutable. The anti-astrology arguments were sound. Checkmate.

The article concerned the Committee for the Scientific Investigation of Claims of the Paranormal—a group of scientists who had gotten together in 1976 to debunk astrology, parapsychology, and other "outdated mythologies." Disturbed by a 1984 Gallup poll that showed the number of young people who "believe in astrology" had increased by over one third since 1978, the committee decided to take action: They sent out letters to all the daily newspapers in the United States and Canada demanding that a warning appear by the syndicated "daily guide" columns. They wanted people informed that astrological predictions had no scientific basis. The chairman of the committee, Paul Kurtz, phrased it this way: "Much the same as we label packets of cigarettes as dangerous to health, astrology columns should carry a proper label concerning their contents."

Why my fear?

Because I was about to go on the air to defend astrology—and I found I agreed with the committee! They were right: most of those columns don't work. As I went on to tell the radio audience, those newsprint predictions are almost invariably trite, and generally erroneous. With their rigidly mechanical view of how astrological forces interact with human affairs, I feel they have done incalculable harm to serious astrologers everywhere simply by distorting in the public mind the nature of our craft.

There are currently about 400 million Librans in the world. What intelligent person can seriously believe that each one of them is destined to "mend fences with a love partner today?" Some of them don't even **have** love partners. I agree with the committee that those newspaper fortune-tellers are misleading. If **that** is astrology, let's wash our hands of it.

Strange bedfellows, the committee and me.

Our honeymoon, I fear, would be short-lived. I agree that the public deserves better information about what astrology can and cannot do—although I suspect my accord with the committee would collapse over the actual wording of that information. Here is the wording they suggested: "The following astrological forecasts should be read for entertainment value only. Such predictions have no reliable basis in scientific fact." Here's mine: "Astrology is humanity's oldest and most precise mind-map. It cannot, however, control you. The planets hold half the cards, you hold the rest. Choices you make within the astrological environment determine what actually happens to you."

We are free. No rigid, fatalistic prediction can bind us. There is no astrological event so baleful that creativity, intelligence, and honest self-appraisal cannot turn it to constructive uses—and there is no configuration so glorious that laziness cannot sour it.

The purpose of modern predictive astrology, long hidden behind ancient veils of superstition, is not to "forecast events." It is to help people make better choices, to clarify the nature of the psychological terrain through which they are passing, and to serve as their ally in the endless, unpredictable task of **creating the future.**

Not fate, but freedom in the real world, a world of hard limits punctuated by the miraculous—that is modern predictive astrology.

This book will teach you how to make accurate astrological predictions—predictions that will stand up to any kind of scrutiny. You will not, however, learn how to predict when you'll get your next speeding ticket, only when you might benefit from being careful of impatience. The aim of modern predictive astrology is to fan the flames of conscious choosing, not to quench them with inescapable prophecy. We predict the shape of the inner terrain, not the outer one.

Astrology is a craft, and like any craft, there is nothing inherently mystical about it. With imagination and a little patience, you can become quite proficient. My aim in writing this book is to offer a clear introduction to the **craft** of practical predictive astrology—the book I wish I could have found twenty years ago when I first began studying astrology myself. *The Changing Sky* is not theoretical; it is, I hope, grounded in the real world of everyday life. Every statement and procedure in it has been tested in my own astrological practice. To the best of my knowledge, every idea and guideline that follows is true. I do, however, see the world through my own eyes. When that world looks different through your eyes, **trust your eyes!** No single person can ever write the last word on astrology.

The Changing Sky is just one more link in a chain that stretches back to neolithic caves, to clear-eyed moon worshippers, to the ancient, intelligent children of the earth goddess. Astrology's endless story meanders through Egypt and China and Meso-America. It washes against the shores of stony Greek islands where Pythagoras walked. Christ came among us at the outset of the Age of Pisces—his birth foretold by astrologers who had "seen His star in the East"— and his followers took the astrological symbol of the fish as their own symbol. Astrology is there in the roots of the intellectual traditions that led to modern astronomy, physics and psychology. It is there in literature and language, in art and music. Despite the groundless assertions of the Committee for the Scientific Investigation of the Paranormal, astrology has made the transition into the Turn-of-the-Millennium worldview. Many fine astrologers are currently assembling an impressive array of hard evidence supporting the scientific basis of astrology. If you are interested in that kind of material, explore the work of Michel Gauquelin for starters.

In the pages that follow, we honor astrology's past but we do not enslave ourselves to it. Astrology is not a religion. Indeed, a large part of what you will read here owes much to one of astrology's rebellious teenagers—modern psychology.

If you are new to astrology, just beginning to find your place in the long chain, you might prepare yourself for the journey ahead by reading my first book, *The Inner Sky*. That book deals with the birthchart itself and introduces you to the basic symbolism. Although I've striven to make this book accessible to beginners, it describes forces that **act upon the birthchart over time**, and is the second in the series, building on the foundation of the first.

My wife and I have also co-authored a third book in the trilogy, *Skymates*, which is about relationships from the astrological viewpoint. But that's another story.

—Steven Forrest
Chapel Hill, North Carolina
Lammas, 1998

PART ONE

CREATING THE FUTURE

CHAPTER ONE

WHO'S IN CHARGE?

When Mars crossed Martin Luther King's Ascendant in October 1960, he was arrested for leading a sit-in demonstration in Atlanta, Georgia. Courageously, he refused to post bond, thereby refusing to acknowledge that his actions constituted a "crime." He was thrown in jail. Several months later, Mars did the same thing to Ernest Hemingway's Ascendant. He aimed a loaded shotgun at himself and pulled the trigger.

Suicide or civil disobedience. Self-destruction or nonviolent resistance. What are the common denominators? What is the **meaning** of the planet Mars?

Historically, Mars is the war-god. It symbolizes the will to survive, that sheer, primeval fire burning in the depths of the human spirit. Mars is the spark smoldering deep in the heart of each one of us, pushing us past the obstacles of daily existence—and past those darker obstacles lurking in the silent spaces of our own innermost selves.

That interpretation accounts for Martin Luther King's brave defiance of racism—but what about Ernest Hemingway's decision to end his own life?

Hemingway's suicide would make perfect sense to the fortune-tellers, past and present. To those who accept fatalistic interpretations of these life forces, Mars is one of the bad guys. They call it a "malefic" influence and associate it with violence, peril, and mean spiritedness. Are they wrong? Not exactly, but the truth is not quite so simple. Mars has its ugly side, and that ugly side is available to all of us at any time. Each of us is free to be cold-blooded, treacherous, and cruel—to others or to ourselves—whenever we please. But that is just one side of the Martial force. The other side of the coin is courage.

Which path will we choose—courage or destructiveness? Will we make a stand for ourselves come what may, or will we run home with our tail between our legs and angrily slam doors? Both behaviors are Martial. Both are consistent with the meaning of the red planet when it ignites a sensitive point on our birthchart. How will we respond? I pity the old astrologers. They felt it was their duty to answer to that question. That is an impossible task. We can study the motions of the planets for a million years and still be no closer to unraveling that riddle. Astrological prediction, in the traditional sense, fails for one critical reason: **Planets do not make our choices for us.** We make those choices ourselves. Ernest Hemingway could have chosen to live. Martin Luther King could have run like a frightened rabbit.

Mars sets the stage, but we all write our own lines.

UNCERTAINTY

"You will meet a tall, dark stranger." Spoofs of astrology invariably involve a line like that, usually uttered by a toothless gypsy. We laugh, as well we should. But when we sit down with that gypsy and she correctly describes how we quit our job last year, then goes on to predict that in three more years our marriage will break up, laughter is not part of the picture. We are fearful, then rebellious, then perhaps resigned. Above all, we feel powerless, as if alien and incomprehensible forces were ruling our lives.

"She really had no way of knowing about my quitting that job... I wonder... Kelly has seemed a bit distant lately..."

Chance alone cannot account for the success of fortune-tellers' predictions. They are correct far too often for that. The most skillful of them might be right half the time, often enough to impress anyone. Fifty percent accuracy. Amazing. But what about the other half of the time, when those astrologers are wrong? That's a fairly impressive statistic, too.

Right or wrong, anyone who looks into your birthchart and tells you your marriage will break up is abusing astrology—and abusing you too, for that matter. That is not what the symbols are intended to do,

nor is it what they do best. You are not a marionette. The planets that
move through your chart year by year are not controlling your strings.
That's the old picture, and it has led to deep misunderstandings as well
as needless worry and fear. The astrological forces are **questions**, not
answers. They pose riddles, and each riddle has many solutions. Some
of those solutions help us lead happier, more engaging lives. Others
might only mire us more deeply in self-defeating existential sinkholes.
The worst of them might see us pointing loaded shotguns at ourselves,
literally or figuratively. Which solution will we choose? The choice is
left up to our own ingenuity, determination, and nerve. We are, in other
words, free.

Freedom. That is one of those magic words. Everybody wants some.
Everybody approves of it, hungers for it, claims to pursue it. But what
is it? All too often freedom is taken to be synonymous with happiness
and peace. Actually, the best synonym for freedom is probably uncertainty. And uncertainty is another one of those magic words—but in
this case, no one wants any. Avoidance of uncertainty is as universal as
avoiding icy mud puddles on a January morning. And yet uncertainty
is woven into the very fabric of astrological symbolism. No astrologer
can say what any one of us will do next. He or she might say how the
stage is set, what the issue of the day might be—and what will happen
if we try to slither away from facing it. The astrologer might also tell us
what we can learn if we respond creatively to that issue and what new
possibilities each path might open—all that, but what we will actually
do? Never.

Fate versus free will? Certainly, the old-fashioned approach to
astrology is the essence of fatalism. "Saturn is approaching your Sun.
Get ready for some rotten luck." Does modern astrology espouse the
opposite viewpoint? Is it all freedom? No, at least not exactly.
Astrology embraces both sides of the paradox. Certain specific classes
of events are "fated;" others remain open to uncertainty and choice.
When, for example, Mars crosses your Ascendant, we know that
you will face stress and that your courage will be challenged.
That much is in the category of "fate." But how you will respond—with
the iron-willed defiance of a Martin Luther King or with your own
version of Ernest Hemingway's shotgun blast—that is as uncertain as
tomorrow's horserace.

Questions, not answers: these are the heart of any accurate approach
to predictive astrology. We honor human freedom and weave it into
our understanding of the astrological symbols. We do that not for
pretty, soothing philosophical reasons, but because the human will is a
mighty force, a power capable of shaping its own future. In short, every

accurate astrological prediction ends with a question mark. It is we, not the planets, who are writing the script. And with that freedom comes uncertainty.

THREE LEVELS

Here's an idea that has proven practical to me in organizing my understanding of predictive astrology. It is the notion that the process of life goes on at three distinct **levels**.

The first and most obvious is the **physical** level. This comprises all that we **do** in obvious, outward ways—trips to Europe, the endings and beginnings of relationships, meetings with "tall dark strangers."

The second level is **emotional** and **psychological**. Thoughts and feelings are the substance of this dimension—all the inner, subjective reactions we might have to the actual events on level one. We quit a job: that's a fact, a level-one experience. But how do we **feel** about it? Scared? Elated? Inspired to new heights? Insecure? That's level two.

Finally, on level three, the **spiritual** level, we find issues of **meaning** and **purpose**. One way to come to terms with level three is to imagine that we are reflecting back on personal events of many years ago. What ultimate significance did those events possess? How did they help us to become what we are today? What we're getting at in level three is a sense of how given events fit into our overall pattern of development. Typically, such reflection inserts into our memory of those events a level of **self-awareness** that did not exist in us then. "Mommy didn't hug us much, but she would always feed us candy when we were good." At the time, we felt happy to be given the candy. Twenty years later, level three awareness might arise, helping us to understand how the Love-equals-Food equation has contributed to our pattern of compulsive overeating. We seem to stand outside ourselves, grasping the patterns of our lives—and that's the essence of the third, or spiritual, level.

Astrology is fabulously accurate at predicting what happens on level three. That is its real purpose and its ultimate strength. Above all, astrology is a study of **meaning**—and meaning exists only in the spiritual dimension. Working on that level, I believe that a skilled predictive astrologer can approach 100 percent accuracy, although in practice the symbolism involved is often incredibly subtle and human error takes its toll. What am I supposed to be learning here? What is the broad purpose of this event in the overall plan of my personal development? How will I look back on this moment two or three decades from now? Those are the questions we ask on level three, and if we want to understand our lives from that perspective, we can seek no stronger ally than a sound knowledge of astrological symbolism.

Moving back to level two, the dimension of emotion, the accuracy of the predictive techniques is still impressive, but not nearly so precise as the descriptions available on level three. How might a person **feel** about facing those spiritual issues? There is a lot of room here for human differences. An astrological event, for example, might arise involving the planet Saturn, always a sure sign that the spiritual lesson will touch on the need for practical, self-disciplined responses to concrete reality. One person might react with renewed personal resolve, self-respect, and determination. Another might experience a sense of inadequacy, followed by feelings of defeat and despair. The lesson itself is in the category of "fate," but the emotional response is something we create ourselves and for which we must take personal responsibility. But what is the nature of the actual **event** which that passage of Saturn triggers? On level two, such a question is of no concern—here we are only interested in feelings and attitudes, not in what "actually happens."

Level one, the physical, is the least predictable of the three. What outward action will an individual take in response to a passing astrological configuration? Certainly, some of that is determined by feelings arising on level two, and they themselves are unpredictable. But even if the feelings are understood, there is still enormous uncertainty. Mars crossed Hemingway's Ascendant. The spiritual lesson (level three) involved the renewing of his sense of courage and his will to survive as a physical and psychological entity. That much is clear. His inner emotional reaction (level two) could have been one of resolution and relentless determination—as was apparently the case when Mars did the same thing to Martin Luther King's Ascendant. But Hemingway took a different emotional course. We cannot know what went on in his mind at that time but we can surmise that he viewed his circumstances as overwhelming, and that he felt elements of fear and anger and destructive violence—Martial contents, to be sure, but of a very different nature than Reverend King's. But even now we are still on level two. To move to level one—the physical—we must imagine what Hemingway could have **done**. Might he have kicked the dog instead of taking his own life? Might he have had a fight with his wife? Certainly. All those actions were possible. His suicide was far from being his "fate." Astrologically, at least, we must view it as his choice—and as only **one** choice out of a thousand possibilities.

To predict which action a person will take in response to a spiritual question is futile and sometimes even destructive. We might be right every now and then, but we will be wrong a great deal of the time. Predicting how someone will **feel** is a bit safer, but even there we will often be surprised. People are frequently far more resourceful and resilient under pressure than we might expect. It is only in predicting the nature of the spiritual issues people are facing that we can achieve dependable levels of accuracy—and significantly, it is there that we can also best help a person to grow in self-knowledge and happiness.

The tragedy of astrology's history is its obsession with level one, the dimension of action. Even its victories in that department seem pitiful in the light of the opportunities missed. It is as if Albert Einstein had decided to be a baseball player.

FIELDS OF PROBABILITY

For centuries, traditional astrologers have been hamstrung by a single disastrous error. They have imagined the future to be already determined. They have viewed our passage through life as a tour of preordained events. At milestone one, you were born; at milestone twenty-three, you married; at number twenty-five, you gave birth to a predetermined child. On and on, until at milestone eighty-two, you slipped on a particular banana peel and woke up in the next world. Step by step, prediction by prediction, life unfolded. All you could do was watch. You were only along for the ride.

Impressive as our gypsy's prophecies sometimes are, that simplistic model of life has two fundamental flaws. One is that it does not account for the **feeling** of freedom and uncertainty that we actually experience when we come to life's crossroads. The second is that the model does not actually predict events particularly well. Those "tall, dark strangers" are notorious for not showing up—and many a marriage endures long after a stable of astrologers has begun auctioning off the wedding rings.

Still, the fortune-tellers get results. So what is really going on? How much can astrology actually tell in advance about what is going to happen to us? Our first step in answering that question is to drop the notion of a predetermined future and replace it with a more workable concept.

A middle-aged businessman has a drinking problem, but has managed to keep his life on an even keel. Suddenly, economic recession hits. His business struggles, then fails. Headaches start, debilitating him. His wife runs off with another man, taking the children. On his fifty-second birthday, the bank forecloses on his mortgage and he loses his home. What happens next? What is your prediction? Certainly it is easy to imagine his life consumed increasingly by alcohol and despair, spiraling down toward the gutter like a falling leaf. Certainly there is a high probability that his future will lie precisely along those lines. But can we count on that? Is his self-destructive descent graven in stone? Absolutely not. That businessman might pick himself up, get involved with Alcoholics Anonymous, find a new job, and begin a new life, perhaps one far more meaningful to him than the one that just collapsed around his ears. That course is perhaps not so likely as the first one, but it certainly exists as a possibility. What determines which path the man will follow? Call it the Grace of God. Call it free will. Whatever that force might be, it is not astrological in nature. Its source lies elsewhere—and if our astrological predictions are to be accurate, we must never lose sight of that wild card.

Fields of probability—these are the keys to unlocking the conundrums that have bound predictive astrology to the Dark Ages. Gone is the notion of the inescapable future. Replacing it we find something far more challenging—and far more in keeping with the way our lives actually feel as we live them from day to day. The future is composed of shifting, interwoven patterns of choice. Possibilities. Probabilities—and improbabilities that we can make happen if we want them badly enough. That businessman was heading for the existential garbage can. That was the dominant "field of probability" he was entering, and if he wanted to wind up in the drunk tank, all he had to do was go with the flow. But other threads were also woven into the tapestry of his future. Magic threads. Unpredictable ones. Threads of self-regeneration and healing—such as his ability to pick up the phone and ask for help. Those threads were his to follow, if only he had the courage and humility to ride them out.

Predictive astrology helps us to distinguish favorable fields of probability from the frightening ones. But it also does something of inestimably more value: this kind of astrology teaches us to transform the frightening fields into allies. When the path of least resistance is a harmful one, we are not doomed to live it out. Nothing can force us to follow a self-destructive course. Nothing except our own laziness, that is. And laziness is a popular pastime. The path of least resistance is a crowded one. That is one reason why the fortune-tellers are so often correct. Woven into traditional predictive astrology is the unconscious assumption that people will always do what is easiest for them. As a view of human nature, that attitude is pessimistic and damaging—but it is also right a lot. Unfortunately, if our goal is to predict what people are going to do, our most effective rule of thumb is probably to assume that they will follow the path of least resistance—we'll likely be right 50 percent of the time. But if our goal is to **help people grow**, then that assumption must change. If our goal is to help, we must recognize the innate capacity of the human will to turn those negative fields of probability into positive ones.

☆ The entire purpose of predictive astrology is to
help people understand how to bend the probability
curves of their lives in the direction of happiness,
personal fulfillment, and growth.

What would have happened if Ernest Hemingway had had a session with a traditional astrologer a few days before his suicide? He would have heard that with Mars arriving at his Ascendent, a hard time was coming, that he was likely to have an accident involving fire and blood, and that he had better batten down the hatches for a short but intense period of conflict and stress. For a person in his psychological condition at the time, that would have been like tossing a drowning man a hungry shark.

But what if Hemingway had come to a truly modern astrologer? What would he have heard? A very different message. Hemingway would have been told that he would soon face a fundamental spiritual challenge. A set of events and attitudes were about to coalesce around him, testing his bravery, his will to live, and his elemental human dignity. His task was to show unflinching determination and courage **for a few days** until Mars moved into less sensitive territory. He would have been warned that the period he was entering contained a high probability curve pushing him toward impetuous acts of destruction and violence—and that only through bravery could he bend that curve in a healthier direction. The choice was his: he could recognize the true enemy—his fear—and make his stand. Or he could turn that Martial energy against himself.

Could that astrologer have saved Hemingway's life? We can never know. People are free—to grow or to blow their brains out— regardless of what kind of input they receive. But we can say with great confidence that the words of the second astrologer might have helped the man keep perspective on his pain, while those of the first would have served only to consolidate his decision to point that shotgun at himself.

Read on and learn to use astrology yourself. This magnificent tool is your natural ally. It will not subjugate you or bind you. Let the signs and planets guide you, but let them guide you gently, not as tyrants, but as trusted friends. Let astrology be part of your freedom, assisting it, illuminating it. Learn to listen to the whispers of tomorrow filtering through the shouting and bustling of the moment. Learn to weave the threads of your life like a master carpetmaker, always attentive to the fleeting details, yet always aware of the patterning and the plan, the larger scheme. Leave prediction to the fortune-tellers and gypsies. Let them make their prophecies. Let them hunger for the events they foresee, or cringe before them. Our task is not to foresee events. It is to create them.

CHAPTER TWO

THE ROOT PREDICTION

You are out grocery shopping one evening. You run into a woman you met at a party six months ago. Smiling, she asks how you're doing. You smile back and answer, "Fine."

Were you lying? Did you mention your backache? What about the cold you're just getting over? And the novel you're halfway through? Or the argument you had with your mother? If you had told her how you were **really** doing, it would have taken the rest of the night and bored the pants off both of you. That, of course, is why we say "fine"—and why we cross the street to avoid those who haven't learned the lesson.

Life is complicated. Ten thousand forces converge on us every minute, besieging, balancing, enhancing the basic qualities of our character. Astrology reflects those forces, helping us to understand them and make the best of the opportunities they offer. That is its great strength. But if we ask our birthchart how we are doing, its response is never a curt, polite "fine." We had better be prepared to spend some time listening; that backache, that cold, that half-finished novel are all part of the answer—and the message they give us may rattle our comfortable assumptions, pushing us one more step down the exciting but often bumpy road of self-discovery.

THE ROOT PREDICTION

Minute by minute, month by month, decade by decade, our mood changes. Now we are intensely involved in our career. Yesterday we buried a relative. Tomorrow we learn to ski. Yet beneath the kaleidoscope, there is something so vast and all-encompassing that it includes the entire tragicomic carnival of life, splicing and interlacing each scene, fusing them into one single, multidimensional **whole**. Metaphysically, we might call that wholeness the **soul**. Psychologically, its name is the **self**. But astrologically, that great unifier is the **birthchart**. Without it, there could be no predictive astrology, because there would be nothing upon which any astrological force could act. Without ears, there is no music.

The birthchart itself is astrology's **root prediction**. It establishes the grand plan of your life, spelling out the spiritual aims that underlie the ups and downs of daily experience, pointing out strategies and resources available for fulfilling those aims, and warning of the shadowy possibilities that arise whenever you opt for laziness and easy answers. **No event or realization that is not "predicted" in the birthchart is likely to have any lasting significance for the individual.** In fact, it is not even very likely to occur at all.

☆ A thorough understanding of the symbolism of
the birthchart is the basis for success in predictive
astrology, and grasping the message of that chart
must always be the predictive astrologer's first step.

Ignoring the birthchart is perhaps the most common error among people learning predictive astrology. The temptation to plunge ahead and hope for the best is always there—and it inevitably leads to disastrously off-the-wall predictions. A stoop-shouldered classics professor with Coke-bottle glasses is not likely to scale Mount Blanc just because Mars is heating up his House of Journeys, nor should he! We must remember who we are addressing, and do our best to understand and respect his needs and aims. Mount Blanc might work as a metaphor, but the mountain that professor is actually facing might have more to do with a convention he's thinking of attending and a paper he would like to present there—if only he could get over his public speaking willies or his fear of flying.

What are the actual circumstances that professor is facing? Without knowing him, we can have no idea, and it is not astrology's business to find out. That would just be more fortune-telling. But by adjusting our language to the natural language of his birthchart, we aim our interpretations straight for his heart, challenging him to stretch and grow. An Arian with Mars conjunct the Sun might feel her soul dancing inside her when we speak of ascending Mount Blanc. Such experiences resonate with her fundamental nature. But maybe that professor is a fourth house Virgo with Cancer rising and Saturn on the Sun. For him, shyness and self-limitation are mountains enough.

Throughout the rest of this book, we explore many specific astrological techniques for analyzing patterns of growth and change. Some are linked to forces that actually rain down on all of us from space—the "cosmic weather," we might say. Others, equally powerful, arise from developmental rhythms inherent in the birthchart itself. All will be covered in detail. All are potent. All shape the tides of our experience. But none are worth a penny without the birthchart. That is the root prediction. If you're fuzzy about the astrological basics, you might benefit from reading my first book, *The Inner Sky*.

TUNING IN

As you sit reading this book, your body is immersed in a fluxing ocean of energy. You are flooded with invisible radiation of every wavelength. X-rays crash through you from pulsars and neutron stars hundreds of light-years away. Gamma rays rush up from decaying uranium in the earth's core. Ultraviolet waves flung out from the exploding heart of the Sun cut into your cells. Not to mention the human stuff—all the penetrating energy put out by WABC and WHFS and WXYC. Disconcerting, huh? Yes, but only when we think about it. Otherwise, we would never notice any of that energy, except maybe the ultraviolet rays that cause our skin to blister after too many hours on the beach. Why? Because we are not tuned in. Our senses do not respond to those wavelengths. If we want to hear the broadcast, we need a radio.

Astrology works the same way. When a full Moon occurs in a given part of a certain sign—say the last few degrees of Sagittarius—one person might stand on her head while another sleeps through it. Looking at their birthcharts, we quickly see why. That degree of Sagittarius is the first woman's Ascendant. For the second woman, it doesn't represent a sensitive area at all—that part of Sagittarius is in an obscure corner of her sixth house and makes no important aspects to anything else on her chart. The first woman, in other words, is "tuned in" to the last few degrees of Sagittarius while the second woman is not. Astrologically, that marks the difference between drifting through a forgettable weekend and moving to Katmandu under a false identity.

If your radio is tuned to 89.3 FM, that is what you hear. All the other stations still continue their transmissions, but they simply pass through you unnoticed. Birthcharts are like defective radios—they are stuck on one station. They pick up every nuance of planetary radiation but only on that particular wavelength. Anything else might as well not exist.

The situation is a bit more complex really. Each chart is actually sensitive to several wavelengths and affected somewhat by all of them, but often so slightly that for practical purposes we can ignore the impact. In a roomful of roaring chainsaws, no one is bothered by the buzz of a mosquito.

☆ If the birthchart itself is tuned to a particular issue, the impact of planetary motions triggering that issue is magnified dramatically.

There is another dimension to our ability to "tune in" astrological forces, one that is often overlooked in traditional texts. Say a woman is born with a chart in which the significance of Saturn is predominant. It lies in Capricorn, conjunct her Ascendant and opposed to her Sun. Saturn, in other words, is always with her, touching every corner of her life. She may respond positively, in a brave and self-regenerative way, learning the lessons of realism, self-sufficiency, and patience. Or she may take the low road, becoming cynical and depressed, as the fortune-tellers would predict. Either way, Saturn is the "master teacher" in her life. That stern, sober hand influences all her affairs, ever-present and uncompromising. She is on Saturn's wavelength no matter what that ringed planet is doing. She responds unmistakably even to fairly subtle changes in Saturn's daily location. Why? **Because no matter what Saturn does, she is listening intently.**

That same woman might have a husband whose birthchart is much less Saturnine. He is a cheery, energetic Leo with a friendly Libran Moon in the first house and a strong affiliative Venus. His Saturn lies in the eighth house and makes no important aspects. He lacks any planets in Capricorn—a sign that is resonant with Saturn—so even that wavelength is blocked. His astrological radio, in other words, can barely pick up Saturn's broadcasts. What happens when Saturn moves through a sensitive area in his birthchart? It would be a grave mistake to assume that the planet would have little or no impact on the man. Most certainly it will. It may jar him quite severely in fact. But in the long run, that period in his life will prove to be much less pivotal than a corresponding time in the life of his more Saturnine wife. She is "majoring" in Saturn. For him, it is only a "minor," like a course in calculus he must endure and then forget as he gets on with his efforts in journalism school.

How will each of them actually behave when Saturn is prominent? We do not know. In questions like that, the astrological factors are only holding half the deck. The rest of the cards are in the hands of the individual. We do know that the woman has been living with the ringed planet all her life. We could say that they are old friends—or at least friendly enemies. Her husband, on the other hand, is a relative stranger to Saturn. He is unaccustomed to that austere, solitary energy. For better or worse, his wife feels Saturn's passage more intensely. Unless she blinds herself with depression and self-pity, she recognizes it as a fundamental, high-stakes turning point in her life. And far more than her husband, she is emotionally and psychologically equipped to make a strong response to the period. Why? Because her birthchart— her root prediction—is built to face exactly this kind of challenge, if only she adopts a positive attitude.

What happens to her husband in the face of Saturn's onslaught? He has as much freedom as anyone else. He can bend the probability curves in his own favor—or he can passively ride them out, thereby fulfilling the negative prophecies of the fortune-teller. We do know that Saturn's lessons are more difficult for him to grasp. Unlike his wife he is not built for this kind of lesson. Suddenly he is confronted with a period in his life when reality itself seems harsher, less benign, more demanding, less compromising. He is more alone than ever before, facing stark black and white choices, unable to melt them as usual into grays and pastels with his charming smile. For him, the Saturn period represents something different than it did for his wife. He faces a challenge of adaptation and flexibility. Although the period is of less ultimate significance to him, it may at the time shake him more deeply than it did his wife. For her, the Saturn time represents an intensification of **familiar** issues and patterns. For him, something **unfamiliar and alien** is striking from an unexpected direction—and even if that force proves less formidable than the one advancing on his wife, surprise and shock may take their toll.

Underlying both these examples we see the inescapable impact of the root prediction—the birthchart itself. The motion of Saturn or any other planet has no independent meaning. Our first step must always be to understand the individual. Only then can we begin to unravel the meanings of the events he or she might experience.

Our examples do allow us to formulate three more general principles in predictive astrology. Absorb them, and the technical material that follows in later chapters will work easily and effectively for you.

☆ The more strongly a planet is configured in the birthchart, the more dramatic is its continuing impact upon the individual's life.

☆ If a planet is prominent in the birthchart, even though its subsequent motion strikes the individual more deeply, he or she is more naturally equipped to respond creatively to the issues it raises.

☆ When a planet that is weak in the birthchart moves through a sensitive area, even though its developmental significance is less, its emotional impact may be greater, since the individual is challenged to develop in new, unfamiliar ways.

Let's tie together all that we have covered so far with a concrete illustration. How do these principles really **work** in everyday life?

General Custer is known to most of us in America for his infamous military blunder at Little Big Horn. Underestimating the power and strategic sense of the massed Sioux and Cheyenne under the effective leadership of Sitting Bull, Custer led over 260 troops into ambush and massacre, giving the Native Americans what was perhaps their most decisive victory of the long war. It is easy for us to see Custer as little more than a comic book character, two-dimensional and foolish. Such is the perspective of history. Let's look at him through a sharper lens, one which reveals him as what he was—a human being, like ourselves, only perhaps a bit more adept at tripping over his own feet. Let's consider his birthchart, then see what kind of astrological forces were bearing upon him on the day he blundered away his own life.

Like most people who lead extreme lives, George Armstrong Custer has an extreme type of chart. He is a "triple Sagittarian," with Sun, Moon, and Ascendant in that sign. As we learned in *The Inner Sky*, those three astrological symbols are the "primal triad." Together they establish the skeleton of the person's individuality. The Sun shows his (or her!) core **identity**. The Moon reveals his underlying emotional needs and motivations—his **soul**. Finally, the Ascendant—and the first house as a whole—indicate the way he expresses all that material outwardly and socially, streamlined into an everyday personality. For that reason, we call the Ascendant the **mask**. With all three in a single sign, we observe in George Armstrong Custer an unusual and extreme situation. Clearly, he came into the world to gather wide experience and to gather it with speed and unrelenting intensity—that's basic to the developmental strategy of the Archer. His Sagittarian resources were exuberance, confidence, and enthusiasm—with good judgment and careful deliberation taking a backseat, that is, if he succumbed to the temptations of the Archer's shadow.

The presence of the Sun and Moon in Custer's twelfth house add an undercurrent of spiritual perspectives, at least potentially, implying rather paradoxically that the existential terrain he was navigating involved learning to transcend his rigid identification with his ego and his pride. Does this mean that Custer was some kind of closet guru? No. We must be careful to remember that houses are only **territories** in life. Whether we navigate them well or poorly is up to us. In a successful navigation of twelfth house terrain, Custer's self-transcendence would have been voluntary and intentional. In an unsuccessful passage, the lesson is enforced by circumstance, hence the medieval view that this was the "House of Troubles." Certainly there were beautiful seeds in this man. He could have been a colorful mystical philosopher, and probably was one in quiet moments. He also shows a disturbing tendency to accelerate around blind curves with both eyes closed and a belly full of beer.

That latter quality is emphasized by the presence of Mercury (the speech function), but more especially Mars (the aggressive function), in his first house. Thus, his "mask" was that of the quick-witted warrior, rough and ready at all times. Uranus, with all its tendency toward explosiveness and impulse, lies in spacey Pisces and makes a tense, unstable square aspect to both his Sun and Moon. Custer's birthchart does gain some balance from having Saturn conjunct the Sun and Moon—normally an indicator of prudence and deliberativeness. Poor Saturn, however, has clearly met his match here. Faced with a primal triad in Sagittarius, along with Mars and Uranus as critical focalizers, even the ringed planet can offer little more than a highly developed sense of tactics.

It is tempting to don our wizard's hat smugly and proclaim that Custer's birthchart was a disaster waiting to happen. The fact that such was ultimately the case does not make that kind of analysis any more appropriate. Even if we cannot respect the man, we must at least respect the miraculous potential that existed within him. He could have learned to stand outside his bluster and extremism, balancing it with perspective and a bit of humor at his own expense. He could have understood his own perilous foibles more clearly, had he only been less addicted to his pride. Apparently he did not take those steps, and thus fell prey to one of the most basic laws of life: **That which we cannot think out, we must live out**. It was not astrology but a stubborn fear of letting life teach him anything that brought George Armstrong Custer to that bend in the Little Big Horn.

What was happening astrologically on that June day in 1876 when Custer led his troops to destruction? Both Saturn and Mars were moving through very sensitive zones of his birthchart. To the medievals, these are "malefic" influences and their simultaneous presence at trigger points is seen as ominous. A modern astrologer would be less pessimistic, but still quick to recognize that some kind of critical juncture had been reached. Custer was at a choice point, and unless he could bend the curves of probability by taking a leap in his level of self-awareness, he was heading for a fall.

Saturn, being the slower of the two, set the stage. It was moving through the ninth degree of Pisces—a hypersensitive zone for Custer for several reasons. It was forming a conjunction with his natal Uranus and simultaneously squaring his Sun and Moon. What could this signify? As we learn in detail in the next section of the book, Saturn's passages always imply some kind of **confrontation with reality**. Grant Lewi, a fine astrological writer of a past generation, called them "the cosmic paycheck," implying that during Saturn periods you get exactly what you deserve, for better or worse. We can dream and scheme and weave a web of soothing half-truths about ourselves—but when Saturn comes to a sensitive point in our birthchart, those phony psychological card-houses come crashing down. Custer, with his Sagittarian primal triad, probably thought he was bulletproof. He had, in fact, had ten horses shot out from under him while receiving only one minor wound in his career. At Little Big Horn, reality (Saturn) clashed (the square aspect) with his brash overconfidence (the Sagittarian Sun and Moon). Reality also met (conjunction) his headstrong impulsiveness (Uranus).

Saturn remains within the orbs of such a set of aspects for many weeks. What triggered the events of June 25, 1876 in particular? Unsurprisingly, the answer lies with the war-god. Mars was in the twentieth degree of Cancer on that day, within the orbs of two highly charged aspects. It was squaring Custer's Pluto and making an opposition to the place it had occupied when he was born—his natal Mars. Each of these holds a piece of the puzzle.

Pluto lies in Aries in the fourth house of Custer's birthchart, the domain of "heroes" and "shadows." With dominant Pluto there in the sign of the Warrior, it is clear that belligerence and the love of command run very deep in this man. Under the transitory pressure of friction (square) from the symbol of aggression and territoriality (Mars), that furnace was burning white-hot. With Mars opposing the position it occupies in his birthchart, his ferocity was at its height, perhaps irritated even further by the frustrating confrontation with reality indicated by Saturn's activity. The disastrous potentials inherent in Custer's birthchart were being pressed toward their limits. Something had to crack. Would it be a breakthrough in self-awareness regarding his own arrogance and impulsiveness, or would the fortune-tellers claim another victory?

What might Custer have done differently? Marching into that strategically dangerous valley, full of confidence and the adrenaline high of a stimulated Mars, was there any hope for him? Absolutely. He could have sobered up, turned around and marched out again, prudently sending a scouting party ahead to reconnoiter. Certainly those actions were possible, even logical. But astrologically there are even more significant questions: What were the spiritual purposes of those passing astrological patterns? What was the man supposed to **learn**?

Saturn was there to teach him a lesson about reality, and through the square aspect to his Sun and Moon, we know that the lesson pertained to how reality sometimes clashes with the blindspots and personal predilections of individuals. Imagine Custer riding along toward disaster— only now he is suddenly struck with a distinctly Saturnine thought: "There are a lot of angry Sioux and Cheyenne around here somewhere. They are led by a medicine man who might very well be a brilliant strategist. They are fighting for their homeland and for the lives of their families. They know we are out to get them. I am leading my men toward a suspicious bend in the river. Now, if I were Sitting Bull . . ."

Add to that the importance of Mars. It was passing through General Custer's seventh house, while opposing his own natal Mars in the first house. Traditionally the "House of Marriage," the real significance of this house is far broader. It refers to anyone whom we view as an equal and with whom we are locked into some kind of relatively stable partnership. In some medieval texts, the seventh house is called the "House of Open Enemies." This is quite accurate. The long-term "worthy opponent" whom we disregard only at our peril, who brings out qualities of excellence and effort in us, is very much a seventh house contact. Anyone who has lived with a mate for long will be quick to recognize this dimension of the House of Marriage.

What kind of evolutionary response could Custer have made to the challenge of Mars? Expanding and specifying Saturn's lesson about facing reality, Mars's message is perfectly clear: "General Custer, **you have met your match.** You, with Mars in your first house, are a mighty warrior. But now, opposing you, there is another Mars, another **will,** equal to you and lined up against you. You need not surrender, but you had better not underestimate your opponent. Respect him, make no mistakes, and you have an even chance." Custer, of course, ignored all this and marched pompously to his own massacre, dissipating the Martial force in bravado and pointless fury. Astrology only asks the questions. People give their own answers. Like the rest of us, George Armstrong Custer was free—and, so sadly, that can be a chilling epitaph.

At the end of Chapter One, we asked ourselves what might have happened had Ernest Hemingway consulted a modern astrologer a week before his suicide. Let's imagine the same about Custer. What would have happened had he been aware of the "astrological weather" bearing down on him? Perhaps nothing would have changed. Truth is useful only if it is heard, and hearing it is often hard. If he were so immersed in his damn-the-torpedoes pride and glory that he could not bear to open his heart even for a moment to the astrologer's words, he would have marched into the valley of the Little Big Horn no matter how eloquently the astrologer had spoken. But what if he was not quite the blunderer we have often taken him to be? What if he was **already close** to grasping the lesson of this phase of his life? What if that wisdom and that change were on the verge of cracking through into his conscious awareness? Would the astrologer's warning have pushed him the final inch—and pushed history down yet another one of the avenues that fan out before it? We cannot know, but questions like these are the blood and soul of modern astrology.

Custer is dead. His choices are made. But we are among the living, and therefore in the realm of the miraculous. The past may be frozen behind us—but ahead stretches not a fate, but a tangled web of probability curves, waiting to be tested, chosen, and shaped. Most of us have chosen rightly many times. But most of us have already marched into our own Little Big Horns, too, seduced by our own pride, victims of our own press releases. Once we have hurt ourselves that way a few times perhaps we can swallow our pride and begin looking for allies.

Friends. Religion. Psychotherapy. Inspiring heroes. They all help. Astrology can help in exactly the same way.

Let's continue absorbing this ancient language, so exotic at first, and yet so strangely familiar. In *The Inner Sky*, we learned how to unravel the root prediction itself, deciphering the symbolism of the birthchart. Now let's take it a step farther and see how that long message unwinds not only over a lifetime, but over minutes and days and months. Our astrological ally has more sharply focused lessons for us. Now let's allow it to speak.

PART TWO

TRANSITS

CHAPTER THREE

TRANSITS I: DEFINITIONS

Earth is like one of those plaster ponies on a carousel, spinning around the center of its merry-go-round, rushing through space at about eighteen miles per second. Its nearly circular orbit courses around the Sun once every 365 days. Only two horses on the solar carousel are faster—Mercury and Venus. The rest move more slowly, their speeds decreasing in order of their increasing distance from the Sun. Mars—the next pony out—takes about two-and-a-half years to get all the way around. After Mars comes still-slower Jupiter, making the circuit in a stately twelve years. The rim of the merry-go-round is fuzzy to us, too far away to see clearly, but so far as we know, Pluto is the last planetary pony, and therefore the slowest, making one long, lazy passage around the solar system every two-and-a-half centuries.

If we could watch this carousel from a starship far above the solar system, all the planets would follow sensible, predictable paths. Our viewpoint, however, is not so lofty. We watch the cosmic merry-go-round from one of the moving ponies, and that scrambles everything. Our own motion gets added to the natural motions of the planets, making them appear to accelerate and decelerate, even to stop dead in their tracks, in seemingly random ways. Although the plan of the solar system is extremely simple, it is no wonder that human civilization took ten or

twenty thousand years to figure out what was actually going on.
See figure one.

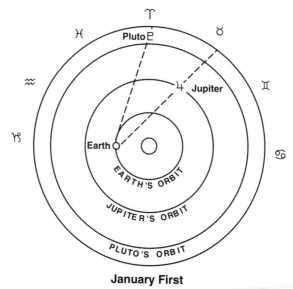

January First

**Earth's own motion affects where we see the planets
against the backdrop of the signs**

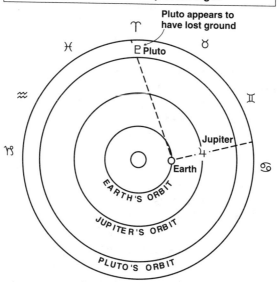

FIGURE 1

Looking into the sky we see Mars "over there," advancing night after night against the backdrop of a particular group of stars. One week it slows to a stop, then begins to backtrack. Meanwhile, Venus has caught up and passes Mars, going the opposite direction. Mars stops again a few weeks later, and sets out after Venus, both of them now heading the same way. Venus is quick, though. Mars loses ground, falling back in the race. Both bear down on slow-moving Jupiter. Venus passes him, with Mars lagging behind. Unexpectedly, Venus stops, turns **retrograde**, hurling herself back toward Jupiter, arriving there just as Mars approaches. A collision? No their varying distances prevent that. But the combination may very well feel like a personal collision for you! What we have here is a **triple conjunction** of Mars, Venus, and Jupiter, and if it falls on a sensitive degree of your birthchart, hold on to your hat.

Observed planetary motions such as these are the workhorses of predictive astrology. We call them **transits**. We'll be exploring them thoroughly in the next few chapters.

> ☆ Transits are the actual, physical motions of the planets around the Sun as observed from the perspective of the Earth.

Just as we can watch the movements of the planets from night to night against the background of stars, similarly we can record that same motion against the backdrop of the birthchart itself. This technique is the heart of predictive astrology.

Other useful techniques exist. Built into each birthchart there are certain developmental rhythms that have nothing to do with current events in the sky. They are called **progressions**, and are the subjects of Parts Three and Four. For now, though, let's decipher the message coded into the nightly dance of the planets. To accomplish that, we turn once again to the fundamental instrument of astrological research: our eyes.

THE FIRST TECHNIQUE

A lot of people don't "believe in astrology," but it is surprising how many of those "nonbelievers" admit to being spooked by the full moon—the old astrological symbol of the emotional and the irrational. Most of us have experienced a certain heightening of our emotional responsiveness at that point in the lunar cycle. Popularly, the full moon is connected with romance. In practice, it also seems to stimulate moodiness, irrationality, and crankiness. For better or worse, it is as if the volume were simply turned up on emotion in general, right across the board. There is even some scientific evidence to support the notion that the moon affects us: In 1966 Leonard Ravitz of Duke University found marked changes in the electrical potential—the degree of positive or negative charge—of schizophrenic patients, changes that were strongly correlated with the moon's phases. Similar changes were also observable in clinically normal people, but not quite so vividly. Ravitz, indirectly supporting one of the oldest premises of astrology, confirmed the ancient belief that the full moon creates special tension and upset among the insane.

The phases of the moon are the most obvious and unmistakable examples of the entire class of astrological events that we call transits. They are current, daily astronomical happenings, in other words, capable of having an impact upon the tone of our mood and the shape of our experiences. It is very easy to imagine our distant ancestors, living with a far more vivid awareness of the sky than our own, quickly noticing the change in the communal mood produced by the full moon—and perhaps in doing so, unwittingly establishing the foundation of the entire art-science of astrology. The concept of the birthchart very likely came along much later. It is vastly simpler to recognize that people get jumpy under the full moon than it is to grasp that one who happened to be born under a full moon twenty-seven years ago is a bit more emotionally reactive in general than the rest of us.

A full moon occurs each month. Sometimes the event just seems to "go by," without having much effect on us personally. Other times, it feels as if the CIA were slipping hormones into our morning cup of tea. Why does one full moon hit us so hard, while the next one fails to touch us at all? The answer lies with the birthchart. Although transits were in all probability discovered first, grasping the concept of the birthchart was what really breathed magic into astrology. As we saw earlier, the birthchart is the "radio receiver," tuned to specific wavelengths. If we are tuned to the middle of Gemini—perhaps by having our natal Moon there—and a full moon occurs in that part of the sky, the emotional, irrational dimensions of our personality make quite a racket for a couple of days. A month later, with the full moon in mid-Cancer, we may be a model of sober good judgment, trying to peel our Cancer friends off the ceiling.

The birthchart, as we learned in *The Inner Sky*, is a "photograph" of the solar system, taken at the minute of our first breath from the viewpoint of the particular place where we were born. Now, as we advance into predictive astrology, we must add another dimension, that of development over time. **The planetary energies that are crystallized in us at birth continue changing as we mature, alternately stressing and enhancing the resources inherent in our birthchart.** That chart, in other words, does not exist in a vacuum. The original "photograph" is just a single frame in a never-ending movie. The birthchart, in other words, is the movie screen and the transits are the movie.

The celestial movie develops day by day, but the birthchart itself remains constant. The pattern the birthchart symbolizes is intricate, representing the potentials of an entire lifetime. Relationships. Responsibilities to the community. Personal style. Aesthetic sensitivity. Children. Spiritual attitudes. All are there in the birthchart, and no matter what kind of movie we project onto that screen, those fixed patterns continue to exist. It takes each of those dimensions to form the multi-layered reality of a human psyche—but there is no way any human being can attack all those pieces of the puzzle simultaneously. One month we might be dealing intensively with career questions. A few weeks later, the job is put on "automatic pilot" while we concentrate on our marriage or our relationship with our kids. Why? What points the finger first at your Venus, then at your Jupiter, asking you to develop this one, then that one? The answer lies with transits.

☆ Transits mediate the unfolding of issues inherent
in the birthchart, timing and triggering their active
emergence into the world of events.

Intricacies abound in predictive astrology. Many of the techniques are subtle. As always, our prime ally is an orderly, methodical approach to the symbolism. If we follow certain defined steps with scrupulous care, the transit's message eventually leaps up at us from the chart. It is much like looking for a brightly colored hummingbird hidden among the blossoming rhododendrons. At first it is impossible to see. Then you pick it out. After that, it is impossible to miss. Transits leap out like that, too, but only if you scan them with order and concentration. You'll be learning to do that soon, once we've gotten our basic vocabulary defined.

Be a little suspicious, by the way, of astrological books that give prepackaged "meanings" for each transit. They can be helpful once you know what you are doing, but at first they promise much and deliver little; just mishmash interpretations, full of contradictions. Why? Because they violate the first law of predictive astrology. They ignore the birthchart.

TRIGGER POINTS

Aspects are simply certain specific geometrical angles formed between planets in the birthchart— or between birthchart planets and transiting ones, which is what we'll be concentrating on here. They represent **certain fundamental qualities of relationship** between various "compartments" of the psyche.

In other words, one's **aggressive, territorial function** (Mars) might temporarily fuse (conjunction) with one's **ability to make clear assessments of reality** (Saturn)—as we see occurring in figure 2. There, we observe Mars moving through a wide arc of the zodiac over a period of a few weeks. Only at one point in its trajectory does the red planet align perfectly with the position of Saturn in the birthchart, forming the conjunction. Later, as Mars continues its journey, those two mental functions might exist in a state of **tension** (opposition) or one of **harmonization** (trine). The accompanying table will serve as a quick refresher if you need your memory jogged.

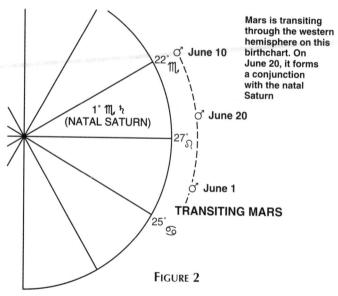

FIGURE 2

A planet always challenges us to attain some heightened level of self-awareness or understanding. It is a realization waiting to happen. As Uranus, let's say, transits through an aspect to that natal planet, that realization is likely to emerge into consciousness—perhaps in connection with some dramatic event. The transiting planet, in other words, serves as a **trigger**. The precise nature of the trigger is determined by the planet's inherent meaning and by the aspect it is forming. Take Sally Ride, for example, the first female American astronaut. I don't know the time of her birth, so I can't show you her birthchart, but I do know that she was born on May 26, 1951. That's enough to let us know that her birthchart features a Sun-Mars conjunction in the early degrees of the sign Gemini. Lacking the birthtime, we don't know what house that conjunction was operating in, but we can be sure that the evolutionary thrust of her life revolves around the Martial process of acquiring courage through the facing of fearful circumstances. Adventure, in other words, is powerful medicine for her. The fact that the conjunction lies in Gemini adds another dimension: her adventures involve intensive mental concentration and a willingness to move into environments which shock, surprise, and challenge her basic assumptions about reality.

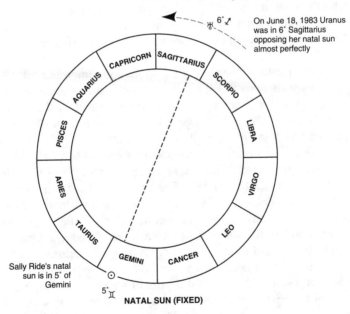

TRANSITING URANUS (MOVING)

On June 18, 1983 Uranus was in 6° Sagittarius opposing her natal sun almost perfectly

Sally Ride's natal sun is in 5° of Gemini

NATAL SUN (FIXED)

FIGURE 3

No astrologer could have looked at her birthchart back in 1951 and announced that she would rocket into earth orbit aboard the space shuttle, but he or she most definitely could have predicted similarly adventurous types of activity for her, thereby illustrating the basic thrust of her chart—and that astrologer certainly would have foreseen the radical intensification of those activities during the middle months of 1983, when she took her historic flight.

How? Uranus was transiting through the early degrees of Sagittarius during that period. You might have slept through it. Your Aunt Isabel might have quietly crocheted her way through it. But for Sally Ride, a transit of Uranus through those degrees was enough to blast her into orbit. Uranus was opposing her natal Sun-Mars conjunction, triggering it into manifestation. And with Uranus taking eighty-four years to orbit the sun, such a transit is a once-in-a-lifetime event, guaranteed to offer some kind of breakthrough.

Exactly how should we go about understanding the transit? First, we attune ourselves to the part of the birthchart the transit is stimulating, in this case, a natal Sun-Mars conjunction in Gemini. Second, we grasp the significance of the transiting planet itself. Uranus: the symbol of individuation, typically operating through explosive, unexpected breaks with the past. And third, we absorb the nature of the aspect which is temporarily linking those planets. (Here we have the opposition: tension, polarization, often stresses and challenges that arise **outside ourselves**, in the external world.) Then we put on our thinking caps.

The exact spiritual meaning of this transit is something fully known only to Sally Ride herself. We can only watch from outside, speculating about events in her inner world. We do know that in the summer of 1983, she faced a critical challenge in her growing individuation, that is, in her effort to develop her full, unique, unprecedented potential as a human being. Uranus makes that clear as crystal through the simple fact of its involvement. Challenges to the evolving individuality are what Uranus invariably means. The planet tells us more—we know that Sally Ride's enemy in this Uranian process was history itself both in the form of communally held assumptions antithetical to her personal aims and in the form of her own internalized versions of those assumptions. How do we know that? Once again, Uranus itself tips us off. Transits of this planet always involve some expression of the tension between **self** and **the tribal myths of society**. The implications of all this for the first woman astronaut are fairly obvious: sexism is easier to deplore than it is to root out. That these challenges placed tremendous stress on her and that they arose outside her, in the world of circumstance, is shown by the opposition aspect. And that a successful response depended upon alertness, courage, quick responses, and the full use of her intelligence under conditions of pressure is shown in the root prediction itself—transiting Uranus was making an impact upon her alert, feisty natal Mars-Sun conjunction in Gemini.

A glance at the ephemeris for May 26, 1951, tells us that no planet occupied early Sagittarius on the day Sally Ride began her life. Yet the passage of Uranus through that part of the sky created an opportunity for her that would serve to support and define her individuality for as long as she lives. Even though that sector of the sky is physically empty in her birthchart, it is far from being devoid of significance. Through the power of the opposition aspect, those degrees of Sagittarius are linked to the most critical focalizer of all: the Sun.

Other degrees are linked to Sally Ride's Sun, too, although for different reasons. The early parts of Pisces and Virgo are tied in through squares, capable of releasing the solar potential by applying **friction**. Early Aquarius and early Libra mesh with her early Gemini Sun through the process of **enhancement or harmonization**, symbolized by the trine. Aries and Leo link in through sextiles, firing the Sun through yet another form of aspectual interaction: **excitation**. The conjunction, of course, is also powerful, but more obvious. It creates **fusion**. Added to that we have the retinue of "minor aspects," less potent, but not without significance. Have a look at figure 4—it shows all the Sun's major trigger-points.

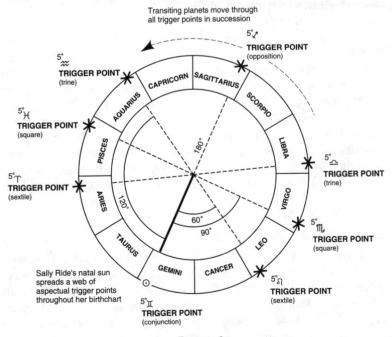

FIGURE 4

And the Sun is just one astrological factor! There are nine other planets, along with house cusps and several more abstract mathematical points, such as the lunar nodes. Like the Sun, each one makes major aspects to seven points apart from its own position on the chart. A transit through any one of those points can fire the natal planet just as surely as if it were passing directly over that planet.

> ☆ Each natal planet spreads a web of highly sensitive aspectual "trigger points' throughout the birthchart, each one awaiting stimulation and ignition by a transiting planet.

If your head is starting to spin, hold on. There are procedures to follow that help us sort out really significant transits from the less important ones. And not all those trigger points are being touched at the same time. There are far more trigger points than there are planets, so not every thread of the web needs to be understood in each situation. Once again, the purpose of transits is to **mediate the unfolding of the birthchart over time**. Just as we cannot handle each nuance of every developmental issue in our lives simultaneously, not every trigger point can be touched at once. Transits, believe it or not, make it simpler, not harder, to be human.

Once again, our primary ally is an orderly approach. Even though there are literally hundreds of trigger points in every birthchart, there are only ten planets to transit over them. At any given moment, several of those are likely to be moving through less sensitive regions of the chart and can safely be put on the back burner. That typically leaves us with just a few really critical transits to consider. Even those can be sorted out and understood methodically.

Transits are not all created equal. Some represent the flesh and bones of life; others are just the clothing. Discerning the difference is simpler than you might expect. All we have to do is see how fast the planet is moving.

THE SLOW-FAST DISTINCTION

As we learned at the beginning of this chapter, the carousel of the solar system has a very strict law governing planetary speed limits: the farther away a planet lies from the Sun, the more slowly it goes. There are no exceptions. Distant planets move much more slowly through space. They also have vastly greater distances to cover. The results are dramatic. As we learned earlier, Mercury, the closest planet to the Sun, rips through space at about thirty miles per second, covering its tiny orbital circuit in about eighty-eight days. Pluto, at the other end of the spectrum, plods along at about one-tenth that speed, completing a tour of its vastly greater orbital territory only once in 248 years.

Planetary journeys around the birthchart of course display a very similar range of speeds, complicated somewhat by the fact that we are watching the carousel from one of the moving "plaster ponies"—earth itself, which is moving at about eighteen miles per second.

So far, all this is smooth and orderly. But there is a hitch. Venus takes 225 days to get around the Sun. We take 365. Mars gets around in 687 days. Then something happens. Jump out to Jupiter, the next planet, and we find an orbital period of about 12 years—a huge increase. After that, the numbers settle back down into a reasonably orderly progression. Saturn at 29 years, Uranus at 84, Neptune at 165, and finally Pluto at its stately 248. In other words, very roughly speaking, we have a pattern of doubling, which holds in a crude but clear way in every case except for the gap between Mars and Jupiter, where the orbital period is multiplied not by two but by six.

For a long time that gap was a mystery. We now have an explanation. There is space for another planet between Mars and Jupiter, but instead of a planet, we find an interplanetary hailstorm—countless thousands of little moonlets, mostly tiny, but a few large enough to be considered "miniplanets." We call them asteroids. The bigger ones have astrological significance, but that is not a topic for this book. (Try *Asteroid Goddesses* by Demetra George.) In a more romantic time these asteroids were viewed as the remains of an exploded planet. That was a colorful notion, but it foundered on the fact that no one could ever figure out precisely **how** a planet might explode. Current theory suggests that the asteroids are a planet that never was, only the raw material, swirled and shredded to such a degree by Jupiter's enormous gravity that it never had a chance to coalesce.

Even if asteroids do not prove to have the same breadth of astrological significance as the planets, they still play a crucial role in our understanding of transits. They represent the boundary between the realm of the inner "terrestrial" planets and the outer ones—all "gas giants," apart from Pluto. Astrologically, that distinction is primarily one of speed, and it leads to one of the most elemental laws of predictive astrology.

☆ The more slowly a planet moves, the longer its transits have to build depth and complexity of

meaning for an individual, and therefore, the more
ultimate significance they possess.

Mercury might transit through the orbs of a square to your Venus in
a few days. It might come into play on Monday, and by Saturday, be a
thing of the past. It has meaning, but how significant can that transit
be? Basic changes in one's individuality or fundamental realizations
about life rarely come bursting out of nowhere. They may perhaps hit
us "in a flash," but if we scrutinize the matter, we generally see that we
were building toward them over months or maybe years—and months
and years are exactly the pace of the outer planets. They establish the
tone of the key issues that engage our attention at length, creating what
we might call "chapters of our lives." Compared to the slow transits of
Jupiter, Saturn, Uranus, Neptune, and Pluto, the meanings of the fast
ones are little more than minor victories and petty annoyances. The
truth is a bit more complex, but grasping this idea sets us on the road
toward creating order in our approach to the predictive techniques.
Even though we cannot leave the fast planets out of our considerations
forever, our first practical step is temporarily to ignore them.

☆ Transits of the slow-moving outer planets establish
the meaning, the circumstances, and the timing of an
individual's long-term development.

Does this suggest that by ignoring the transits of the Sun, Moon,
Mercury, Venus, and Mars, all we lose are insignificant day-by-day
details? Not exactly. The inner planets play a central role in transits
theory. It is just that their role is different from that of the outer ones.
We cannot ignore them. That will not work. They do have meaning of
their own, and that meaning is not of a "minor" nature, safely
forgotten. Their speed may rob them of the ability to generate
long-term themes like the outer planets, but it gives them another role,
in some ways a more colorful one. They help determine **when** those
long-term themes are going to come crashing down out of the world of
potentials and into the world of events.

☆ Transits of the fast-moving inner planets trigger
into action the great fields of potential indicated by
the theme-generating outer planets.

Outer planets typically remain within the orbs of a critical aspect for several months. Jupiter is usually the quickest of them, occasionally passing through an aspect in as little as a couple of weeks. Pluto, the slowest, can remain in a sensitive zone for three or four years at a time. All of them, owing to retrogradation, have a tendency to make multiple passes through a trigger point, thereby extending their stay. Throughout the period in which a slow transit is in effect, the individual is gradually incorporating some new wisdom, perspective, or skill into his or her character—or at least that opportunity exists. But such steps typically require **rites of passage** to cement them into the person's awareness. These "rites of passage" usually take the form of events that crystallize in some distinct action the significance of an entire period. To time them and to describe how to make use of them successfully we turn to the transits of the inner planets. They are to the outer planets what directors are to producers in the film industry—they handle the actual creation of the product that the outer planets have defined and declared necessary.

Mercury, for example, was transiting through a conjunction with Sally Ride's natal Sun-Mars conjunction on the day the shuttle blasted off. It served as a trigger, **fusing** (conjunction) an intensified element of **intelligence, alertness,** and **adaptability** (Mercury) with her basic identity. That same transit had touched her a great number of times in the past, generally doing little more than brightening her wit for a few days. On June 18, 1983, it served a deeper purpose. Why? Because on that day Mercury had something deeper than itself to trigger—it grasped onto the long-term transit of Uranus, and simply said, "Now!" The same logic applies to our analysis of General Custer's debacle at Little Big Horn. Saturn squaring his Sun and Moon by transit established the basic theme of that chapter of his life. Mars served as the trigger, pointing out that particular period of a few days as a critical "rite of passage" within the larger cycle. In his case, a bit too critical.

WHAT ABOUT RETROGRADATION?

Close your left eye. Now hold your index finger out at arm's length. Open the left eye, and close your right. What happens? Your finger seems to jump to the right. Alternately blink your eyes and the finger oscillates back and forth. Now let your finger drift slowly to the right. What happens now? Basically the same thing. As you blink your eyes, the most obvious motion of the finger is still its oscillation. It gains an inch to the right, then loses three quarters of an inch, then gains another inch, and so on, very gradually making progress toward the right.

Planets operate the same way. In the six months it takes Earth to get from one side of its orbit to the other, Pluto's real position changes by less than a degree. But that's not quite what we see. Pluto seems to advance more rapidly than that—but then during the following six months, it loses much of what it has gained. It is as if one side of our orbit is our left eye and the other side is our right. We are blinking at the slow-moving outer planets, superimposing on their real motion an apparent oscillation that has nothing to do with them directly. When our own motion makes the planet appear to be losing ground, we say that the planet is **retrograde**. When their motion appears normal, we say they are **direct**. And when they are standing still, about to turn either retrograde or direct, we say they are **stationary**.

A retrograde planet in a person's birthchart suggests that the normal outward flow of that planet's energy is partly **reversed**. The psychological function it symbolizes becomes more internalized and personal, sinking deeply into the character, but sometimes at the expense of easy outward expression. In transits, retrogradation works in a similar way. The retrograde period in a transit often represents a relatively quiet phase of the growth process, one in which the breakthroughs and developments are primarily internal and attitudinal. It often coincides with a period of reassessment and reflection.

> ☆ When a planet transiting over a trigger point turns
> retrograde, the developmental process it symbolizes
> tends to turn inward, unfolding independently from
> the context of outward events.

In practice there are exceptions to this rule. It really represents a trend more than a hard-and-fast law. Very little occurs inwardly without having some outward, visible effect, just as very little can happen outwardly without touching us inwardly in some way. We must also consider other transits occurring simultaneously with the retrograde transit. Mars might trigger the cusp of someone's seventh house while Saturn is retrograding through a conjunction with her Venus. The slow transit of Saturn suggests a period in which she is realistically evaluating (Saturn) her relationship status (Venus), and in this retrograde phase, that evaluation is tending to be mostly private and subjective. Mars, however, heats everything up in an outward and visible way through its entry into her House of Marriage. Events seem to take over, forcing her to reveal her hand despite her subjective feeling of "not being ready" or of "things moving too fast." Life is like that sometimes—and so are transits. The retrograde planet does not **want** to come out and take a stand just yet, but other transits may **demand** that it do so.

Stations also play a role in understanding transits. When a planet stands still, about to turn either retrograde or direct, events tend to come to a head. There is often a "turning of the tide" in the matter the transits represents. Just as a stationary planet on a birthchart represents a particularly powerful—and perhaps particularly stubborn—dimension of an individual's character, a transiting planet making a station usually represents an **intensification** of the developmental drama.

There is one more general principle to grasp before we can weave our theory of transits into a coherent whole. This last notion is a fairly obvious one, and has to do with **aspectual orbs**—those broad zones within which an aspect is operational. Refer back to figure 3 for a moment. Sally Ride's natal Sun is in the fifth degree of Gemini. When the space shuttle blasted off, transiting Uranus was in the **sixth** degree of Sagittarius—a little past the perfect opposition. That was still close enough for it to work. In fact, Uranus could have been several degrees away from the precise trigger point and still been effective. In transits, nothing "clicks on" or "clicks off." Like most processes in life, transits have a gradual, flowing feeling about them—they build slowly, then fade out like long summer evenings.

Here is our general principle:

☆ The more precise a transiting aspect becomes, the more powerful are its effects.

Orbs can never be defined with perfect accuracy. Attempting to do so is like attempting to define exactly the beginning of "the modern period" or "the day I grew up." A rule of thumb is that you should consider that any of the fast planets are within the orbs of a transiting aspect when they are roughly 6 degrees from the trigger point. With the slower, outer planets, reduce that orb considerably—4 degrees is about right. What if someone argues with you for lesser or greater orbs? Smile, agree with them, and walk away. They are right, too. It is purely a question of where we want to set our limits. Since transits are typically complicated, I personally prefer to set fairly tight orbs, thereby limiting myself to those planetary configurations that are most momentous and pressing. I cast a wide-mesh net, in other words. That way I catch only big fish. If you have a taste for minnows, spread those orbs more widely.

What have we learned? Putting it all together is a subject for later in the book. Right now, we are still untangling the basic symbolic threads woven into these sky changes. Just as with birthcharts, we must first learn the words before we try to write the sentences. Don't worry if you are wondering how you could apply all this in practice. That comes soon enough. For now, let's quickly review what we have just seen about peaks and troughs within the activity of a particular transit.

Saturn approaches a trigger point. When it is about 6 degrees off, its effects begin to be felt, building radically as the orb narrows. Events begin to occur that crystallize the meaning of the period through various rites of passage ignited by transits of quicker planets. The transiting aspect becomes precise, then wanes as Saturn moves on. A crisis has passed. Perhaps that is the end of it. But let's say Saturn now slows to a stop, making a station, about to turn retrograde. Once again, some kind of crisis is reached— the volume is up on the issue. With Saturn retrograde, whatever is going on in the person's mind has some tendency to become quieter and more subjective for a while. He is "biding his time"—or at least trying to. Trigger effects from fast planets continue to ignite events, but now he is more hesitant, a bit unsure of himself in the new psychological territory. Circumstances might press at him, but his attitude is now more reflective and quiet. Tactics of delay appeal to him and are actually often a good strategy now. Then the aspect becomes precise again. Another peak is reached, but now that peak is focused primarily in his **inner world**. Retrogradation continues, with the significance of Saturn fading until another station is reached, whereupon events speed up actively and outwardly, rushing toward a final explosion and culmination when the planet once again moves through the precise trigger point.

This is a neat picture—neater, probably, than life will ever be. Still, it serves as a guideline, giving us some sense of the broad outlines of a typical outer planet transit. Most fit roughly into this pattern, although the overlay of fireworks from the quick planets sometimes obscures it. Other factors get involved, too. You might, for example, have a transit of Neptune coinciding with that Saturn passage, but with its own peaks and troughs occurring slightly out of phase with those of the ringed planet. Finally, there is a purely human factor. Sometimes, for reasons we can never detect astrologically, an individual is particularly "ready" for the lessons of a certain transit. Generally such a person responds quickly and decisively, often forcing all the relevant outward events right at the beginning of the period. Other times, a person is extremely resistant to the transit's message, postponing the real developments until the very end—or perhaps never truly absorbing them, thereby dissipating the transit in a lot of noise and static, missing the point entirely. Such dimensions are purely personal and cannot be foreseen or understood astrologically. Once again, we are not machines. We are people.

WHEN THE PARTY'S OVER

What about when a transit is finished? What then? This is a critical question, often overlooked in traditional astrology books. There is a temptation to think that when a transiting planet at last moves out of the orbs of an aspect, its effects are over and done. In truth, those effects are only beginning. A planet may stop influencing the birthchart for a while, but the significance of its passage over a trigger point remain with us forever. If we have made a strong, self-aware response to the issues the transit raised, **something within us has permanently changed**. We are not the same person we were when it began. Those new realizations and skills remain with us always.

Reading these words is effortless for you. You are not even really conscious of reading them. Your attention is with the concepts themselves, not with the mechanics of how they are being conveyed to you. It was not always like that. Some years ago you had to put very considerable labor into acquiring the skill of reading. Even that step rested on a foundation of far greater effort—you spent the first tenth of your life grasping the rudiments of language. The effects of all that struggle are with you now, but unconsciously so. They are taken for granted, having become part of your essence as a literate adult. That is precisely how transits work.

> ☆ Once an individual has made a positive response
> to a transit, those new strengths and insights remain
> latent within the personality forever, ready to be
> activated effortlessly and automatically whenever
> circumstance demands.

If it were not for this final principle in transits theory, the process would be empty. We would be no more than existential Ping-Pong balls paddled around by random and impersonal astrological forces. But life is an evolutionary process. Through the medium of memory our very essence is transformed minute by minute, always evolving toward more knowledge, more awareness. Like getting married or starting out in a profession, a transit is an **event**. And like any event of consequence, we **remember** it, not only in the obvious way of recalling outward details but in the far more profound way of being **changed by the experience**.

Let's allow transits to teach us how to create meaningful, lasting change in ourselves. We need not limit ourselves to predicting the ephemeral. We can become architects of permanence.

CHAPTER FOUR

TRANSITS II:
TEACHERS AND TRICKSTERS

Sun, Moon, and planets. As we learned in *The Inner Sky*, they stand for **psychological functions**. Much like the ego-id-superego model Freud developed, they represent a universal road map to processes within the human mind, applicable to anyone. The main difference is that the astrological model is vastly more precise than Freud's. Where he saw the mind divided into three "compartments," astrologers see ten. We might for example become interested in how a particular woman expresses her assertiveness and territoriality. Immediately we turn to her **Mars**—the planetary symbol of those aggressive functions. In what sign does it lie? In what house? What aspects does it make? How does that Mars fit in with the general tone of her chart? Quickly a picture emerges. Mars lies in Aries. The "god of war"—her assertiveness function—is motivated by the sign of the Warrior: hot stuff. But it lies in her fourth house, opposed by Saturn and the Moon—that warrior is hidden and controlled. Broaden our focus now: What about the rest of her chart? She is a second house Pisces with Capricorn rising—a strange framework for fiery Mars. The pattern leaps out: her blade is sharp, but she keeps it in a silk scabbard. Her fires burn white-hot, but they burn inwardly.

That woman's Mars is alive, and like all living things, it can change and grow. We cannot know how she will unravel the riddles the red planet has set before her, but we can perhaps help her by describing how that Mars would operate if she were healthy and happy—and warn her about getting tangled up in its more shadowy expressions. Such insights might be useful to her at any point in her life. Why? Because we are speaking of her birthchart, and planets in the birthchart remain constant throughout a lifetime. Our responses to those planets may mature, but the basic issues—the strategies, the resources, the shadows—endure from our first breath to our last.

In transits all that changes. We use the same planets and they still stand for the same key ideas. What differs is our focus. We move from the general to the particular, from the abstract to the immediate, from the lifetime to the days and minutes and seconds of which it is composed. If a planet on the birthchart is like a husband or a wife, then a transiting planet is a lover who shocks us and shakes us and then moves on. That lover may teach us something about life, or perhaps leave us with angry scars. Either way, the lover is gone, and what we make of the experience—wisdom or loose ends—is our own business.

Personifying the transiting planets—thinking of them as lovers or teachers—has always been an effective strategy for me. Perhaps the ancient Greeks and Romans were not so far from the mark in calling the planets "gods." In a way, each one does have a personality. Like ourselves sometimes, the planets are half angel, half devil. Which side of the transiting planet's character will touch us? That is up to us.

Let's meet these Tricksters and Teachers individually. We'll begin with the outer planets, the slow-moving "theme generators." As we learned in the previous chapter, they are the ones that create the **evolving framework of issues** that gives shape to our months and years.

JUPITER THE TEACHER

Glyph: ♃

Orbital Period: Twelve years.

The Gift: **The ability both to envision and to seize upon new possibilities and potentials for the future.**

The Challenge: **Can you recognize something better than you have ever known, utterly new and positive, that now lies within your reach— and can you devise a way to grasp it?**

Expanding into the future—that is the spirit of Jupiter as it transits over trigger points in a birthchart. To the medieval astrologers, Jupiter was the "Greater Benefic." They tended to see its passages in the most encouraging light. The truth is more subtle, as we see when we explore Jupiter the Trickster, but this planet does bring **opportunity** to our doorstep. The question is, Can we recognize it? To take full advantage of a Jupiter transit, we must lead with our imagination. Some **new possibility** now lies close by. Where is it? What has changed? How are we underestimating ourselves? When Jupiter arrives at a trigger point, some dimension of our character—as indicated by the planets, houses, signs, and aspects involved—is due for **healing and regeneration** through an influx of hope, luck, and self-confidence. That healing may come in the form of a crisis, something that old-fashioned astrologers often miss. A bankruptcy, a separation, the death of an oppressive parent—I have seen all these under the "lucky" transits of Jupiter. The face of good fortune is sometimes benign, sometimes fierce. Learn to recognize it either way and to seize the gifts it offers—while it still offers them. That is how to make mighty Jupiter your Teacher.

Albert Einstein, with Hitler's anti-semitism close at his heels, saw the handwriting on the wall and seized the opportunity to flee Germany for the United States—all with Jupiter transiting through an opposition to his Sun. Under Jupiter's transiting conjunction to the Sun, Eubie Blake, the famous ragtime pianist and composer, saw a crack in the wall of racism in the America of 1914, and succeeded in publishing his first printed musical composition. Under the opposition to his Sun, Ted Turner saw the new, untapped possibilities in the recently launched SATCOM satellite and began his fabulously successful national cable TV network. These men each let Jupiter manifest as the Teacher and moved into a new realm of potential in their lives. But it did not have to be like that. Jupiter has another face, one we should never allow ourselves to meet.

JUPITER THE TRICKSTER

The Trap: **The temptation to let ourselves be lulled into lassitude and foolishness while basking in the warm feelings created by mere glitz, overconfidence, arrogance, or still-incomplete success.**

The Lie: **Don't worry—everything will take care of itself.**

Jupiter the Trickster strikes not with reversals and misfortune, but with the inner enemies we create with our own egos. After that, we create the reversals and misfortunes for ourselves. Under a Jupiter transit, we may feel lucky. We may in fact **be** lucky—but perhaps not as lucky as we feel. We get lax, missing "details" that may later get us into trouble. We may also fall prey to some "all that glitters is not gold" scenario, falling for mere appearances. High-handedness, pomposity, overextension, underestimation of adversaries, these are all possible if we succumb to Jupiter's deceptions. It is as if the prison guard has mistakenly dropped the keys right outside the dungeon door. All we have to do is reach out, grab them, unlock ourselves, and flee. But we decide to savor the moment for awhile. We have been saving a piece of chocolate for a breakthrough just like this one. Let's gaze at those keys for a few minutes while we slowly suck all the goodness out of that chocolate. No need to be hasty.

John DeLorean's well-publicized cocaine bust occurred as transiting Jupiter conjuncted his Saturn. His overconfidence (Jupiter) collided with reality (Saturn). Going back many centuries, when Charlemagne's rearguard was overwhelmed and massacred by the Basques at Roncevalles—later mythologized as Moors in the famous *Song of Roland*—Jupiter the Trickster was busily at work, squaring his Uranus. Overconfidence (Jupiter) created a crisis (square; friction) in his sense of freedom and individuality (Uranus). With Jupiter conjuncting its own natal position, Henry David Thoreau proposed marriage to one Ellen Sewell—and was rejected. Overconfidence again.

Either way, Teacher or Trickster, Jupiter can exert a powerful influence on our lives. Remember above all that no aspect or sign makes Jupiter into the Teacher. What does that is our own willingness to think positively without allowing that positiveness to slip into arrogance and pride.

SATURN THE TEACHER

Glyph:	♄
Orbital Period:	**Twenty-nine years.**
The Gift:	**The ability to see reality clearly and to respond to it effectively and decisively.**
The Challenge:	**Can you push aside wishful or fearful thinking and respond to concrete issues with self-discipline, patience, and practical strategies—and if necessary, can you do it alone?**

Saturn times are typically viewed with horror by traditional astrologers. I must admit that when I see one coming in my own life, I sometimes wish I were someone else. But in retrospect, those visits from the ringed planet perhaps do more for us than any other planetary passage. The gifts they leave in their wake are typically of the quiet but precious variety, gifts such as **maturity, dignity, and self-respect**. No matter how much growing and learning we do inwardly, there always comes a time when we must translate that inner growth into **concrete, outward terms**—and that is what Saturn transits are all about. Saturn is the planet of **reality**. It refers not so much to what we might **feel** as to what we actually must **do**. Its transits are always a **call to action in the real world**. Classically, Saturn is "Father Time." Its transits always involve a theme of potential **maturation**. Time for the planet Saturn is touching to "grow up," to adjust to its advancing place in the life-cycle, and to "give up childish things." When Saturn approaches a trigger point, first consider what part of you (which natal planet, in other words) it is contacting. Then think: What kinds of behaviors in this department of my life continue to take up my time even though I know in my heart that I have outgrown them? Then temporarily forget about nostalgia, sentiment, and self-doubt and plan a realistic, effective program of behavioral change for yourself and stick to it, even if nobody rushes to your side to congratulate you. A mountain looms before. Climbing it will be exhausting — but failing to climb it will imprison you in a place you have outgrown.

Cesar Chavez, leader of the famous five-year "grape strike" among the migrant workers in California, saw the **reality** of anger and resignation threatening to overthrow his ideals of nonviolence. Inspired by Mohandas Gandhi, he endured a twenty-five-day fast in a successful effort to reinspire his followers—while Saturn was transiting through a conjunction with his Sun. A heightened sense of self-discipline (Saturn) fused with his self-image (Sun). Mother Theresa, known for her work among the destitute in Calcutta, received her inspiration that she must leave the convent and make real her Venusian ideal of Christian love while Saturn was transiting over her Venus. With Saturn transiting over his myth-making Pluto, George Lucas **crystallized** his uncanny sense of myth and fable—and permanently affected the unconscious of a generation—in the release of his history-making film *Star Wars*.

SATURN THE TRICKSTER
The Trap: **The temptation to slip into despair and frustration when reality seems to turn against us.**
The Lie: **You can't win.**

Saturn the Trickster is perhaps the most embittering of all planetary enemies. He builds a mile-high wall across the road of our life, filling us with a sense of impossibility and self-pity. We stare at that wall, convincing ourselves that we are permanently stuck, with no possibility of going on. What we often miss when the Trickster has us in his clutches is that even though that wall is high, it is not very wide. We can go around it—but only if we alter the course of our road to adapt to changing circumstances. Inwardly we have become something different. Outwardly we have not. That maturational course-change is necessary—but frightening. Orchestrating some kind of **collision with reality** is always Saturn's way, whether he is the Teacher or the Trickster. The Trickster's strategy, relying on our stubbornness and inflexibility, is to depress and devitalize us, thereby **trapping us in our narrow, sorrowful subjectivity**, and robbing us of the energy we need to face that reality effectively. Saturn the Trickster relies heavily on the fact that real change always feels unnatural to us at first, using that to put us off the track. His dark art lies in deceiving us into believing that we have painted ourselves into a corner— and thereby drawing our attention away from the fact that we have sprouted wings and ought to be concentrating on learning to fly.

General Custer's inflexibility in the face of reality was the subject of the latter part of Chapter Three. His debacle at Little Big Horn occurred while Saturn was squaring his Sun and Moon. Charlemagne's losses at Roncevalles happened under Saturn square Uranus, complicated as we just saw by transiting Jupiter squaring Uranus, too. Saturn was crossing Charles Manson's Ascendant when his followers murdered Sharon Tate—and the reality he had created got out of hand and quickly came crashing down around his ears. Under pressure for his alleged "mental problems," Thomas Eagleton withdrew his candidacy for the vice presidency when Saturn transited through a conjunction with his Jupiter. Did the Trickster rob him temporarily of his expansiveness, confidence, and hopes for the future (Jupiter)? We cannot say—but that certainly would have been our warning to him during that difficult time in his life.

□ □ □

URANUS THE TEACHER

Glyph: ♅
Orbital Period: **Eighty-four years,**
The Gift: **The ability to distinguish our true individuality from the desires and fantasies about us held by our family, friends, and associates.**
The Challenge: **Can you stand up to the pressures of conformity, asserting your right to be yourself in the face of censure and rejection—and in the face of whatever social conventions you may have unwittingly internalized?**

In certain traditions, Uranus is viewed as the ruling planet of astrology. I think this is quite accurate. Astrology and Uranus share a common purpose—to free us from anything that limits the full, healthy expression of our natures. Society—in the form of pressures placed upon us by others—is an arch offender here. From the moment of our birth, we are given an all-embracing set of instructions regarding how to go about being human. What is success? What is failure? How long should you make eye contact with a stranger? How far should you stand from her? On and on, until every nuance of our lives is flavored with the spirit of the "tribal" society into which we happened to be born. It would be foolish in the extreme to claim that all that instruction is damaging. Culture is a blessing and we should be thankful for it. But some of that instruction is not natural to us and if we are to be happy, we must be purged of it. And that purging is the essence of the transformation demanded by a Uranian passage.

The secret of grasping Uranian transits lies in understanding that even though they often involve some fireworks in our relationships with the people around us, those fireworks are secondary. Our primary concern must always focus on how we have allowed phony descriptions of ourselves to gain power in our own minds. Uranus offers us freedom, step by step, battle by battle, realization by realization. More than any other planet, Uranus symbolizes change; the enemy this Teacher fears most is the antithesis of change: habit. For all our talk to the contrary, something within us hates to change. We are embarrassed by it, so addicted are we to our habitual patterns. Imagine a friendly mockery between you and a long-standing friend. She loves murder mysteries. You swear you would never waste your time with one. One day, while waiting for a bus, you find yourself getting into a copy of *The Thin Man*. How quick are you to confess that to the friend?

It is a silly thing. Nothing. But if she is coming over for a visit, you put the book in the bedroom, out of sight. Why? To avoid the embarrassment of having been caught in a present that is inconsistent with your past. Grappling with the effects of history and culture are certainly Uranian processes, but as always, we are often quicker at recognizing the outer enemy than the inner one. It is this inner enemy—our own addiction to the status quo, and the pride we take in maintaining it— that we must recognize and defeat if we are to make Uranus our Teacher.

Cesar Chavez offers us a fine example of a man standing up for his individuality in the face of a particularly gross kind of social pressure. While Uranus was transiting through an opposition to his Sun, he faced an assassination plot mounted against him by certain commercial agricultural interests in California, which were upset by his successful unionizing activities. In the previous chapter we saw how the same transit represented a personal breakthrough for Sally Ride—and, through her, a symbolic breakthrough against the entrenched cultural notions of femininity. Jimmy Carter, long before he was elected to the presidency, gave an impassioned speech in his Plains, Georgia church in favor of admitting black people to the congregation. In the summer of 1965, in the rural South, such sentiments did not always receive rave reviews. What indicated his break with tribal tradition? Uranus was transiting through a conjunction with his Sun.

URANUS THE TRICKSTER
The Trap: The temptation to submit to the herd instinct because it is practical to do so, because the rewards are high, and because the alternatives are impossible.
The Lie: You can't fight city hall.

Getting trapped by Uranus the Trickster can have a catastrophic impact upon a person's life. With the planet's eighty-four-year cycle, its transits quite literally represent once-in-a-lifetime chances. If we blow them, they're gone forever.

Throughout so much of life, we are just cruising, living out the consequences of decisions we've already made. It is as if we were walking down a long hall, unable to alter our course. We made a decision to have a child—so naturally we have twenty years of active parenting ahead of us. We got a degree in electrical engineering—so it will be tough to get work as a psychotherapist. But when Uranus comes to a trigger point, it signals us that we've come to the end of the hall. We are free, ready to move on into a chamber full of doorways. If the trigger point is really a critical one—say, a conjunction with the Ascendant—we are challenged to **reinvent ourselves**. Why? Because our old style of living has burned out. We are done with it, ready to put those years behind us and to move enthusiastically and creatively into a new phase of our life. If we succeed, we are rejuvenated. But if we allow other people's resistance to those changes—or our own fears—to freeze the process, then we remain trapped in the past, living lives that have become irrelevant to us.

Early in his career, comedian Richard Pryor attempted to keep his performances within the bounds of "decency" as it was then defined by society. His natural inclinations were more earthy and ribald, but for a while he allowed Uranus the Trickster to convince him that he had no choice but to play by the rules. In October 1967, the tension came to a head. Pryor was in the middle of a seventeen-day gig at the Aladdin Hotel in Las Vegas, doing his act, when he spontaneously began to express himself more according to his natural style—and was fired on the spot for "obscenity." Transiting Uranus (his true individuality) was opposing (tension, crisis) his Ascendant (outward appearances). Although this episode marked a creative breakthrough for him, it must have been agonizing personally. Astrologically, our question must be: What was he doing in Las Vegas in the first place? Couldn't he have made this step more harmoniously? In the dramatic, painful clash between how Richard Pryor was perceived and who he was actually becoming, we see the unmistakable hand of Uranus the Trickster.

NEPTUNE THE TEACHER
Glyph: ♆
Orbital Period: **One hundred and sixty-five years.**
The Gift: **The ability to experience serenity, inspiration, and transcendence in the face of life's dramas; the ability to receive a Vision**
The Challenge: **Can you intentionally enter an altered state of consciousness, opening your awareness to what we might call God or your deeper self?**

Mystical language is difficult to avoid when we speak of the transits of Neptune. These are typically dreamy periods, vivid as we pass through them, often hard to express or even to remember in retrospect. The human psyche is vastly deeper and more complex than the version of our "personalities" we carry around in our heads. We have deep roots that link us to a realm of mystery. Where do dreams arise? Or artistic inspirations? Or flashes of insight? Those experiences seem to come out of nowhere, revitalizing and refreshing us, often in ways we cannot understand logically.

When Neptune touches a trigger point, it is like a signal arising in that hidden psychological territory. It tells us that our outward personality has become too stiff, too preoccupied with itself, too rigidly convinced of its own rightness. Inner and outer have drifted apart, exposing us to the danger of blindly and mechanically pursuing a course that feels increasingly devoid of real feeling or spiritual relevance. The inner world is attempting to reestablish the lines of communication—before the outer stretches them so thin that they snap.

What is the first action we should take when Neptune approaches a trigger point? **Forget about taking any action**. Just relax. There is nothing we need to do, though we may feel restless and hypersensitive. **Doing**, in fact, is the very obstacle that Neptune the Teacher is attempting to surmount. Our task is only to **feel**, to get "in tune with ourselves." A good beginning is to admit that we need a Vision for our lives, that we are lost somehow. When Neptune strikes a chord, remember this: You are the problem. Something precious within you has become dissociated from your biographical life. Meanwhile, however, your outer self is going merrily along its way, trying to pretend that those old patterns still have life in them. Listen to that deeper voice. Allow it to guide you. Imagine. Dream. Flow. Whatever the nature of the issue, the resolution arises **outside** the personality, coming in a flash of inspiration originating in the deeper self. If a solution is going to arise, it comes only when you stop pumping up that old, tired description of yourself and **listen**.

How do we do that? We meditate. We spend time alone, cultivating a contemplative, receptive state of mind. We allow our deep self to **play**, expressing itself through art and fantasy. Perhaps we seek out psychic counselors. Maybe we get interested in astrology, or any other symbol system that allows our unconscious to speak to us. We avoid our memorized cycles of thought, scrupulously weeding out all our private clichés and certainties. Why? Because if we want new wine in the jug, we must first empty the old. We can't create a miracle, but we can at least make space for one to happen.

Peggy Fleming enchanted the world with supernatural Neptunian grace as she figure skated to her Olympic gold medal in 1968. Neptune's pure inspiration flowed through her and out into the world as it transited over her Ascendant (outward appearance: "style"). With Neptune trining his Sun, Miles Davis began his career as a jazz musician in New York. Inspiration (Neptune) enhanced (trine) his self-image (Sun). And here is one man's way to ensure himself some quiet time for contemplation: With Neptune fusing with his Sun through a conjunction, Thor Heyerdahl spent a hundred days floating across the Pacific Ocean aboard the famous raft, Kon Tiki. The ancient "god of the sea"— normally a metaphorical reference to the "sea of consciousness"—took on a literal meaning in his case, becoming part of his identity through the Neptunian-solar contact.

NEPTUNE THE TRICKSTER

The Trap: **The temptation to deceive or undo ourselves with glamorous falsehoods and easy, self-destructive patterns of escape.**

The Lie: **Eat, drink, and be merry, for tomorrow you may die.**

Neptune the Trickster is a shrewd and insidious foe, sounding our characters for any weakness. Like a cunning judo master, he waits for us to move, then efficiently exploits our efforts, turning them against us, never raising a bead of his own sweat. He works with our wishes and with our fears, those deep-seated and frequently irrational emotions we learn to keep buried within ourselves—buried, that is, until Neptune hits a trigger point in our lives. Then, if we are smart enough to avoid the Trickster, it is time to trundle those feelings out to reabsorb them in a new way, thereby allowing our outward personalities to catch up with the steps our deeper self has already taken. That, at least, is the theory. The Trickster has other plans. He knows those feelings have not previously had any direct contact with reality. They have not known its checks and balances. They are naive, and immature—and hungry. He lies in wait for them like a practiced hooker awaiting a ship full of cadets.

Hype—that is the Trickster's favorite weapon. He loves to blow our needs and fears out of proportion, taking a truth and twisting it into the most convincing and devastating kind of lie. He loves glamour, which casts its spell of inflated desirability over the most tawdry objects and options, enchanting us into foolishness and waste. When Neptune comes to a trigger point in your birthchart, before you act, make every effort to think realistically. When you get a "fantastic idea," cool down for three days, then reconsider it. Neptune passages are far more useful as times of **reflection** than as times of action—and getting us to forget that point is the Trickster's aim. He loves to get us to overuse alcohol and drugs because of their tendency to fill us with irrational enthusiasms. He likes self-destructive emotional and sexual entanglements a lot, too, for exactly the same reason. And pride—that's the one he will pick every time he can get it. Once we have developed an irrational enthusiasm for our own ego, the Trickster has us in his grip.

Eubie Blake found himself playing piano in a whorehouse when he was fifteen years old. With all those "glamorous temptations" around, it says a lot about Blake's character and drive that he managed to get out of that environment with his creative energies still functional. The Trickster really gave him his best shot—transiting Neptune was simultaneously trining his Sun, conjuncting his Jupiter, and squaring his Uranus during that period. John DeLorean didn't fare so well. When his cocaine dealings were being secretly tape-recorded by federal agents, Neptune (self-deception) was sitting right on top of his Mercury (communication and alertness). Score one for the Trickster.

PLUTO THE TEACHER

Glyph: ♇ or ♀

Orbital Period: Two hundred forty-eight years.

The Gift: **The ability to heal one's soul, recovering the energy needed to find an altruistic mission in life, thereby filling one's consciousness with a sense of ultimate purpose.**

The Challenges: **Can you face your deepest wounds and fears? Can you recognize some inner vision or gift that life has given you, and do you have the courage humbly to submit yourself to the task of exploring it?**

So far as we know, Pluto is the last of the planets, and therefore it represents the most remote and inaccessible state of awareness of which we can conceive. We climb the ladder of growth, becoming ever wiser, more loving, more uniquely expressive... then what? Who cares? What does it all finally **mean**? That is Pluto's question. Against the backdrop of centuries, against the incalculable forgotten sufferings of humanity, against the glorious victories no one remembers—of what significance is your existence? When Pluto transits over a trigger point, you had better have your answer ready, and that answer had better be sincere. Nothing less than absolute sincerity can survive this Teacher's withering scrutiny.

Submission—that is the key to letting Pluto be the Teacher instead of the Trickster. But submission to what? The answer is easy to say, but very difficult to live: We must submit ourselves to our mission. We must become so completely identified with some larger moral framework of purpose that we lose our natural preoccupation with ego. In doing so, we attain a transpersonal state of consciousness, more identified with humanity and with the process of history than with our own more narrow pursuits.

Transiting Pluto does not always put us on the six o'clock news. The planet can do that, as we will see in our examples. For most of us, however, its action is quieter, working through us to affect the **roots** of change on the cultural or historical level. Congress acts and everyone yawns. But in the wee hours of a hot Tuesday night aboard a bus running between Dallas and Houston, a young man discusses arms control with a stranger. The stranger later shares the conversation with a friend, who passes it on to another man he meets casually on a flight to Chicago. And that man plays golf with the President the next day, at a time when he is receptive to new ideas about arms control. The young man on the bus to Houston is undergoing a Pluto transit. He of course has no understanding of the cycle of events he has set into motion. No matter. His response to the transit is strong anyway. Why? Because he took the risk of expressing himself to a stranger on the level of moral principle.

A woman suffers exhaustion and various privations in order to open a home for battered wives. Why? "Because she just felt like **doing something** with her life"—a sentiment that immediately puts our attention on transiting Pluto. Perhaps the need for that home existed across the continent from where she was living. Pluto pulls the strings to get her there. Circumstances beyond her control arise and move her, offering her a Plutonian opportunity that she may understand only in retrospect. Once again, just as with the man on the bus to Houston, **understanding** is not the point. All that matters is that the woman surrender her instinctive concern with purely personal needs, moving into a broader, more altruistic framework.

Regeneration and **transformation** are words we often read in connection with Pluto's transits. In order to have the energy we require to face the soul-challenges we've outlined above, we often have to do some serious "soul-retrieval," going down into our own inner hells and facing whatever has wounded us in our lives: the humiliations, lies, and abuses we have endured. This process is not for the faint-hearted, but Pluto presses it upon us. The whole subject is so complex that I wrote a book about it. If you're interested, have a look at *The Book of Pluto*.

Bruce Springsteen, who struck a deep chord in the mass mind, signed his first recording contract with Columbia while Pluto was transiting over his Sun. His personality (Sun) was transformed into a symbol on the cultural, historical level (Pluto). Precisely the same transit occurred in Jimmy Carter's chart when he was nominated and elected president. Like Springsteen's, Carter's personal vision was **amplified** and **accelerated** to the point where it could make an impact upon the process of history. Abraham Lincoln was an Aquarian by birth and therefore was inherently attuned to the Aquarian-Uranian ideals of individual liberty. When transiting Pluto opposed his natal Uranus, circumstances outside his control (Pluto **and** the opposition aspect) pressured his sense of the rights of the individual (Uranus) into action: Fort Sumter was attacked, the Civil War began, and Lincoln issued the Emancipation Proclamation, freeing the slaves.

PLUTO THE TRICKSTER

The Trap: **The temptation to allow rigidity, dogmatism, and power tripping to narrow our perspective, isolating our egos in a spirit of cynicism, despair, and nihilism. The compulsion to reenact whatever dramas have wounded us in the past.**

The Lie: **Look out for number one.**

Pluto the Trickster is perhaps the most pitiless of any of our planetary enemies. He corrupts and erodes the very roots of the human spirit, and he does so in a particularly vicious way. Where other planetary Tricksters work on us with lies, Pluto damages us with truth. Pluto gives us too much truth too fast, more than we can handle. Then he stands back and watches us rip ourselves to shreds. His truth? "This is a vast, icy universe in which the only certainty is death." From there, we take over ourselves, formulating two laws Pluto the Trickster never utters but whose seeds he planted within us: "Look out for number one," and "Get it while it's hot." Narrowness, petty opportunism, and fear control us, blinding us to the transpersonal possibilities that are the true answers to the questions Pluto raises.

In considering Pluto the Teacher a few paragraphs back, we imagined a woman who was moved across the country by forces beyond her control or understanding in order that she might have the opportunity to open a home for battered wives. What form could those forces take? We can never know specifically, but Pluto has an affinity for operating through broad social or historical pressures that overwhelm the individual. Maybe that woman's husband was in the steel industry. When foreign competition began to squeeze it down, he was laid off—and moved with his family across the continent to seek another job. If Pluto wants her in Los Angeles, then Pluto will get her there by any means necessary. This is true of both the Teacher and the Trickster. But once that woman has been moved, she is on her own. Perhaps she transcends herself and recognizes the needs and opportunities that now lie before her. What if the Trickster wins? Then she descends into existential despair, bemoaning her move to the West, feeling cheated and ripped off by the brutal randomness of life, entering a frightened, hardened, contracted mental state in which self in all its richness and multidimensionality collapses like a black hole into mere egoism.

Once that Plutonian collapse has occurred, the psyche chooses between a passive road and an active one, both of which lead to misery. On the passive road, the individual quietly simmers in feelings of pointlessness and futility, slipping further into existential resignation. On the active road, Pluto's despair is released as rage. In a desperate attempt to reclaim a sense of meaning, the personality attempts to aggrandize itself with conquest and tyranny, lording over anyone foolish or defenseless enough to put up with it.

Underlying all this misbehavior and self-inflicted misery is a very simple principle. During a Pluto transit, whatever has hurt us in the past reemerges into our lives. If we were abandoned as a child, for example, we'll feel the drive to abandon someone — or to arrange to be abandoned again. If the Trickster wins, those bleak, submerged feelings surface and dominate our actions. Under Pluto the Teacher, we may still feel those impulses, but instead of repeating the past, we create a different kind of future.

Adolf Hitler is the classic example dark Pluto.. All through the Second World War, transiting Pluto was squaring his Sun. A sense of futility (Pluto) was infuriating (square: friction) his ego (Sun). As the war drew to a close, the Trickster was moving into a conjunction with Saturn: his self-aggrandizement (Pluto) crashed against the brick wall of reality (Saturn).

Mohandas Gandhi serves admirably as an example of the Teacher's effect in almost every case, but we do know of one period in his life when the Trickster gave him his best shot. Deep in the period when Gandhi's idea of nonviolent resistance was sweeping through India, frustrated, angry British soldiers indiscriminately massacred a large group of men, women, and children at Amritsar. The moral principle of meeting violence with nonviolence was sorely tested. Pluto the Trickster (narrowness and cynicism) was squaring Gandhi's Sun (the very basis of his identity), perhaps tempting him into abandoning his ideals. He held out, the murders created a global scandal, and the rest is history.

Those are the Teachers and Tricksters, the great theme-weaving outer planets that wheel so slowly around our birthcharts. A thorough understanding of their gifts and their lies is a prerequisite for doing effective predictive astrology. Even if we ignored the quick, triggering action of the inner planets, a knowledge of these outer ones would still give us a clear perspective on the general topography of a period of years. But by leaving out the transits of the fast planets we would lose precision in the timing of specific events—the **rites of passage**—through which those larger themes are made concrete.

That loss is not catastrophic, but it is also not necessary. As an adjunct to our understanding of the Teachers and Tricksters, the fast planets can be a great help. A transit of Saturn might suggest that for a while you should make every effort to show patience, self-control, and realism in your job or profession. It might, however, tell you that the advice applies to a period of eight months. That is useful to know, but knowing that the third week of June looks especially critical in that department is in some ways even more useful. Sustaining an unnaturally high level of "good behavior" for a few days is one thing; trying to sustain it for months is another.

Now let's take a closer look at the quick-moving trigger planets.

MARS
Glyph: ♂
The Trigger: **The immediate, intentional use of will in a courageous way; the effort to survive as a physical, psychological, spiritual entity; the right tactical use of assertiveness and aggression.**
Backfiring: **Frozen by fear, awareness turns to self-destruction or to pointless attacks upon targets which are both extraneous and relatively defenseless.**

The transits of Mars are remarkably potent triggers, precipitating the dramas implied by the motions of the slower planets. Above all else, a Mars passage is a **call to decisive action**. We must face a fear, striking an effective blow against whatever stands between us and our legitimate goals. Nerves may be frayed. Finer shadings of emotion may be buried. No matter. Sensitivity and introspection have very little to do with the red planet. Effective action is all that counts. We do what we **must** do and lick our wounds later. Do you need to have a little talk with your mate, one that you do not expect to receive cheerful reviews? Now is the time, if Mars is crossing through a sensitive zone.

What about that leak in your second-story roof? It's not going to heal itself, despite your fear of climbing up that ladder and scurrying across those loose, canted shingles. With Mars, all we can do is take a deep breath—and then do what is necessary. Maybe the situation explodes in our face, but only maybe. If we do not take action, that explosion is **certain** and will probably be even more destructive when it finally does detonate.

A backfiring Mars transit is about as comforting as a snarling German shepherd with glazed eyes and a foaming mouth. We feel **overwhelmed**. Sometimes we suffer terrible reversals, physical or emotional pain that seems to strike us randomly, through accidents or other people's malice. Such self-pitying analysis rarely stands up to close scrutiny. "But I cut myself washing the dishes—it could have happened to anyone!" Tempting logic. Perhaps it's true sometimes. But be careful! Why did you happen to cut yourself on that particular night? Is Mars opposing your natal Venus? Are you steamed up at your mate or business associate over some issue that needs to be discussed? Were you taking it out on those knives and glasses? The right expression of legitimate anger is a Martian strategy for sure—but often that process must begin a step earlier, with the recognition of precisely who or what is the true target of our rage or frustrated assertiveness. Clues exist in the birthchart. What is Mars triggering? What have we bottled up? Are we really that incensed over the little gift our neighbor's dog left on our lawn—or does our real target lie elsewhere, scaring us so badly that we would rather bleed off the pressure by making an ugly scene with the people next door? Questions like these guide us through Martial times, but only if we have the courage to ask them. Otherwise, ego either implodes into depression and a sense of "being a victim," or it explodes into waves of ignorant, arrogant, cowardly destructiveness.

Examples abound of acts of courage connected with the triggering effects of transiting Mars. Sally Ride flew the space shuttle with Mars transiting through a square to her Saturn. Courage (Mars) applied friction (square) to her sense of personal limitations (Saturn). Eugene Cernan, another astronaut, rode Gemini 9 into Earth orbit with Mars squaring his Moon—then took Apollo 17 to the base of the Taurus Mountains near the lunar crater Littrow six years later with Mars trining the same point. Thor Heyerdahl launched his famous Kon Tiki expedition on the day Mars opposed his Sun. Fear (Mars) challenged (opposition) his very identity (Sun). With Mars trining his Mercury and sextiling his Jupiter, Admiral Peary became the first human being to stand on the North Pole. Under those harmonious Martial aspects, courage (Mars) enhanced (trine) his intelligence (Mercury) and excited (sextile) his natural exuberance (Jupiter). The list of Mars-inspired acts of bravery goes on and on.

But there is a darker list, too. We saw in Chapter One how Ernest Hemingway committed suicide with Mars crossing his Ascendant, and in Chapter Three we observed how George Armstrong Custer met his fate at Little Big Horn while Mars was both opposing its own natal position and squaring Pluto, filling him with arrogance when he should have been feeling caution. Fidel Castro offers us a look at both sides of Mars. The red planet co-rules (with Pluto) his Scorpio Ascendant, so he is particularly sensitive to all its transits. After battling Batista's corrupt dictatorship of Cuba for many years, he marched triumphantly into Havana in January 1955, with Mars transiting through a square to his Sun. Later, with Mars conjuncting his Sun, he was perhaps not so courageous. He had foolishly allowed the Soviets to place nuclear missiles on his soil. The price he paid was the United States blockade of his ports during the infamous Cuban missile crisis—all of which could have been averted had he stood up to Soviet demands. One final example: With Mars passing through a square to his Sun, Salvador Allende, the elected president of Chile, was murdered and replaced by a brutal dictatorship in a shameful CIA-inspired coup. Was he simply an innocent victim of the red planet? I do not rule out such possibilities—but I have learned that so often some convenient slip on our own part sets the stage for Martial disasters. Could Allende have responded more decisively to the pressures he faced and perhaps saved his life and Chilean democracy? Given the circumstances, we may never know.

VENUS
Glyph: ♀
The Trigger: **The discerning of an opportunity for rest and regroup-**
                ing; the recognition of the possibility of aid arising
                from another person; the cementing of alliances.
Backfiring: **Lulled into lassitude, awareness dulls itself with**
                torpor and self-indulgence, seeking ego reinforcement
                while manipulating others with slickness, flattery,
                and charm.

If dodging Tricksters gets wearying sometimes, then stretching out under the guidance of a Teacher is plain exhausting. Although a

Teacher rewards our efforts, while a Trickster only robs us and mocks us, either way our emotional resources can be strained toward their limits. Even when those outer planet transits are heated up, there are breaks in the bombardment. When peaceful interludes arrive, we must be quick to recognize them. We need those breaks just as surely as we need sleep. If we fail to take full advantage of them, then we fail to refuel ourselves—and when the pressures return, our fatigue makes us more susceptible to the Trickster's wiles. How do we recognize those chances to regroup? We watch the transits of Venus. She is the goddess of peace, and if we cooperate, she triggers in us the process of **restoration and recovery**. Sometimes she accomplishes this by shaping circumstances in such a way that positive action becomes temporarily impossible. The ball is out of our court for a while. We might as well rest until it bounces back in again. Other times, Venus shows us another of her ancient identities: the goddess of the arts. She may offer a chance to restore and refresh ourselves through contact with beauty. A night at the theater, an evening listening to music, a morning walk in the dewy woods—or, even better, an idle afternoon spent with our watercolors or strumming our old guitar.

As the goddess of love, Venus brings yet another grace: We realize that we are not alone. These are times when we must turn to our allies. Friends. Our mate, if we've got one. Benevolent strangers. Why? Simple creature comfort is part of it. A hug, a kind word, an expression of concern or encouragement—none may be of direct practical value, but they do serve to soothe us and to strengthen our resolve. Masters of brainwashing and interrogation understand this well: when they want to break a spirit, solitary confinement is always a favored ploy. No matter how difficult a time we might be facing, the transits of Venus always show a break in that solitude—if we are willing to accept one. **Receptivity**—that is the key. Those allies often bring more than reassurance. Many times they bring wisdom, some new perspective or suggestion which lies outside the realm of our awareness. Without their input, we might, for example, spend hours searching our pockets when the papers we lost are actually out in the car where our friend saw us leave them. Perhaps what these allies have to say is threatening to us. Maybe it is simply unappealing. Whatever form it takes, Venus transits warn us that we don't have all the pieces to the puzzle we are trying to put together. If we want to complete it, we had better lie back, take a deep breath—and make an effort to be receptive to love and assistance.

How can the Venusian trigger turn sour? One way is that we simply fail to recognize it and it passes by, unused. We remain frantic or overextended, even though the chance for a much-needed rest is staring us in the face. Another risk is that out of pride we refuse to accept help, thereby consigning ourselves to a continued futile search of our pockets. Those are the passive responses to Venus, the ones in which we hurt ourselves only by refusing to help ourselves. There are bleaker possibilities. Venus can push us toward self-destructive extremes as we overreact to its call for a rest. In the midst of a tough week on the job, Venus may offer us a quiet night at home curled up with a cup of tea. We may instead stay out until the wee hours drinking Budweisers and smoking Camels, only to wake up the next morning more exhausted and devitalized than ever. We may also take foolish advantage of the magnetism or charm that the transits of Venus bestow on us, dissipating the chance to receive **real help** in a manipulative campaign to receive mere **ego reinforcement**. The transit passes, and instead of bailing our boat in the calm eye of the hurricane, we wasted the opportunity by preening before the mirror, checking to see that we had every hair in place. And before we know it, the wind is howling again, our hair is a mess . . . and our boat is sinking.

Albert Einstein's special theory of relativity was published in the summer of 1905. So deeply did it challenge the basis of our understanding of the universe that it produced very extreme reactions throughout the scientific world. The debate over the validity of his ideas went on for fourteen years—and would have gone on for fourteen centuries had not Einstein had allies who offered him a kind of support that he himself could not generate alone. A British expedition to the southern hemisphere was mounted. Its purpose was to study a solar eclipse in an effort to detect whether the sun's gravity could warp starlight that passed close to its blackened disk. If it did, then Einstein was correct. If not, then he was wrong. Einstein was, of course, vindicated, and his name became synonymous with genius the world over. What was going on for him astrologically at the time? Venus alone could not produce such a turning point. Like the other quick planets, it is only a trigger. Both transiting Pluto (the ability to affect history) and transiting Jupiter (triumph and opportunity) were fusing with Einstein's Ascendant (public personality) at the time of the eclipse, setting up a powerful field of **potential**, awaiting some kind of signal. Transiting Venus rushed into the same part of the zodiac— Einstein's early Cancer Ascendant—as the British expedition was setting up its equipment, and was just a few degrees past that point when the eclipse occurred—triggering the effects of Jupiter and Pluto through the Venusian tactic of affecting us through our ability to cooperate with allies.

Einstein shows us the other side of Venus in a rather humorous way. Hungry as he was to have his theories proven, he was distinctly unprepared for the fame that followed. The expedition kept its findings under wraps for a few months while the results were carefully checked. The eclipse had occurred in May 1919. In November, the announcement was formally made. Einstein, to his shock and dismay, "awoke to find himself famous," his peaceful, reclusive existence shattered forever. Pluto was still on his Ascendant, amplifying and accelerating his self-expression— but transiting Venus (personal magnetism) had now moved into an opposition (tension) to his Sun (identity and self-image). He reaped as he had sown, with Venus triggering the fame he unwittingly earned.

MERCURY
Glyph: ☿
The Trigger: **The opening of the mind to new possibilities; the active use of intelligence and logic; the stimulation of our willingness to learn.**
Backfiring: **Confused by its resistance to new information, the mind accelerates out of control, experiencing nervousness and a tendency to chatter and to flit about aimlessly.**

As the Teachers and Tricksters set their puzzles before us, one commodity becomes increasingly precious: information. The world "out there" is infinitely complex. Perhaps we will never fully fathom its mysteries. As we live, we build a second world, an inner, subjective one, modeled on the external world but differing from it in details, erring from the truth by whatever degree to which we have accepted and internalized falsehoods and by whatever information we lack. As much as we like to believe we are living in the real world, the actual fact is that the world we really live in is that second one, the mental world we have constructed. Jack and Jill have a date to go to the movies. Jack thinks Jill is angry. The truth is, she is quite pleased with **him**, but she has a headache she is not mentioning for fear of ruining their evening. He takes her quiet mood to be evidence of her anger and responds defensively, which makes her headache worse. The situation spirals out of control, all because of attitudes and actions based on their subjective models of the world, models that in this case have nothing to do with the objective truth.

How do we align the two worlds? The process is arduous and ongoing. Despite its obvious rewards, we often resist it. The mind must remain eager to learn, open to change and redefinition, hungry for new experiences. It must be wary of its instinctive tendency to pour energy into **defending old** models of the world instead of using it to **stretch into unprecedented new models**. The transits of Mercury over trigger points represent **mental crescendos** in this process of aligning ourselves with the objective truth.

When Mercury backfires, the mind becomes overwrought. We tend to get nervous. We chatter. We run around in circles, accomplishing very little. Why are we so frantic? Usually because we are resisting some critical new concept, desperately trying to hold together our old model of the world rather than allowing ourselves to flow into a clearer, more mature picture of life and of our place in it. One of the psyche's favorite tricks at this point is to talk . . . and talk and talk and talk. Even when no one is listening, the talk continues inwardly. It is as if we are attempting to maintain the outdated, erroneous description of our circumstances through the sheer force of language and repetition. That compulsive verbal litany works, too. The truth "out there" remains the same—but we often succeed in ignoring it, condemning ourselves to another cycle of pratfalls and unpleasant surprises.

Many of us have read Carlos Castaneda's books describing his work with the Yaqui Indian "sorcerer," don Juan. Castaneda's mental picture of life before his apprenticeship began was apparently a typical one for an academic anthropologist in the early 1960s—logical, linear and "reasonable." When he began his field work with don Juan on June 23, 1961, he was confronted with a view of life which was entirely alien and new to him. Mercury was involved, as we might suspect, but only as a trigger for far deeper events brewing in his chart. Some of those we will only understand when we are in a position to grasp the significance of **progressions**. But even through transits alone, evidence of some basic, enigmatic change is apparent. Pluto (the ability to make an impact on history) was fusing with Castaneda's Neptune (experiences of higher reality). Neptune itself was highly stimulated, having moved into a sextile (excitation) with its own natal position. And a confrontation with reality is indicated by a very special Saturn event which we will consider in detail in Chapter Seven—the ringed planet had completed precisely one circuit around his birthchart. Into that volatile, latent mixture marched Mercury. It triggered this remarkable turning point in Castaneda's life by transiting through an opposition to his Sun, placing tension (opposition) on the basis of his identity (Sun) by shocking him with a new and more complex level of information about life (Mercury). His vacillation between acceptance and rejection of don Juan's picture of the world is a case study in both the triggering and backfiring effects of Mercury.

SUN

Glyph: ☉

The Trigger: **The ego itself confronts the world — or vice versa.**

Backfiring: **Stubborn pride, selfishness, and conservatism spoil an opportunity to move forward in both our outward circumstances and in our inner life.**

Transits of the Sun give us perhaps our purest, most undistorted view of the elements of our birthchart. Whatever the Sun touches is simply **emphasized in our awareness** by the contact. Although the Sun has its particular significance just like the other nine planets—the formation of identity—that significance is so broad that it seems to exist in a category all its own. Just as the Sun is so distinct from the planets astronomically, it plays a unique role astrologically as well, representing the raw impulse of life that is taken and channeled into nine mental "circuits," stimulating and vivifying them into existence. When the transiting Sun hits a trigger point, it is as if all the intensity of our life force were focused on that particular dimension of existence. Why then is the Sun relegated to being a mere triggering influence? This sounds grander, more like the stuff of Tricksters and Teachers. It most certainly would be, except for one tragic flaw—the Sun moves too fast for its transits to build up the depth and complexity of meaning characteristic of the passages of the slower planets. Its journey around the chart takes only one year. It remains within the orbs of an aspect only for a couple of weeks at the outside.

The best way to view the transits of the Sun is to think of them as a big, celestial searchlight. It plays a hyperintense **beam of self-awareness** over us, cutting through the overlapping webs of planetary trigger points spread throughout the chart. Whatever part of the mind it hits is temporarily centralized in the ego, occupying our attention and expressing its needs. With solar transits, ego plays its hand, for better or worse. It might, for example, trigger our Jupiter. Perhaps we have been keeping that part of our planetary makeup reasonably healthy lately. We are fully extended into the world, not arrogant but quietly assured and confident of ourselves. Then, during that solar transit across Jupiter, we feel bright and expansive. We take some positive step, and the world responds, sending around a limousine for us. On the other hand, perhaps we have allowed ourselves to develop an arrogant attitude—a Jupiter disease. The Sun hits, and that arrogance is hung out like so much dirty laundry. Or maybe we had a different Jupiter problem—an underinflated ego. The Sun brings that out in the open, too. We finally express our irritation with those who have been "bossing us around," perhaps giving everyone a guided tour of the chip we have been concealing on our shoulder.

Henry David Thoreau began his famous retreat to Walden Pond very close to his birthday (under a conjunction of the transiting Sun with his natal Sun, in other words). The crisis of identity (Sun) that had been simmering within him came to the surface and demanded some expression into the world of action.

MOON
Glyph: ☽
The Trigger: Unintegrated, repressed, or misunderstood emotions
                 demand expression and inclusion in the conscious
                 mind; wholeness is restored.
Backfiring: Moodiness overwhelms us; shadowy, childish
                 dimensions of our character temporarily usurp control
                 of our behavior.

Transits of the Moon are rarely dramatic in an outward sense. It is unusual for them to trigger events of lasting importance. Consistent with the law that creates the distinctions between slow, theme-weaving planets and quick, triggering ones, the transits of the Moon, being the fastest of all, have very little time to generate deep meaning. The Moon might, for example, stay within the orbs of a sensitive aspect for about twelve hours—hardly enough time for truly profound realizations to gel within us. Can we ignore the Moon's transits? If our focus is on major developments in a person's life, the answer is probably yes. But if we want to observe the second-by-second **microstructure** of personal growth, an understanding of the Moon is indispensable. The transits of the Moon illuminate the daily impact of the unconscious mind upon the ego, of soul upon personality. The Moon, as always, symbolizes our emotions—and emotions are the telegraph line that links us to all the fragmented and suppressed psychological material that arises as we streamline ourselves enough to cope effectively with daily experience. Watch the Moon's transits carefully, and they help you stay in touch with the parts of yourself that get "left out" as you make the inevitable emotional compromises of adult life.

Is there some sense of joy or personal triumph you have been too busy to sit back and feel? When the Moon passes over your Jupiter or your Venus, you will be humming a blissful tune while you do the dishes and carry out the garbage. Why? Because you are in the process of **integrating into consciousness** a happy emotion that you have not yet fully accepted. The pattern is always the same: Ego and feelings tend to get out of line with each other. It is the Moon's job to bring them back into harmony.

Historical examples of the Moon's action are difficult to find. Its tone is unremittingly subjective, having little to do with outward events and everything to do with **what those events mean to us**. By its very nature, the Moon is **irrational**, often bringing out distinctly childish dimensions of our character. Create your own examples. Watch the Moon's transit around your birthchart. It passes over all your trigger points once each month, never allowing the gap between conscious and unconscious to have time to grow wide. Monitor your feelings, especially when they seem to be pulling at you, forcing you into a mood—a strong mood of any sort is always a sure indicator of lunar activity in the birthchart—and then correlate that mood with the position of the transiting Moon. Soon you will have a solid grasp on this most mysterious and evanescent of the astrological forces.

CHAPTER FIVE

TRANSITS III: THE CYCLE OF HOUSES

So far, we have paid little attention to the houses of the birthchart. In transits just as in birthchart work, houses supply the same pivotal piece of information: **Where** is that sign-planet dynamic being released? As always, they refer to actual **arenas** of life—work, marriage, family, and so on.

Take a look at figure 1. Here we have a graphic representation of the twelve houses as they appear on every birthchart, along with a key word or two for the meaning of each segment.

How are houses affected by transits? (Toward the end of this chapter, we'll spell out the interpretive process step by step, but for now let's look at a simple example.) Mars might pass through a conjunction with your Arian Mercury. We know from previous chapters that such a passage temporarily **fuses** (conjunction) an element of **assertiveness** with your already rather forceful **style of communication** (Arian Mercury). That much we understand without reference to house symbolism. Now, **where will that verbal assertiveness appear?** To answer that question, look to the house position of the conjunction. Is it in the tenth house (career and communal role)? Then that transit is connected with your public life. You might have a confrontation with someone at work or speak out at a city council

The Twelve Houses

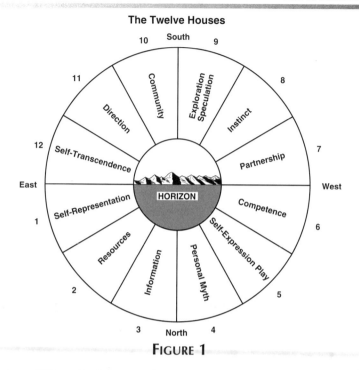

FIGURE 1

meeting. What if the conjunction occurs in your second house (personal resources)? Now the scene shifts: instead of career, we recognize that the Martial trigger is affecting a particularly touchy area—your self-confidence, and perhaps your wallet. During the few days in which the transit is in effect, a situation arises in which you must assert yourself verbally **to prove yourself to yourself**, but you must be cautious about coming across as if you had a chip on your shoulder.

If we shape the probability curves in our favor during a given transit, turning the planet into our Teacher, then the houses involved tell us where to expect our reward. But if we are not alert enough to avoid the Trickster, then the transit symbolizes something like a disease process within us—and the houses tell us where to expect its symptoms.

Apart from conjunctions, all transits involve two houses. The natal planet lies in one house, and since the nearest major trigger point, the sextile, lies 60 degrees away, the transiting planet must be in a different house. (There are occasional exceptions for people born at very high latitudes.) Thus most transits link two distinct and unrelated **wheres**, tying them together for a period of days or perhaps years.

Have a look at figure 2. A woman has Venus in the fifth house of her birthchart. If she is to be all that she is capable of being, then her

creative instincts (Venus) must learn to manifest themselves concrete-
ly (houses!) in the department of life we call **self-expression,
performance, and enjoyment** (fifth house). In other words, her
Venusian sense of harmony and balance should express itself fluidly
and effectively in her **behavior**. Let's say she has made a strong
response to that birthchart configuration—she is a painter. One
summer, transiting Jupiter enters her ninth house ("long journeys over
water") and makes a trine to her fifth-house Venus. Some **opportunity**
(Jupiter) of a ninth house nature (travel, education) arises and
enhances the potential (trine) of her Venus. Perhaps she is offered a
scholarship to study painting in Italy. Does she take advantage of it?
Only if she lets Jupiter be her Teacher, recognizing and seizing the
chance he has given her. If she allows him to show his darker face, then
she lets the **opportunity slip through her fingers**, lulled by the
peacefulness of the trine and by the overconfidence of Jupiter, probably
convincing herself that such scholarships are now to be expected often
or that she was too advanced to benefit from the teaching. Either way,
ninth house possibilities become relevant to her fifth house Venus—
for a few weeks. After that, those linkages disappear.

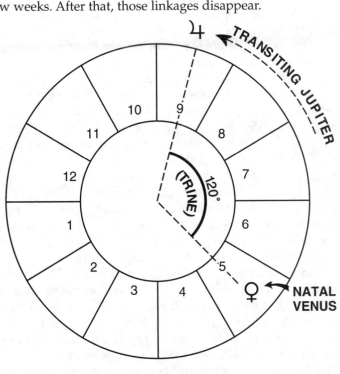

FIGURE 2

CYCLICAL PATTERNS

A cycle is any fixed pattern of development that repeats itself over a period of time. For example when a baby is born, he or she enters the human life cycle. Barring unexpected events, that child grows, enters adulthood, experiences midlife followed by old age, and then finally dies. Those are the phases of the aging process. What we do with them is open to endless variation, but the phases themselves do not change. Similarly, each planet has an orbital cycle, passing through the signs— or phases—of the zodiac in an essentially regular way. Taurus follows Aries, Aries follows Pisces, and so on. Planets must traverse them in that order. Retrogradation may complicate the pattern a bit, but those complications are only ripples on the surface. The basic pattern remains as immutable as our own physical aging. In Chapter Six, we explore these planetary cycles in detail. Now we must recognize something even more basic: The houses themselves represent the primary developmental cycle inherent in any life process. As we follow a given planet through the twelve houses, we observe a cyclical pattern of phases common to the passages of any other planet. The transits of Mercury, of course, express those developmental steps on a **mental** level, those of Neptune, on a **spiritual** or **psychic** level. The mental function differs, but the steps remain the same, just as certainly as thin hair follows thick in the course of human life.

In *The Inner Sky*, houses were presented in a static way. Each one was seen as representing a particular **terrain**. If you were born with a planet there, then throughout your life you were bound to that terrain, although hopefully your navigation of it would become more successful over the years. That viewpoint is fine—so long as we limit ourselves to the study of birthcharts. As soon as we enter predictive astrology, everything changes. Each house, whether or not we have a planet there in our birthchart, plays at least a passing role in our experiences. By moving through empty houses, temporarily enlivening them, transiting planets often face us with opportunities and challenges that have little to do directly with our birthcharts. The "shrinking violet" sooner or later is faced with a roomful of people whom she must address. At some point, the "rascal" collides with a situation in which he must make some kind of moral statement—or lose all dignity and self-respect. Those events may have relatively small impact on the whole life pattern—they are not part of the "root prediction"—but they do occur. What significance do they have? Typically, their work is to set the stage for later events that are more closely related to the birthchart. They are phases in the developmental cycle, and the lessons they teach prepare a person to navigate richer, more directly relevant terrains later on.

There are three critical concepts to remember here:

> ☆ As a planet cycles through the houses of the birthchart, it faces us with a cumulative developmental process composed of twelve critical phases.

> ☆ If we respond successfully to the issues a planet raises as it transits through one house, we are prepared to respond effectively to the issues it raises in the next house.

> ☆ If we fail to respond effectively, then the cycle partially aborts and the expression of its subsequent phases is weaker, in proportion to the degree of our failure.

Those three ideas are the heart of our understanding of houses in predictive astrology. Think of it like this: A woman is born with the **potential** to be a great violinist. The mere existence of that potential, however, offers no guarantees. Before the woman can even begin to express herself on that level, she must **grow up**, passing successfully through the preliminary developmental phases of the human life cycle. She must, for example, gain control of her body. She must learn to read. She must develop some degree of self-confidence. On and on. Each phase is essential. Each one must be navigated. In each, the possibility of failure exists—and if that failure is radical, then there is no hope for the expression of the potential with which she was born. Houses operate the same way. Success in the second house does not guarantee success in the third, but rather creates the **possibility** of success there.

Let's take another look at the astrological houses, seeing them in a different way than we did in *The Inner Sky*, not as isolated territories to be navigated, but as the tightly interlocked phases of life's most elemental cycle.

THE FIRST HOUSE

Phase: **Beginnings; emergence; renaissance.**
Process: **Invention; improvisation; creation.**
Ally: **Courage.**
Abort Sequence: **Collapse under pressure, followed by shell shock
                  and self-abandonment.**

(Note: The first house follows the twelfth and cannot be understood
fully outside that context. You might read this section again in a few
minutes, after you have read through the others.)

Consciousness faces a blank slate. Nothing exists but the urge
to create a new reality or a new set of circumstances, independent,
unprecedented, and discontinuous with the past. The first house
period is necessarily a "selfish" time, oriented around ego and the power
of the will. It symbolizes a time of radically enhanced **freedom**—and
freedom is always synonymous with uncertainty. We do not know
exactly what we are doing, but we feel a compulsion to act, we feel
urgency. During this phase of the life process, we are aware of our
power—but we often have no clear sense of how it should be used. A
new beginning is crystallizing in our lives. We have a tiger by the tail.
All we can do is hang on and trust our intuition to guide us, all the
while remembering that in the first house period, **action is everything**.
We are planting the seeds of a new cycle of experience—a new
identity—whose full nature will only be revealed gradually as we
move through the subsequent houses.

One morning you wake up sensing that something is wrong. Odd
yellow light is flickering on the other side of your closed eyelids. You
open them. Torches. A drafty medieval chamber. Someone approaches
you deferentially. "Good morning, your Highness." Uh oh. You went to
bed as a waitress in Chicago. You have awakened as the Queen of
England. What do you do? You improvise! You pretend. You fake it.
You act as if you **believed** you were the queen. Why? Because that is
the reality in which you now find yourself. Adapting to it is
disconcerting and stressful—but failing to adapt is unthinkable. If you
start babbling about being a waitress from Chicago, you will be doing
ten-to-twenty in the Tower of London before you can say *Twilight Zone*.
Later, perhaps, there will be time to reflect on what has happened. Now
the pace and pressure of events prevent that. Now all energy must be
directed into the adaptive process of **reinventing yourself**. That is
precisely how the first house period in any planetary cycle feels.

By its very nature, this process of creating a "new self" always feels unnatural. No more waiting on tables. You are the queen now. The King of Spain has proposed an alliance. He wants an answer. Today. It's exhilarating—and scary.

THE SECOND HOUSE

Phase: Solidification; sustainment; momentum.
Process: Follow-through; building inner and outer
                    resources; gaining confidence.
Ally: Conviction.
Abort Sequence: The loss of nerve, followed by retreat into the past.

    The first house phase is a roller coaster. Everything is happening so quickly that we have little time to deliberate about it. We are busy—and we are also improvising as we go along. Between the two, our days are very full. By the time we arrive at the second house, the dust has settled. We are beginning to feel more comfortable within the new patterns. Being the Queen of England is starting to feel natural to us— and suddenly we have the luxury of becoming terrified. We are threatened by a massive failure of nerve. "Oh my God, what have I gotten myself into?!!" We feel like an impostor in our new role. We question ourselves, feeling awkward and uncertain. Often we look back longingly at the security of the past—even to the security of a thoroughly miserable past. "How I miss getting up at four A.M. to serve those omelets!" Sometimes our self-questioning leads to an obsessive desire for guarantees, such as money and prestige. Whatever happens, we must **keep going**. There is no returning to times gone by. As much as we may long for it, that door is closed behind us. We must **follow through** on what we have begun. How? By establishing a **resource base**—both inwardly and outwardly—appropriate to our new circumstances. Sometimes the ancient "House of Money" notions come into play here—we rearrange our finances to accommodate our new direction. Other times, those confidence-enhancing resources take the form of advisors and patrons, or perhaps of inward, attitudinal changes supported by new skills and tools we acquire. Conviction and confidence are the keys—we must prove ourselves to ourselves, convincingly and beyond the shadow of a doubt.

THE THIRD HOUSE

Phase:	Reconnaissance; information gathering.
Process:	Becoming aware of the environment; searching; asking questions.
Ally:	Curiosity.
Abort Sequence:	Overextension, followed by dissipation and loss of focus.

If our passage through the second house has been a successful one, we are now filled with a sense of legitimacy and authority. We have proven ourselves to ourselves. We now become curious and communicative, eager to learn—and eager to teach. Restlessness and mental activity become dominant features of character. The third house phase is typically a busy period, full of new ideas, interesting strangers, and much moving about in the world.

Although we are rarely conscious of much more than a dramatically heightened level of activity in our lives, our larger self understands that its new vehicle of expression is fully functional and that it must now seek some kind of purpose or direction. But where? The old formulas have failed—that was what the first house phase was all about. No clear answer emerges, so awareness takes the only logical step: it casts about **at random**, trying to get a taste of everything. The strategy is effective—but its danger is that we can overextend ourselves to the point of nervous exhaustion. Many times, if we go down that road, we end up releasing our tension through aimless chattering and obsessive, pointless activity.

THE FOURTH HOUSE

Phase:	Strategic withdrawal; immersion in the deep self.
Process:	Attunement to the roots of awareness.
Ally:	Feelings.
Abort Sequence:	Emotional self-indulgence, followed by psychic paralysis.

In the third house, we exist in a universe defined by **information**. In the fourth, we enter one defined by **feelings**. We turn inward, seeking our psychic roots. The trouble is, we can become so entranced by our own inner conundrums that we forget to live. Even if our navigation is sound, we still must now enter a protracted period of self-administered psychoanalysis. We are trying to discover what our souls have become.

We rummage through the memories we have stored up through the first three phases. "Heros" and "Shadows"—those inflated wishes and fears we met in *The Inner Sky*—emerge into awareness. Often we are drawn back into deep contact with our families at this time; once again, the search for roots is the theme. Although we may not understand it, we are in the process of recreating a myth of ourselves, a constellation of basic values, visions, and inspirations that will underlie and motivate all our actions in the remaining eight phases. To accomplish that, we need peace and quiet. We must to some extent, withdraw from the world. Invariably we cut back on the frenetic activity of the previous phase. Either way, in outward terms, the fourth phase is an obscure period—but in the life of the mind, it is a pivotal one.

THE FIFTH HOUSE

Phase: **Self-expression; self-revelation; psychic refueling.**
Process: **Playful, unpremeditated celebration of self.**
Ally: **Spontaneity.**
Abort Sequence: **Debauchery and ego tripping, followed by**
                   self-loss in a maze of childish personal dramas.

Fertilized by our contact with the deep self in the fourth phase, we are now hungry to **reveal what our souls have become**. In the fifth house, we begin to **create**—and that creativity takes the form not only of art, but also of flamboyance and playfulness. The time has come to **celebrate ourselves**. How? By creating outward, visible symbols of the inner terrains we explored in the fourth house. Suddenly we appear with a sportscar or a sailboat or a fancy French cookbook.

Many times, new friends or lovers—our "playmates"—come into our lives at this point, helping us break our addiction to the past. Don't let the word "playmate" fool you into thinking our business with these people is not profound. **Playfulness** is our key now, and it is something we must relearn. Only in **playful spontaneity** can our crusty egos allow new material to break through the walls of habit and routine. Although our active relationships with these playmates are often brief, their task is a critical one: they encourage our spontaneous, unselfconscious self-revelation. They help us do what children do instinctively—that is, to use play to prepare ourselves mentally for "adulthood." They are our cheerleaders. If we accept their help, they midwife us out of the fourth house womb and send us spiraling onward out of our "childhood."

THE SIXTH HOUSE

Phase: Acquisition of skill; submission to larger purpose.
Process: Learning to be useful.
Ally: Competence.
Abort Sequence: Sense of inadequacy, followed by drudgery and resentment.

In the sixth house, we react against the essentially selfish orientation of the fifth phase. Again, consciousness is filled with restlessness, seeking some larger framework of significance. We begin to hunger for **meaningful responsibilities** rooted in what we have learned in the previous five phases. We are filled with a desire to **express a new level of competence**. The sixth house represents a deep crisis: pure self-interest no longer sustains us, and whatever we have been avoiding facing in ourselves tends to catch up with us. That ego-oriented universe has become too narrow. We begin to recognize that we are dependent upon other people for the maintenance of our own identity and self-respect. We stretch beyond the narcissistic preoccupations of the fifth house, seeking to establish lasting relationships by making ourselves necessary to others—or we fail and descend into drudgery, trying to earn love but only creating resentment and contempt. That type of relationship-forming strategy is a crude one in many ways, but it sets the stage for the deeper alliances that arise in the next phase. How? By offering us two gifts that make the sustainment of loving relationships between adults possible: humility and a sense of responsibility. There is something tentative here, something that feels uncertain, like a prelude. Often the sixth house echoes the second house in that once again we are full of uncertainties and questions regarding our own ultimate value. Generally this phase involves a lot of plain hard work and self-sacrifice as we begin to share all that we have learned in the first half of the house cycle—and to prepare to crash through the barrier into the second half.

□ □ □

THE SEVENTH HOUSE

Phase:	Cooperation; interdependency; recognition of the "other."
Process:	Selection and establishment of long-term partnerships.
Ally:	Love.
Abort Sequence:	Addiction to another person, followed by loss of self.

The second hemicycle begins. What was hinted in the sixth phase now becomes clear: From now on in the cycle of houses, the narrow framework of ego-oriented personality is insufficient. Other realities, usually symbolized by other people, begin to nourish our growth. In the seventh house, we recognize our **inability to make further progress alone**. We are stuck. The insights we created in the first six phases may be good ones, but they do not add up to an answer. What can we do? **We must learn to love**. New partners enter our lives now—and standing relationships are called into scrutiny, reevaluated. We create—or recreate—lasting bonds with life partners, people whom we can count upon to remain with us for extended periods, serving as reliable sources of support, understanding, and **insights into ourselves that we could never generate alone**. The people we meet now are distinguished from our fifth phase "playmates" in that these seventh house bonds are less "giddy;" they feel normal and familiar, almost from the beginning. Compared to fifth house contacts, they involve less insecurity—less need for assurance and reassurance—and do not falter over mundane issues such as determining whose task it is to take out the garbage or do the dishes.

Recognizing our need for honest, equal partnerships is the first step, and the humbling crises of the sixth house prepare us to take it, helping us to move past the ego-oriented perspectives of the fifth house. The second step is to learn to pick out our natural allies. Who are they? Most of us have fallen in love from time to time, only to look back in befuddlement at the choice we made. Often, in retrospect, we realize we experienced a subjective need for partnership, then pasted that feeling right over the face of some convenient target. In the seventh house, we must confront that problem. The essence of this phase of the cycle is to develop the capacity to **see other people clearly**, free from the addictions and distortions introduced by our own needs and fears, while never losing track of our own identity. Romance can be a legitimate part of the seventh house, but the essential lessons are **respect, acceptance, real communication**—and inevitably, **compromise**.

THE EIGHTH HOUSE

Phase: Integration; intensification of feelings; psychic
                    housecleaning.
Process: Absorption of psychological undercurrents.
Ally: Honesty.
Abort Sequence: Resistance, denial, and fear, followed by mental
                    depression.

Paralleling the processes of the fourth phase, our awareness once again turns inward, seeking revitalization and self-validation in the labyrinths of the unconscious. But now those labyrinths run deeper. We face a spiderweb of inner dimensions that are at once extremely personal and yet also universal. We enter the realm of **instincts**—and often their emergence fills us with moodiness and brooding. Material conveniently "left out" of our field of attention during the previous seven phases now arises, often tempestuously. We become aware of our own motivations and psychological ambiguities as never before.

As astrologer Stephen Arroyo has pointed out, the eighth house process often feels like a passage through purgatory—which, in a sense, is exactly what this house represents. We are being purged. By this phase in the cycle, ego has become strong—maybe too strong. No longer the feeble, uncertain creature of the first few houses, it now has the dangerous capacity not only to lie to itself, but successfully to sustain a lie. The eighth phase cannot always cure that problem—we can resist the deep material and descend instead into a period of depression. The point is to **realign personality with its roots in the unconscious mind**, and our greatest ally in that process is the courage to be honest with ourselves and face the legitimate growing pains of deepening maturity.

All instinctive psychological processes come to the forefront emotionally at this point in the cycle. For example, those bonds of love we formed in the seventh house deepen now, and are tested. If they survive, we are **imprinted** on the other person, thereby encountering the power and true meaning of the sexual instinct. We also become instinctively aware of our place in the aging process, and therefore develop a gut level awareness of our own mortality. Sometimes deaths occur around us during this period, serving as reminders that life gives us little time to waste playing games with ourselves or others. Often we tune into latent dimensions of spiritual or extrasensory awareness at this phase, instinctively sensing that there is more to this life than meets the eye. Always the eighth house theme is the same: You are ready now for a taste of **wisdom**, but you must purchase it with courage.

THE NINTH HOUSE

Phase: **Expansion; exploration; education; the attainment of perspective.**
Process **Breaking up routines.**
Ally: **A sense of wonder.**
Abort Sequence: **Dogmatic rigidity, followed by stultifying boredom.**

In the film, *Coal Miner's Daughter*, Sissy Spacek, playing the role of Loretta Lynn, is accused of being stupid. Her petulant retort is, "I'm not stupid. I'm ignorant." Very much the same sentiment fills us as we leave the claustrophobic, close-focus atmosphere of the eighth house and enter the expansive terrain of the ninth. Once again, consciousness has been fertilized by its passage through one of the "deep" houses. In the fourth phase, we made contact with the more personal parts of the unconscious mind—and that led to bursting creativity and self-expression in the fifth phase. Now, after passing through the more explosive, compulsive territory of the eighth house, we emerge hungry for nothing less than a **quest for vision**. What does life mean? What is my ultimate purpose? What is Right—and what is Wrong? We may not know the answers, but we are ready to dispel our ignorance.

Boredom—often that is the dominant mood after the relentless self-scrutiny of the eighth house. We are tired of psychology, tired of mental mazes. We want something larger, more substantial. We fear it, too—change is always spooky.

Assuming our navigation is successful, the ninth phase is a time of stretching and exploration. Often we travel. Frequently we educate ourselves. Almost invariably, we encounter fascinating people from outside our normal circles—"foreigners"—who face us with novel, challenging ideas. In the eighth phase we purged ourselves of unprocessed mental residues left over from earlier periods. Now, in the ninth phase, we are ready to break up the time-worn routines of action and thought that those residues created. **Make it new**—that is the spirit of this house. We need a broader perspective. The time has come for us to recover our sense of wonder. Our task, in a nutshell, is to let life amaze us.

□ □ □

THE TENTH HOUSE

Phase: **Empowerment; declaration; going public.**
Process: **Interfacing self and community.**
Ally: **Integrity.**
Abort Sequence: **Pretense, followed by entrapment in a limiting role.**

With our ninth house education behind us, we are now ready to play a more direct part in the process of society. We have skills. We have a supportive network of relationships. We have a set of values. The time has come for us to "get a job," or to make some public, communal statement of our identity. Often there is an emphasis upon career development, but the scope of the house is larger than our professional concerns. It takes in the entire concept of **community** and our role in it. Who are you? That is the question, provided we remember the viewpoint from which it is asked. Our intimate friends might have one answer. But now the inquiry is coming from the community as a **whole**. While career is typically the tenth house focal point, I have often seen people get married under tenth house transits. Their **relationship** may have formed under seventh house influences, but their marriage ceremony is a statement to the community—tenth house material. Any rite of passage that requires public observation for it to be meaningful immediately places our attention on this house. Whether that rite of passage involves praise and recognition or rebellion against social norms is irrelevant; **public visibility** is the key. This is a time of blossoming. Whatever private, inward inspiration germinated within us back in the first phase must now come out in the open, make its stand, and face its reviews.

THE ELEVENTH HOUSE

Phase: **Self-direction; goal setting; the establishment of strategic alliances.**
Process: **Pathfinding.**
Ally: **Clearly defined priorities.**
Abort Sequence: **Hesitation to choose, followed by drifting.**

The cycle of personality development we have traced through the previous houses culminates here. The eleventh house represents a time of completion. Long ago, back in the first phase, we set goals for ourselves—but we would have been hard-pressed to define them clearly then. They were intuitive feelings. Now, having established our public identity in the tenth house, we experience a sense of fullness, of self-knowledge. Our first phase improvisations have now crystallized; we play a known role with poise and assurance. The future opens up before us, and in a sense, our dreams are coming true. Subjectively, the experience is not like that—the eleventh house doesn't feel dreamy— but that is precisely what is happening. If we dared, back in the first phase, to dream only small dreams, then the fruits we taste now may be meager. If our dreams were larger and we stuck with them through the previous houses, then this is a time of applause and rewards—and of critical decisions. Where will we go next? Now that we have this power, how will we use it? Simply "growing up" was a full-time job, enough to absorb us. Now that we have attained maturity, now that all these expectant eyes rest upon us, where will we commit our energy? Decisions. Goals. Strategies. "Now that you have your Ph.D., what's next?"

Answers to such questions must come straight from the heart. Only we alone can determine what overriding goals and values will shape our lives. Setting priorities—that is the skill we must develop in this phase. How important is honor and prestige? Where does the balance lie between family life and professional advancement? These are decisions that hammer out the broad contours of a life—and they are the choices we face in the eleventh house.

Strategic alliances play a critical role here. We determine our goals alone—but we often require assistance to attain them. Typically, such assistance comes from people who share those same aims. Whomever we meet, the eleventh house phase represents a time of guidance received and guidance given, carrying us closer and closer to the full realization of what we began so vigorously—and with such naivete— in the first house.

THE TWELFTH HOUSE

Phase: **Dissolution; surrender; self-transcendence.**
Process: **Letting go.**
Ally: **A sense of the eternal.**
Abort Sequence: **A terror of change and of psychic nakedness, followed by bitterness, confusion, and escapism.**

If the Force-That-Shaped-the-Universe were a middle-of-the-road psychologist, there would be only eleven astrological houses. The cycle would end there. We would have done what we set out to do, having "realized the meaning and purpose of life" by creating a self-actualized identity, operating within a network of healthy relationships, adjusted to sexual realities, and comfortably and creatively integrated into the community. What more could there be—to a middle-of-the-road psychologist? But that life-shaping Force plays by different rules; it has one more trick up its sleeve, one more house for us to experience. Now that we have sweated and strained to create that self-actualized identity, we must let it go. We must recognize that each of the eleven phases had only one ultimate purpose, and that **was to create some permanent change in the quality of our awareness**. All the outer events were just phantasmagoria, insignificant in and of themselves, useful only in that they changed us.

What a shock! In the twelfth phase, the rug is pulled out from under ego. What ego thought was important turns out to be empty, only a joke. The prize it earned with such labor, the prize it was finally awarded in the eleventh house, now lies in the gutter—unwanted and unlamented. What has happened? We have **outgrown** the goal we set for ourselves in the first phase! Now that the goal is attained, it no longer has any meaning for us. Why? Because the point was the process itself, not the attainment of the goal. Attainment is anticlimax—that is the twelfth house formula. And to ego, it is the ultimate rip-off.

Do we have to **be** ego? If so, then the medievals named the twelfth house well when they called it the House of Troubles. But we are more than that. We are also the **consciousness that observes the dramas of ego**, absorbing them reflectively, distilling them into wisdom . . . then, their usefulness spent, forgetting them. If we have that **sense of the eternal** within us, then the twelfth house period is a rich one, "the last for which the first was made." But if we try to cling to dying circumstances and to an old myth of ourselves, then it is a painful, confusing time. We are at the end point of the cycle: we need privacy. If we interact with the world at this time, we are often absentminded and prone to foolish accidents. Our heart is elsewhere, drawn back into the depths. The flower has bloomed, now it withers, falls from the vine. But deep in the earth, in the roots, something is stirring, moving, breathing.

(Note: Now that you've seen all twelve houses, take a minute to go back and reread the material about the first phase. Astrologically, life isn't an endless line; it's an endlessly spiraling circle.)

HOUSES IN PRACTICE

Two factors shape our practical application of all that we have learned about the cycle of houses. The first is the **nature of the planet** passing through them; the second is **how quickly that planet is moving**. Knowing the nature of the planet tells us what part of our character is facing the lessons of each phase. If Saturn, for example, transits into your twelfth house, then your Saturn function **as you have defined it** has outlived its usefulness to you; there is something too fixed about your self-discipline and something too stable and limiting in your assumptions about reality (Saturn stuff). Those old patterns will not help you any longer—they have entered the twelfth phase of their cycle—but you are probably quite accustomed to them, inclined to take them for granted automatically and without thinking. Until you recognize and eliminate those outworn dimensions of your behavior, you are prey for Saturn the Trickster. His lie, as always, is "you can't win"—and until you change, he is right. Your capacity for discipline has gone awry; your sense of reality has holes in it. Perhaps you are working too hard, disciplining yourself too rigidly, smashing your head against walls which no longer lie across your path. The walls haven't changed—but your path has. You must allow yourself temporarily to surrender, to gather perspective on your Saturn functions, **recognizing that certain trusted patterns of behavior in that department are now burned out, running on vapor and momentum, and ready to be reabsorbed and redefined.**

Saturn is a slow planet, taking twenty-nine years to complete a circuit of the houses—and that leads us to our second critical factor: speed. As we learned in chapter 2, the more slowly a planet moves, the longer its transits have to build depth and complexity of meaning. That same law applies to their passages through the houses. The slow planets generate basic themes as they gradually phase through the cycle, while the quick ones work on the surface of life, triggering events that help us crystallize the messages of the theme-weavers. Even if our life is long, Saturn's orbit allows it only three passages through each house—and each passage is of profound significance. Pluto is even slower. In a typical lifetime it touches maybe four houses—and knowing **which** four, and **when** each one is entered, tells us much about changes in the larger framework of meaning (Pluto) upon which that person must invariably hang the fabric of his or her destiny.

In contrast to the ponderous rhythms of the outer planets, the inner ones sparkle and dance like fireflies. The Moon slips around the entire circuit in just a month, averaging only two and a half days in each house. One day, we feel (Moon) energized, ready to start new projects (first house). A couple of days later we are following through on what we began (second house). Then we get restless and curious for a couple more days (third phase), followed by a brief mood of withdrawal and reflection (fourth). We emerge from a quiet Wednesday and Thursday, ready to play (fifth house) on the weekend. Monday brings responsibilities (sixth house). Wednesday we have lunch with an old friend (seventh house). The next couple of days we are withdrawn, brooding over some complicated feelings that old friend brought up in us (eighth house). Those feelings unraveled at least partly, we now feel the urge to stretch out and do something different—with the moon in the ninth house, we skip our favorite television show one evening and go for a long, random walk through town. It clears our head. We figure something out, gaining perspective—and two days later, with the Moon in the tenth house, we write a letter to the editor about a toxic waste dump near town. Next, all fired up about that letter, we join a citizen's group worried about the dump (eleventh house). Finally, with the Moon in the twelfth house, we put a dent in our car—and that jogs us into realizing that while that waste dump is a serious problem, some of our passion over it stemmed from unprocessed anger at our old friend. Admitting that is humbling, but we are soon filled with a desire to make ourselves new . . . (first house again).

If you live a normal lifespan, you will pass through that lunar cycle about nine hundred times. Each time the dramas are different, yet like any cycle, the core phases remain constant. Only your level of self-awareness changes—that, and the larger environment of meaning created by the transits of the slower planets. In our example, great emphasis was placed upon that conversation over lunch with the old friend. Why? Perhaps Jupiter and Uranus had just entered your seventh house, signaling a period of expanded horizons (Jupiter) and rebellious redefinition (Uranus) in your intimate relationships (seventh house). A tremendous potential was brewing in you; the Moon came along and triggered it—and the whole lunar house cycle that month is flavored by the far more momentous entry of two slow planets into a new phase of their far longer cycle.

TRIGGER POINTS IN HOUSES

Each house contains a web of highly charged trigger points. When a planet contacts one, a button is pressed and events occur that reflect and illuminate the meaning of that phase of the cycle. These trigger points come in three varieties: those created by aspects to other planets in other houses; those symbolized by natal planets that actually lie in the house; and finally, the very critical trigger point symbolized by the **cusp** of the house itself. Each of these needs to be understood before we are ready to leave the subject of house symbolism.

The first variety of trigger points—aspectual ones—were the

subjects of Chapters Two and Three. As we learned at the beginning of
this chapter, houses simply add precision to what we learned earlier.
They help us define where those passing planetary configurations are
unfolding. Now that we have a deeper grasp of houses, we can
amplify that understanding.

Refer back to Figure 2 (page 73) for a moment. There we see
transiting Jupiter hitting a trigger point in a woman's ninth house—
arriving at a point that trines her natal fifth house Venus. Perhaps a
little bit farther on, that transiting planet hits another trigger point, this
time linking it temporarily to her Ascendant through another trine.
Thus, when Jupiter moves through that part of her ninth house terrain,
it almost simultaneously triggers her Ascendant through the process
of harmonization or enhancement. Deeper in her ninth house, that
transiting Jupiter might make a square to her Cancer Moon in her natal
twelfth. Later still, it might sextile her eleventh house Neptune,
stimulating that dimension of her basic character by creating Jupiter
events of a ninth house nature that are temporarily relevant to her
permanent eleventh house Neptune issues.

With ten planets, each one casting a net of seven distinct aspectual
trigger points throughout the birthchart, it is easy to see how each of
the twelve houses contains many such sensitive zones.

Many of the houses of a person's birthchart contain planets—natal
ones, that is. These planets, shaped by the signs in which they lie and
operating through houses, are the basic "bits" we learned to unravel in
The Inner Sky. Ten such "bits" go together to create the unique personality of the individual chart. Each of them is a gold mine—or mine
field—of meaning, giving special importance to the house in question,
making its successful navigation one of the keys to happiness and
fulfillment for the individual in question. Clearly, when a transiting
planet contacts that point—either directly, or through major aspects—it
strikes a deep chord. How do we understand such an event? First, we
grasp the meaning of the "bit" itself. Second, we understand the nature
of the transiting planet that is stimulating the "bit." Third, we look at
the **aspect** that is linking the two planets—what is the nature of the
process occurring between them? And fourth, we observe the house
through which that planet is transiting—**where** are the events
occurring that are stimulating the natal "bit?"

A minute ago we considered a transit of Jupiter through a woman's
ninth house. We observed that during the course of that transit, a
square aspect would be formed between Jupiter and her natal twelfth
house Moon in Cancer. Let's apply our rules and try to understand
what is going on here.

Step One: Analyze the "bit."

Moon in Cancer in the twelfth house. It's always risky to look at any part of birthchart in a vacuum, but let's proceed for the sake of the example. From looking at her birthchart, the woman's emotional, subjective function (Moon) is propelled primarily by an urge to create a safe environment for nurturing deep feelings and memories—the "self-administered psychoanalysis" of Cancer. The process is expressed in the department of life we call the twelfth house—eternal, transcendent, spiritual perspectives. Her disposition clearly contains mystical, romantic elements—as well as strong themes of withdrawal and self-protection.

Step Two: Understand the nature of the transiting planet.

Jupiter. As Teacher: confidence, new perspectives, the ability to seize opportunities and move boldly into the future. As Trickster: self-undoing through overconfidence and pride.

Step Three: Grasp the aspect linking the transiting planet to the "bit."

Square: Friction; conflict; the aspect of "natural enemies," threatening each other but also demanding growth and excellence from each other.

Step Four: Understand the house through which the transiting planet is moving.

Ninth house: Expansion; exploration; education; the attainment of perspective. With Jupiter transiting through this phase of the house cycle, we see a time of renewing, enlivening enthusiasm coupled with an awareness of previously unforeseen potentials (Jupiter stuff.) It stretches the woman's spirit by offering her novel opportunities for travel, for learning, for philosophical expansion, and for the breaking up of old routines (ninth house terrain).

So what happens? As always, the woman herself is holding half the cards in the deck. The precise natures of the possibilities that coalesce around her and certainly her responses to them cannot be foreseen astrologically. We do know that some great ninth house Jupiter opportunity comes to her during the time of the transit—and that it frightens her shy, inward twelfth house Cancer Moon worse than watching an Alfred Hitchcock film all alone on a stormy night in a Gothic bedroom where a murder had happened. Jupiter's gift, in other words, applies friction (square) to all the issues locked up in her lunar "bit." What may seem like a boon to everyone else fills her with foreboding and ambiguity. Lightning strikes—she wins a contest she entered six months before. The prize? An expense-paid trip to India. She has always been fascinated with yoga and meditation. But now, amid all the cheering and celebration, the quiet, reclusive voice within her begins to worry: Foreigners/strangers to meet/dangers/weird customs/ bugs in the food....why did I ever enter that stupid contest? If she goes, her Cancer Moon is forced by the friction of the transiting Jupiter square to take an evolutionary leap, transcending those weaker dimensions of its nature that might limit her overall development. That's Teacher work. But maybe the Trickster wins, comforting her, lulling her, filling her with soothing rationalizations—while she lets the trip to India slip away from her like a dream she never really believed.

The third class of trigger point we need to recognize is a very simple one: the **cusps** of houses themselves. Cusps, of course, are the beginnings of houses, their "gateways," we might say. Normally, cusps are defined quite precisely—usually down to fractions of a degree. In practice, they are relatively wide zones, spanning about a 3-degree arc centered on the technical cusp. If, for example, your third house begins in 13 degrees 39 minutes of Taurus (Remember 60 minutes= 1 degree), once a transiting planet moves to within about a degree and a half of that point—say 12 degrees, 9 minutes of Taurus—it starts to stimulate third house activity and events. And it does so very powerfully. Cusps represent the most sensitive zones of any house. Houses, in other words, begin with a bang. Aspectual trigger points within the house might modify this principle in practice, but the general rule is that **the independent, internal energy-structure of any house peaks at its cusp, then gradually trails off**. Look to the entry of a transiting planet into a house for some of the most dramatic and characteristic events of the phase.

Within the internal energy-structure of houses, one more pattern can be discerned, although this one is somewhat less reliable than the "law of cusps." **Often, in a given transit, there is a second peak of activity when the planet nears the end of the house.** It is as if the psyche suddenly realizes that time is running out. Unfinished business comes to a head. Events—and especially realizations—are intensified. The house goes out just as it began—with a bang.

And those are the houses. In the next chapter we take our final step with transits—understanding the inner cycles of individual planets— and then we are ready to move on into new territory.

A word of encouragement—we are learning a new language here, just as we did in *The Inner Sky*. Once again, our first step is to absorb vocabulary and grammar. Only then are we ready to start forming sentences on our own. If you don't yet feel prepared to apply what we have been learning in a practical way, don't worry. You are right on target. Predictive astrology is a puzzle with many pieces. We must learn their shapes before we try to put them together. Synthesis is a subject for later on.

CHAPTER SIX

TRANSITS IV:
THE CYCLE OF LIFE

Would you predict "career developments" for a five-year-old or a sexual blossoming for a bedridden old lady who remembers Franklin Roosevelt's inauguration? Such predictions ignore the person's place in the human life cycle, and as a result, they tend to fail, generally in a comical way.

In the previous chapter we drew an analogy between the astrological houses and the normal human life cycle. Maturity follows adolescence, just as the tenth house follows the ninth. Both are **fixed patterns of development**, though the choices we make at each stage are our own.

But what about the life cycle itself? What about the fact that each of us starts out as a child and moves on from there?

> ☆ Every astrological prediction must be seen in the
> context of the human life cycle, and must draw part
> of its meaning from the fixed realities associated with
> each individual's chronological age.

This rule is a powerful one, but it must be applied with delicacy and sensitivity. Times are changing. Our decisions and life patterns are not as prefabricated as they were a century ago. Courtship issues can be relevant to a fifty-year-old man. Sexual questions can press upon a seventy-year-old woman. Age is not quite the determinant of behavior that it used to be. Modern astrology must recognize those social changes, but simultaneously strive to grasp what is truly essential to each phase of life. Few dimensions of predictive astrology are as significant as this—and few are as subject to distortion by the astrologer's own prejudices or narrow-mindedness.

Common sense, combined with the experience of living our own lives, is a potent tool here. If you are reading this book, then you have at least passed through your own early childhood. If you are an elderly person, then almost the whole panorama of life lies behind you; your position is a very strong one when it comes to understanding these patterns. Those of us in the middle of life must speak partly through experience, partly out of imagination and personal familiarity with people who are farther along in years.

Beyond personal experience, we tap into all the wisdom humanity has accumulated over millenia—wisdom about the life cycle often transmitted to us through clichés and catch phrases. "The terrible twos." "Adolescent rebellion." "Midlife crisis." "Second childhood." People are not clichés, but each of those ideas does convey something universal that underlies the unique experiences of each individual.

Astrology can deepen that understanding even further, not only by adding vitality and richness to the clichés, but also by precisely timing our arrival at various turning points in life. To understand this vein of astrological theory, we must add one more element to our growing picture of planetary transits. We must recognize the cycles inherent in the orbital periods of the planets themselves. Not Saturn's relationship to the birthchart, but Saturn's evolving relationship to itself. A person might, for example, be born with Saturn in Leo. His "natal" Saturn stays right there, of course, but his "transiting" Saturn moves on through all the signs, making a series of aspects to its own natal position, eventually returning to its starting point.

Planetary Cycles

Depending on the nature of the individual birthchart, most astrological events can occur at any time in a person's life. Slow-moving Neptune, for example, can oppose one person's Venus when she is seventeen years old—the two planets were nearly aligned when she was born; seventeen years was enough to complete the aspect. Another person might wait until she is fifty-four to experience that same transit— Neptune had farther to travel in her birthchart before it arrived at that particular Venusian trigger point. A third person might **never** experience it. Why? Because Neptune takes 164 years to get around the Sun (or the chart!). With such a long orbital period, certain Neptunian aspects never form unless the person gets old enough to qualify as a human interest story. There just isn't enough time. For this reason, there is a certain "randomness" about when various transits occur.

One special class of transits is an exception to this rule, and it provides the key to unlocking the riddles of the human life cycle. Even though we have no idea when Neptune will oppose someone's Venus, **we know roughly when it will oppose itself**. We know, in other words, when transiting Neptune opposes natal Neptune. How? Simply because we know how long Neptune takes to get around the whole birthchart—164 years. In about half that time, it arrives at the halfway mark in its journey—and forms the opposition aspect to its own original position. Even if we have no knowledge of a man's birthchart, the bare fact that he is in his eighty-third year tells us, at least roughly, that he is experiencing transiting Neptune opposed to natal Neptune. By similar means, we know that when that man was around forty-one, Neptune squared its own natal position. How? Because forty-one years is one quarter of Neptune's orbital period, and we know that the planet has then moved about 90 degrees, or one quarter of the way around his chart. Since orbital periods are constant for all planets, the same logic applies to each of them. The result is that certain chronological ages correspond to certain very particular astrological events. Weaving them together gives us an astrological picture of the human life cycle—a picture that each one of us holds in common. What emerges is the elemental human drama, the life of "Everyman," the fundamental **biopsychic script** programmed into each one of us by the mere fact of our birth. Superimposed on that pattern, we find the far more personal—and therefore more random—cycles of development indicated by other kinds of transits.

It's essential to note here that planets speed up and slow down as they follow their elliptical orbits around the Sun. As a result, we can't simply divide up their orbital periods into halves and quarters to determine when we reach these aspects, as in the above example. That gives us the rough picture; the precise details will emerge later.

"Everyman's" life presents us with a highly complex astrological picture. As usual, it's best to pick out the most important elements, then later decide if we want to get the details, too.

To understand one planet's cycle is not very difficult. But to try to keep all ten of them straight at the same time seems more likely to give us headaches than wisdom.

Simplification is a necessity. Which turning points in the life cycle are truly critical ones? We faced a similar dilemma when we began introducing transits—figuring them out was like trying to count swarming mosquitoes. The distinction between slow and fast planets came to our rescue, and that same distinction rescues us again. The quick planets—Sun, Moon, Mercury, Venus, and Mars—can also be ignored as we tackle the question of the human life cycle. Why? Because their scope is too narrow. Even in the course of a decade, they repeat themselves many times over. Such transits might tell us how we feel this weekend, but they have nothing to say about what this year means in the overall course of our development.

That leaves us with Jupiter, Saturn, Uranus, Neptune, and Pluto—the slow planets. It is they who weave the web of Everyman's life. Teachers and Tricksters, they move predictably into critical aspectual relationships with their own birthchart positions, creating the challenges and dramas, the melodramas and pratfalls, which shape the pattern of the human life cycle.

Each planet has its own rhythm. Owing to differences in their orbital periods, when one planetary focus "peaks," the others are typically relatively quiet. Throughout much of life, when Jupiter is on center stage, Saturn is still in the dressing room. When Uranus is holding our attention, Pluto has retired to a dark corner of the birthchart. Their cycles are of different lengths; most of the time they are out of phase with each other. We do, however, find certain times when the cycles overlap and reinforce each other. Such events, as we will soon see, represent crisis—and opportunity. We can lose the threads of our lives, or we can seize the chance to leap boldly into new and happier futures.

The slow planets spin their cycles around us, swirling in and out of sensitive zones, going in and out of phase with each other, one disappearing as another reappears—until we enter the middle of our ninth decade of life. Then there is a vast planetary convergence, paralleling the circumstances of birth. (Look at figure 1). Although a few of us live longer and many don't survive that long, it is very difficult to escape the notion that at some archetypal astrological level, it is at this great convergence in our middle eighties that we complete the life cycle. We go out as we came in—with a bang.

PLANET   ORBITAL PERIOD, YEARS

Jupiter	11.88	Seven cycles = 83 years
Saturn	29.42	Three cycles = 88 years
Uranus	83.75	One cycle = 84 years
Neptune	163.74	One-half cycle (opposition) = 82 years
Pluto	247.7	One-third cycle* (trine) = 83 years

FIGURE 1

*Pluto's cycle is complex: see page 111.

Each of these planetary cycles has distinct meaning; each refers to the evolution of a different dimension of character. Yet the **phases** of each cycle are exactly the same. At the **conjunction**,we always find an **intensification** of the planet's impact upon our attitudes. Something is **seeded** within us. At the **sextile**, there is tremendous **vigor** in the development of that function. We have begun to mature in a new way and feel surges of new—and often uncontrolled—power. We are like young lions. At the **square**, the young lion meets his match. We hit a wall. Our vigor is checked. We must begin to adapt to reality—there are other lions out there, bigger than we are and with different plans. At the **trine**, we again feel **energy and opportunity**—but now in a more mature form, tempered by the events that occurred under the square. After the trine comes the **opposition**. At the opposition we challenge reality itself. We have extended ourselves outward into complex circumstances, building, stretching, conquering. The seed that germinated at the conjunction has now blossomed. The young lion is at the peak of his power. It is now or never; he must challenge the king. Perhaps he wins; perhaps he loses. Everything depends upon his preparations. In other words, everything depends upon how well he has learned the lessons of the first half cycle.

Next we move into the waning cycle. Gone is the **outward** stretching so characteristic of the waxing period. Conquest is no longer our goal. We no longer seek to impress ourselves upon the world, leaving our mark. Now we long for home. During the waning phases, the mind is reaching back toward where the cycle began. It is returning, perhaps victorious, perhaps not, but always with one set of thoughts preeminent: What did my journey mean? How can I use it in the long run? What can I **learn** from this experience? If the waxing cycle represents

action, or extension into the environment, then the waning cycle symbolizes **reflection** or the process of integrating the experience into our preexisting memories and concepts. The waning period is no less energetic than the waxing one, but the energy is less visible, directed toward the process of **sorting out** the events of the waxing cycle, weaving them into the fabric of character. At first, this integrative process flows harmoniously (the **waning trine**), though we risk falling asleep, forgetting and falsifying the threatening elements of what we have been through. After that comes a time of conflict, the **waning square**. We feel "out of sync." We resist redefining ourselves in the light of experience. If that resistance is total, the waning square can feel like a vicious, losing battle with reality. Then comes the **waning sextile**— ideally a time of excitement and stimulation as the newly integrated experiences vitalizes us. Thus empowered, we slip back into the **conjunction**. A **new seed** is planted, and the endless cycle spins outward again, freshly or repetitively, depending on whether we learned the lessons the first time around.

Each planetary cycle can be understood according to this waxing-waning paradigm, adding a new level to our understanding of aspects. Squares, for example, are still squares; their basic significance, **friction**, does not change. But now we see that the friction of the waxing square is created by thrusting our will into the outer world. In the waning square, the friction exists between the new circumstances we have now created, and our old self-image which probably hasn't yet caught up inwardly with its own outward accomplishments. In the waxing aspects, in other words, we interact with our environment. In the waning ones, what we have learned from that environment interacts with us.

Neptune and Pluto move so slowly that between them they only form a handful of these aspects in the course of a lifetime. Because of their relative rarity, each Neptunian or Plutonian aspect is important. Jupiter is much faster, completing its whole cycle of seven major aspects in just twelve years. Each one has significance, but to deal with all of them complicates our picture to an unacceptable degree. Since our aims in this book are more practical than theoretical, some weeding is necessary. Over the years, I have found certain of these planetary turning points to be highly charged emotionally and developmentally. Others seem to fade into the background. We will concentrate on the really essential ones. Generally speaking, conjunctions are always powerhouses of meaning. Given Jupiter's speed, we will consider only its return to its natal position (the conjunction), giving us a crescendo of Jupiterian activity every twelve years. The same logic applies to Saturn, with a peak every twenty-nine and one half years. Next in strength after conjunctions come oppositions, followed by squares. With Uranus, we widen our scope to include those phases, too. Neptune, with its 164-year cycle, rarely moves into its waning phase before a person reaches the end of life; because of that slowness, each of its aspects has time to build depth and complexity of meaning. Each must be scrutinized. The same logic applies to Pluto, which rarely extends as far as the opposition.

One more note before we go on to look at these planetary cycles one by one. Planetary orbits are nearly circular, but not quite. Technically, they are ellipses—"stretched" circles. As a result it takes them a bit longer to cover one part of their orbit than another. The effects are slight for Jupiter and Saturn, but for Uranus, Neptune, and Pluto they begin to become quite noticeable. The practical result of this variation, as we mentioned earlier, is that knowing when the various aspects will form is not as simple as dividing the orbits into halves and thirds—almost that simple, but not quite. To be sure in individual cases when these outer planet turning points are reached, it is necessary to look them up in the ephemeris, a book which lists the planets' positions over a period of decades. Use the approximations presented here only as guidelines—they're close to the truth, but only represent average figures.

Let's explore each of these cycles individually, then tie them together chronologically, seeing how their interplay creates the basic biopsychic melody upon which each one of us improvises the counterpoints and grace notes of individuality.

SATURN
The Cycle of Identity
Orbital Period: 29.42 years

Traditional astrologers often use the word "limitation" in connection with Saturn. Logically, that is an accurate assessment of the ringed planet's effect, but emotionally, it's misleading. Unthinkingly, we view a limitation as an annoying existential roadblock. The truth, however, is that limitations often **feel good** to us. Like coming upon a reassuring road sign on a rainy country lane in the middle of the night, they help us realize who we are and which way we should turn. That is precisely the purpose of the Saturn cycle—to clarify, define, and strengthen our identity **by confronting us with a series of limitations**.

Only when we succumb to Saturn the Trickster and to his "you can't win" lies is that process a bitter one.

Baby Sally awakens one morning to a profound realization: "I am a girl." That, in a way, is a limitation, just as being a boy is a limitation. She has found one of her road signs. Barring surgical interventions, she is likely to remain a girl, the experience of maleness is closed to her, off limits. Is she sad? Perhaps. But more likely she's happy. Her sense of her femininity becomes one of the bulwarks of her identity. In grasping that basic limitation, she feels more secure, more **defined**. Later she realizes other limits: her race, her country, her religion. Each feeds the process of identity building. Each is a road sign—and a gift of the ringed planet. As she matures, Saturn spells out her road signs more specifically, defining her identity more clearly—and limiting her more drastically. "I am a feminist vegetarian Democrat for arms control." More road signs, more limits. The process continues, of course, until she dies. Every day she delimits herself with more precision. But there are peaks in the process. Critical moments arise when she must redefine herself in some elemental way, perhaps dumping worn-out definitions as she does so.

Two such Saturn events called **Saturn returns**, mark crescendos in what is arguably the most primal of all the astrological cycles. These "returns" occur whenever Saturn completes a cycle around the birthchart (or an orbit around the sun—they're the same) and returns to its natal position. The first Saturn return occurs when we are looking at turning thirty; the second when we are facing sixty. They divide life into three Saturn cycles, and provide us with our first key to unlocking Everyman's biography.

During the first Saturn cycle, we are in the process of delineating our **personal** identity, seeking a Vision for our lives. Throughout this phase, our roadsigns are insights into our own personality and destiny. Their purpose is to lead us eventually into maturity. They are dreams of **who we might be**. Early in the cycle, those dreams are unrealistic, full of glorious, impossible mythology—"Who are you, Timmy?" "I'm Superman!!!" A four-year-old playing out the role of one of his heroes is not just wasting time; he is establishing the basic neurocircuitry that will later enable him to assume grown-up responsibilities. But a sixteen-year-old playing the same game is in trouble; his or her dreams should be converging more closely with reality. Superman is out, but "I'd like to be a rock star" is a legitimate dream, if it's inspiring. Being a "rock star" may not be his true destination; but in the midst of his first Saturn cycle, that dream is his best road sign.

Eventually, dreams must make a deal with reality—and reality is a notoriously hard bargainer. Superman does not exist. For every rock star, there are ten thousand starving musicians. At the Saturn return, the time has come to strike a bargain. Maybe that aspiring young "rock star" decides to become a music teacher. He has compromised; but the heart of his youthful vision remains intact.

At the Saturn return reality confronts us, sobers us, challenges us, demands that we **grow up**. Typically, it is a difficult time, a classic "identity crisis" as we make the transition between youth and midlife. Even if our dreams have matured, there are still likely to be adolescent elements in them: we want fame, fortune, a perfect marriage, enlightenment. And even if those things have been missing from our lives so far, we have always had a comforting escape clause: we could still say, "When I grow up . . ." At the Saturn return, that escape clause breaks down. It is a deep psychic shock: "Oh my God—I'm turning thirty." We **are** grown up, and something deep inside us knows that—but doesn't know what to do about it.

Saturn does not ask us to cease dreaming; the point is that since we have now grown up, we must figure out a way to **make our dreams real**. Personally, professionally, philosophically, the Saturn return is a time of **commitment**. Commitment to what? To real possibilities, consistent with our dreams—possibilities that can only be made concrete through self-discipline, honest self-appraisal, reasonable compromise, and the acceptance of reality.

After the first Saturn return, we still dream—but now our dreams are tempered. We have not surrendered to practicality. Instead, we have struck a bargain with the real world, sealed it with determination and patience, and are now ready to move into the next major phase of life. Astrologers view that phase as the second Saturn cycle, but most of us simply call it **maturity**.

People who successfully navigate the Saturn return are able to maintain intensity and a quality of mission or inspiration in their lives. Why? Because the adult identity they have created reflects the Visions of youth, modified and partly compromised, but still recognizable. If the construction of personality is the goal of the first cycle, the goal of the second is the construction of destiny. These successful navigators are ready: they have made Saturn their Teacher. The teenage boy who fantasized about being a guitar hero—and practiced hard—now teaches music in a university; the little girl who played at being a nurse—and studied biology—is now a master neurosurgeon; the child who read Hemingway—and has completed two unpublished novels of her own—now writes a bestseller. Much could be said in praise of such people, but perhaps the most succinct way to express their accomplishments is to savor this single, simple idea: they don't hate Mondays. Why? Because the adult life they have created for themselves reflects the soulful inspirations of youth. What they face on "Monday morning" is intimately connected with who they are. They are living their vision.

The horror of a failed Saturn return is that it is so often hidden behind veils of "maturity" and "practicality." We are looking down the barrel of turning thirty—and we fall apart. We surrender. "I used to dream, but now I cope." The lines that begin to form on our faces suggest chronic tension, the appearance of one who is braced against the next blow. What dreams we have left become unreal, quixotic—or limited to fantasies about Hawaiian vacations, flashy Porsches, or sexual adventures. A curious blend of nostalgia and cynicism about our own youth begins to enter our awareness, and our picture of midlife becomes one of noble futility in the face of failing systems. "I used to worry about saving the world. Now I worry about saving my ass"— such is the motto of Saturn the Trickster, and our motto, too, if he succeeds in tricking us at this pivotal juncture.

Young people in their first cycle who encounter individuals who broke down under the pressure of the Saturn return often view them with contempt, calling them empty, boring, materialistic. Those of us who succeed in keeping our dreams alive into midlife usually take a more compassionate view: We know what a close squeak the Saturn return can be. We know how easy it is to let the Trickster rob us of our vitality. Those of us who make Saturn our Teacher are less quick to judge—and quicker to understand.

The second Saturn return around age fifty-nine has much in common with the first. Once again, we come to a turning point. Once again we must shift gears and move into a new phase of life. Once again our whole organism is challenged to **accept reality**. In our first Saturn return, we were challenged to move from adolescence to maturity. Now, at the second, we move from **maturity to old age**.

Wait a minute. Do we really turn "old" at age fifty-nine? Is a twenty-seven-year-old an "adolescent?" Not really. These are only convenient labels, aimed at crystallizing something of the spirit of each phase. The point is that the third and typically final Saturn cycle **begins** as we near sixty. The seed is planted then—and when it blossoms, we have become one of the "village elders," enjoying that phase of life just as we enjoyed the previous two.

Such blossoming is not automatic. The complaining, embittered old man or woman, cursing the present, living in romanticized, falsified memories of the past, has missed the lesson of the second Saturn return. Our goal here is to make a graceful transition into the latter third of life, learning to accept the new rules by which we now live. In the first cycle, we live in the personality. The natural emphasis of life then is upon self-discovery. We spend a lot of time staring into mirrors. In the second cycle, those practices do not disappear, but our emphasis shifts. Now we are concerned with destiny and the products of our self-discovery. Accomplishment is the centerpiece of the second cycle of life. We work. Perhaps we raise a family. If we navigate well, we symbolize something to the community. Then comes the second Saturn return and the beginning of the third cycle: What now? What comes after "destiny?" The end of life is closer, but the vital force is still strong in us. Where must we direct that energy? Certainly we are not ready for the rest home yet.

The third cycle of life is the cycle of **spirituality** or of **immortality**. Terrified deathbed conversions to Christianity are not the point. Our task is to **leave behind some evidence of our existence** in the hands of those come after us. We must teach what we have learned, passing on the wisdom we have acquired. Why? Because this is eternally the natural task of an **Elder**, and because that is where our satisfaction now naturally lies. In a very broad sense, we can say that we are preparing for death, though that suggests a somberness that is quite inappropriate here. The master violinmaker now seeks apprentices, willingly surrendering his secrets. The brilliant psychotherapist now writes her book. The wealthy industrialist endows a Foundation. The grandparents start a savings account for the grandchild's education. All of this implies a process of **passing the torch to the next generation,** which is the essence of the third cycle. Is altruism the motive? No. Not altruism, but enlightened self-interest. We are getting older. Death will overtake us, sooner or later. We must begin to **let go** of what we have created, enjoying it not by hoarding it, but by offering it freely to those who come after us. Like the mythic Vedic kings of old India, the time has come for us to renounce our kingdoms, passing them on to our sons and daughters, and to shift our own attention from the transitory to the eternal.

Many fail. Many are frightened of getting older, and their fear distorts the wisdom folded into their genes and chromosomes. "Oh my God—I'll be sixty soon!" Saturn the Trickster has a field day. The businessman leaves his wife of thirty years, buys a red sportscar, and has his heart broken by a twenty-eight-year-old woman. If we are filled with an attitude of denial rather than acceptance, then this is a perilous time.

How about some examples of the Saturn return from real life? It's such a dramatic time, they're easy to find.

Muhammad Ali was stripped of his heavyweight boxing championship for refusing the military draft during the Vietnam War. After slowly fighting his way back up the standings, he finally was given a bout with the man who currently held the championship, Joe Frazier. Ali fought him during his Saturn return—and lost. He later went on to reclaim the championship, but in that moment, he hit the wall of reality. Some of his cockiness gone, he persisted, trained hard, and was able to win back the title. Sometimes our rite of passage through the Saturn return involves some great work, a bid to be taken seriously as an adult. For many people, it is a doctoral dissertation. For Diana Ross, it was the shedding of her Barbie Doll image in her surprisingly gritty portrayal of singer Billie Holiday in the film *Lady Sings the Blues*. For director George Lucas it took the form of his first important movie, *American Graffiti*. As tradition has it, Gautama the Buddha left his father's palace at age twenty-nine and went on seeking Enlightenment in the jungles—the Saturn return again.

Tristan Jones was a writer and explorer with a long list of adventuresome exploits, mostly undertaken alone in small sailboats. He spent, for example, nearly two years alone except for his dog, Nelson, frozen into the Arctic seas near Greenland. At his second Saturn return, he hit a limit of a dramatic sort for a man of his temperament: he had a leg amputated. How did he react? As I wrote these words, he was sailing his trimaran *Outbound Leg* around the world to draw attention to the organization that he established to help crippled men and women overcome their handicaps and have their own adventures. At age sixty, this remarkable Welshman was a living illustration of a healthy response to the third cycle. He found a way to pass on his torch.

URANUS
The Cycle of Individuality
Orbital Period: 83.75 years

The planet Uranus seems to bear a special kinship with the human race. As the astrological symbol of genius, of individuality, of rebellion against limitations—and of plain headstrong idiocy—it appears temperamentally closer to us than to the bears and otters and goldfish with whom we share our planet. As if to clinch the relationship, we observe that the eighty-four-year orbit of Uranus around the sun corresponds rather closely to the length of human life. It is as if the Great Spirit decreed that Uranus would give us every chance to break free, making every aspect possible on our birthcharts—once.

Freedom—that is the primal Uranian concept. Society trains us, grooms us, teaches us manners and skills, language and morality. For that we should be grateful. But there is a worm in the apple. So often society turns us into marionettes, replacing direct experience with posturing and style, real human encounters with memorized rituals. Uranus is the antidote to that tribal programming, sounding the trumpet of rebellion within us, making us suspicious of authority, honest to the point of outrage, and zealous in mischief.

At about age fourteen, transiting Uranus forms the waxing sextile to its natal position. The **excitation** characteristic of this aspect fills our nascent individuality with its first glimpse of real Uranian freedom. As many a mom and dad will affirm, our first efforts with this explosive energy are often clumsy. Puberty is advancing. The sexual imperative drives us suddenly into complex social situations that rapidly accelerate the development of our individuality. We are unprepared, but ripe for learning. **Separation from home** is the critical lesson here. Sensitive parents must make an extra effort to grant their sons and daughters the right to be taken seriously at this stage, for the Uranian sextile is truly the aspect of "childhood's end."

The next Uranian turning point, the waxing square, comes at an age that society recognizes to be critical: twenty-one, more or less. **Friction** exists between our growing individuality and our awareness of the limits that culture imposes. At this phase, we are ready to recognize that absolute rebellion against society is self-destructive. Something full of grandiose childish tantrums dies within us at the Uranian square, adapting us to the realities of sharing life with 6 billion other people. There are grave dangers here. If the process goes too far, spirits can be broken at this juncture, leaving the young person emotionally flat and resigned to conventionality. Or perhaps the childish fire refuses to mature, and the individual embarks at this point on a course of crime, insensitivity, and ultimate self-ruin.

The trine comes around age twenty-eight, preparing the way for the Saturn return. Individuality has matured further now, readying itself for the leap into life's long middle that comes the following year. We feel our personality beginning to operate in harmony with social reality and yet expressing itself successfully through the rituals and metaphors of whatever society into which we happen to be born. The fabled "awkwardness of youth" begins to fade at this point—unless we slip away to our own Walden Pond as did Henry David Thoreau when this Uranian aspect formed for him.

Of all the Uranian aspects formed in this Cycle of Individuality, the most significant is the opposition. This occurs around age forty-two, although it oscillates a bit, and corresponds to the classic "midlife crisis." Under the extreme tension of the opposition, we are simply tired of being told what to do. We sense that we are now looking at the second half of life—and that spooks us into action. Uranus fills us with a desire to do as we please, for a change. Our individuality has matured: it seeks expression. If we are caught in a job that feels irrelevant to us, or a marriage that feels like an artifact of our youth, this is likely to be an explosive period as those structures are dynamited. "I am what I am"—that is the spirit of this wrenching, but exciting, time. Under its auspices, Timothy Leary was in the early stages of his LSD experiments, on the way to getting himself thrown out of his professorship in Harvard's psychology department. Ted Turner left his media empire in the hands of others, and went sailing, winning the America's Cup in the yacht *Courageous*.

Now the Uranian cycle begins to wane. Individuality becomes more reflective, less inclined to "act out" its dramas. The waning trine around age fifty-six is a more mellow period, as the experiences of life begin to gel within us. We know ourselves well, and feel perhaps more at ease with our own natures than at any other point in the cycle so far. We are gathering strength for the second Saturn return, due in two years. Whatever our gender, the Italian expression of fond respect— "a man with a belly"—suits us now. Thin as a pretzel or sporting a paunch, we now move with natural authority. Our individuality is at home in the world, even if *Mademoiselle* or *GQ* are not approaching us to appear on their covers.

The waning Uranian square comes around age sixty-three. This transit can be a real shock. Once again, friction arises between ourselves and society. We sense that we are being "moved out" in favor of younger people. Often we feel physically weaker, less able to defend our turf. To make a positive response to the challenges this aspect presents, a man or woman must redefine his or her individuality in a way that is less dependent upon social approval. Enthusiastic retirement, with plans for many private projects, is a common healthy answer to the Uranian question. There are other answers, but all involve scrutinizing our own motivations and weeding out those that are connected with collecting brownie points from society.

The waning sextile around age seventy heralds what we might call the "golden years." Here, we often find a new burst of vigor. "The fiery old man," "the spirited old woman," these are the archetypes that are trying to emerge into our personalities at this point.

We return at last to the beginning, to the conjunction, at age eighty-four. Symbolically, this is the end of life—though a few of us live on through a kind of rebirth into a new Uranian cycle. What that cycle means, I'll leave for the nonagenarians to tell me. The conjunction itself represents the **completion of our individuality**. We have come full circle. We have seen it all. A beautiful old man and woman, with the fullness of life behind them, with nobility of spirit and generosity of heart, with absolute ease in their own individuality, with nothing left to prove, with no one to impress, with benign respect for all and yet sly humor regarding any kind of pretense, with peace already made with their dying and therefore no urge to hold on to anything, not even memory—that is the spirit of the Uranian return, and the goal of life, at least at the psychological level. Few arrive, but those who do inspire us all.

Eubie Blake, the ragtime composer, is a fine example of such a man. In his middle eighties he enjoyed a renaissance. Columbia Records released the very successful album *The Eighty-Six Years of Eubie Blake*. Was it only his art that inspired people? The man **himself** became a symbol of the imperishable dignity and humor of the human spirit.

The other side of the Uranian coin can be seen in the dictator of Iran, the Ayatollah Khoumeini, who under this transit escalated the Iran-Iraq war to the point where young children were being handed automatic weapons and sent to the frontlines. His Uranian ego, the shadow of real individuality, raged out of control, fuming like a volcano. The utterly egocentric old man or woman, boring us with endless descriptions of their physical maladies, criticizing the morality and lifestyles of those around them—that is the failed Uranian conjunction. In the Ayatollah we see that failure blown up to world-twisting proportions. Uranus—Teacher of genius, Trickster of determined idiocy—rolls on in its ageless circuit about our star.

Neptune

The Cycle of Spirituality
Orbital Period: 163.74 years

Neptune's long orbit limits the number of turning points it can generate. Unless we live to be about 110 years old, none of the major waning aspects ever forms. For practical purposes, the opposition at very approximately age eighty-two represents the end of the human life cycle. Other than the opposition, we must consider only the waxing sextile, square, and trine. Following our general principle that the slower transits gain their power from the fact that they have time to develop depth and complexity of meaning, we immediately know that whatever Neptune might trigger in us, the leisurely pace of the planet guarantees that it must be very deep and very complex indeed.

As we learned in *The Inner Sky,* Neptune is the planet of **consciousness itself**. In chapter three of this book, we introduced Neptune the Teacher, the transiting planet that opens our hearts to what we might call our inner voice, or perhaps the voice of God within us. Transcendence, serenity, openness to inspiration—these are his gifts. But the Trickster is alive too, as we also saw in chapter four. He deceives us with the temptations of glamour and hype, beguiling us to escape down a path of slow moral erosion, lassitude, and mental decay.

Each of us is more than a personality—that is Neptune's message. Beyond us lies a world of mystery, a real world, accessible to us if only we know how to turn the key. And the secret of the key lies in recognizing that our awareness can go places where our egos cannot go. Subtle shifts in attitude are needed here, shifts away from our normal ego orientation, shifts that can be brought into being by the use of certain Neptunian techniques—meditation, prayer, hypnosis, trance, staring into space. When Neptune arrives at one of the trigger points in its long cycle, we are ready to move one step closer to that cosmic perspective. Or that cosmic perspective is ready to move one step closer to us—with ego suspended, the two experiences are indistinguishable. Either way, we are ready for a quantum leap in consciousness—or if we fail, for an embarrassing period of poor reality testing, escapism, and foolishness, the dark gifts of the Trickster.

Neptune gives us plenty of time to sort the Teacher from the Trickster. Unlike Saturn and Uranus, the slowness of these transits and the fuzziness of the issues they generate often extend the duration of the Neptunian turning point well over two years, sometimes as long as three. The chronological ages we give below refer to the peak periods in the planet's activity. Remember to consider the previous year and the following one in the light of the ideas we are about to develop, and to recall that the actual timing varies a bit from person to person.

The waxing Neptunian sextile occurs around our twenty-eighth year of life, coinciding with the Uranian trine, and often overlapping the early stages of our first Saturn return. Astrologically, the late twenties are clearly emerging as critical years. We are then making many decisions, both practical and philosophical, which determine the shapes of our adult lives. To the Saturnian and Uranian stew, Neptune adds the spice of spiritual maturity, or at least the possibility of it. Through the excitation of the sextile, an eagerness arises in us for some larger perspective on life.

Some enter psychotherapy. Some abandon a youthful rebellion against the church and return to the fold. Some begin practicing meditation. Often, an external trigger appears at this point, deepening our mystical sensibilities. Such was the case for Carlos Casteneda. Under his Neptunian sextile, he first encountered don Juan.

The great peril of the Neptunian sextile is its tendency to excite within us an urge to escape into oblivion. Here, under the mesmerizing gaze of the Trickster, the "kid who likes to drink" becomes the full-fledged alcoholic. Or the gullible young man or woman follows some ersatz guru down the road of sweet promises. The sextile, as always, symbolizes a giddy energy, powerful, but tending toward excess.

Many years elapse before another Neptunian aspect forms, and once more, we find that when it occurs, the aspect again coincides with a Uranian turning point, giving the period a particularly momentous quality. The Neptunian aspect is the waxing square, typically centering roughly around our forty-first birthday—and running into the "midlife crisis" suggested by the powerful Uranian opposition around age forty-two. The square, true to form, applies friction to our growing spiritual sensibilities. We are hungry now, eager for some **direct experience** of God or Truth or Higher Reality. We want **proof**, and the Uranian energies make us suspicious of easy "Santa Claus" answers handed out by figures of spiritual authority. The seeds of doubt are planted; faith can he shattered—or leap to a new level. As always, squares require **effort**. Forces arise that call our faith into question. To endure, that faith must grow, often through some "great work." Cesar Chavez, under the waxing Neptune square, had his nonviolent spiritual values pushed to their limits during the darkest days of the United Farm Workers grape strike in 1968. He could have given up, but instead he pushed through to a new level of inner strength—he fasted continuously from the thirteenth of February to the tenth of March, inspiring his followers and reinspiring himself. Three weeks later, he turned forty-one, deeper, wiser, and with a successful navigation of this tricky passage off to an impressive start.

The next phase of the cycle, the waxing Neptunian trine occurs around age fifty-five, a year before the waning Uranian trine. Another "good" aspect according to the medievals, the Neptunian trine does suggest the possibility of spiritual harmony arising in us, filling us with peace. Guaranteed? No—the risk with trines is our tendency to sleep through them, missing the chance they offer us. Under the dual Uranian and Neptunian trines, these years often have a mellow quality—the "man with a belly" phase. The risk is that they can be **too** mellow. Lethargy and lassitude put us to sleep, aided sometimes by a few shots of expensive Scotch. Perhaps that wouldn't be so bad— except that the Neptune trine is immediately followed by the second Saturn return. We hit the wall, asleep, at seventy-five miles an hour. Properly navigated, these are years of **preparation**. It is now that the spiritual basis for the third Saturn cycle must be established. Now, when it is easy. Now, before the pressure rises. Help, inner guidance, "angels"—all are available now, brought by the trine . . . if only we **wake up**.

Sir Francis Chichester, the pioneering British pilot and yachtsman, gives us a useful example of the mysterious side of the Neptunian trine. In 1957, under this aspect, he was diagnosed with advanced lung cancer. Fatality was presumed. He chose to enter a spiritually oriented "nature cure" hospital—and was miraculously restored to health, living nearly a decade longer.

Cancer is scary. What is so "mellow" about being told you have six months to live? Typically, the Neptunian trine does not have such an edge. That is more common with the square. We must remember, however, that the life of Everyman is simply the backbone of our experiences—other cycles, connected with the internal logic of our own particular birthchart, overlay these broader patterns. When Sir Francis was diagnosed with lung cancer, more was going on than the trine; he also had transiting Uranus applying friction (square) to his natal Mars (courage, fear, survival instinct). That complicated the picture, refining our understanding of how the "generic" Neptune trine applied to this specific individual.

The opposition of Neptune to its natal position occurs in average terms around our eighty-third year, right in the midst of the great planetary convergence we introduced a little while ago. Again, this represents an endpoint. Final exams. **I am not this body. I am not this personality. I am consciousness.** Those are the feelings trying to break through into awareness now. Spirit exists independently of biological processes—that is the Teacher's message. But if the Trickster has his way, then the floodgates of the deep self are opened, drowning the personality in a sea of disconnected images. Self-inflicted senility is the dark side of the opposition, wisdom is the goal.

I once saw a filmed interview with the great mystical Swiss psychologist, Carl Jung, conducted just before his death. At that point, he was in the very early stages of his Neptunian opposition. The interview went briskly, Jung answering complex theoretical questions lucidly in his Germanic English. Only once did he hesitate. The interviewer asked, "Professor Jung, do you now believe in God?" Jung looked away, thought for a moment—and responded, "Now? Difficult to answer. I know. I don't need to believe. I know."

For Jung, as for all who successfully navigate this final Neptunian turning point, the existence of the "beyond" is no longer conjectural, it becomes as real and as palpable as the touch of the night wind. And stepping through that door—again, if our navigation has been successful—is no longer a source of alarm. It is a source of wonder.

PLUTO

The Cycle of Destiny; Cycle of Soul Retrieval
Orbital Period: 247.7 years

Pluto drifts through the signs at such a tortoiselike pace that in a lifetime, it rarely develops as far as the opposition. That gives us only four Plutonian turning points—the relatively rare opposition, the trine, the square, and the sextile. Each one touches us for three or four years, giving it plenty of time to build significance. Those who respond positively to the Plutonian call are swept up by it, carried beyond the world of purely personal concerns into a larger **communal** or **historical** framework. Those who cling to narrower perspectives are often temporarily overwhelmed by a sickness of spirit, a sense of the ultimate emptiness and futility of all they might do. As always, icy Pluto turns his penetrating gaze upon us; he challenges us to trans personalize ourselves by seizing our larger **destiny**.

Complications in Pluto's orbit make it difficult to link its phases to chronological ages. Throughout most of its 248-year cycle, it moves very slowly, never presenting a person with even its first challenge—

the sextile—until he or she has reached the early forties. Pluto's motion is much faster now—and by "now," we mean the latter half of the twentieth century and into the twenty-first. Life is accelerated. Individuals born around 1950, for example, experienced their Plutonian sextiles along with their Saturn returns way ahead of Everyman's schedule, giving them a taste of "midlife crisis" as they finished up their adolescence. Why? Because Pluto's orbit is very elliptical, and therefore its speed is the least constant of any planet. For reasons best deciphered by philosophers and theologians, life has woven these differing time frames into the biopsychic script, letting each generation play a variation on the fundamental Plutonian theme. To know exactly when the aspect occurs for a given person, it is absolutely necessary to refer to an ephemeris.

No matter when it occurs, the cornerstone of the Pluto sextile is **excitation**. But this excitation occurs in a new way: Everyman is stimulated to make his mark in the world. He feels the urge to do something big—and simultaneously he is haunted and driven by a frustrating sense of life's absurdity. "Is this all there is?" The Trickster answers, "Yes, that's all"—thereby imprisoning us in a narrow, pointless existence as we burn off the energy of the sextile in power struggles at work, among friends, or in close relationships. As always, with Pluto there exists that danger of blindly reenacting old wounding dramas. Even if our heart is with the Teacher there is still a "now or never" aura about this transit. Fired by the buzz of the sextile, a voice inside us exhorts us to "do something!"—and that "something" must be more than buying a new car. Like a stone tossed in a pond, it must send ripples out into the community, signaling our presence to the larger world.

Cesar Chavez offers a clear example of a strong response to this phase. The famous California grape strike began under his Plutonian sextile, vaulting him from obscurity into the realm of the history shapers. Mohandas Gandhi's inspiration of the Indian people reached such a frenzied level under this aspect that the British finally had to take notice—he was invited to London.

"Drive, drive, drive" is the Plutonian litany under the waxing square. Precisely **when** it occurs again depends on our historical period, and must be looked up in an ephemeris. The average age is sixty-two, but in contemporary times the aspect occurs much earlier. People born in the middle decade of this century, for example, experience the square in their late thirties. Whenever it occurs, the **friction** can be extremely energizing—the trick is to recognize that **such**

energy must be harnessed. It must be given a mission. Mere ego gets into enough trouble without fueling it with this kind of Plutonian fire. Under the square, pressures rise. Life squalls at us, insisting, demanding something of us—but in a foreign language. To move successfully through this test, a man or woman must learn a new existential vocabulary, leaping beyond self-orientation and behaviors programmed by old hurts, submitting himself or herself to self-transformation through altruistic effort and psychotherapeutic healing, whether self-administered or otherwise. Why? Not because "it is right," but because "it feels right." At the square, whether we have realized it or not, our happiness is more dependent upon improving our soul and our community than upon improving our figure or our income. This Plutonian mission need not be grandiose. We don't need to be a Cesar Chavez or a Mohandas Gandhi. But we must crystallize in some **idealistic rite of passage** our evolution past the narrow, psychologically-determined motivations of youth and into the broad framework of meaning appropriate to the second half of life.

Geraldine Ferraro was blasted onto the track of her larger destiny by this square. With its occurrence, against all odds, she was nominated for the vice presidency of the United States. As we so frequently observe with Pluto, events **beyond her control or understanding** seemed to go over her head, **drafting her into the process of history**. On a less colorful scale, we often find this transiting Plutonian aspect leading people into volunteer work in churches or community organizations—or, if the Trickster has his way, into bleak periods in which life seems to lose all meaning.

Following the square, the trine suggests a flowing time. If we have laid down a strong foundation at the previous Plutonian turning points, our destiny is on a sleigh ride now, accelerated by forces of a collective or historical nature. Charlemagne, propelled by the larger destiny of the European people, was crowned Holy Roman Emperor under the trine. Typically, it occurs late in life—as part of the great convergence in the middle eighties. Once again, contemporary people seem to be leading "pushed" lives—the trine will be appearing as early as the late fifties for people born in the middle of the century, with the **tension** of the opposition reserved for the great convergence.

What is the significance of the Plutonian opposition, this aspect that so few of our forebears ever faced? Two centuries ago Pluto was moving as quickly as it is now—but how many people then saw their sixtieth birthdays? This is a riddle we must figure out for ourselves, and the answer says something not only about Everyman, but also about these times. **Tension**—that is the theme. With Pluto finally opposed to the position it occupied at our births, a kind of judgment day has come. Life stares questioningly at us, asking, "What great work did you do? What do you remember with **transpersonal** pride and satisfaction? What mark did you leave behind?" These are the inquiries most of us reading now will have to answer, not in the presence of some judging Old Testament God, but in the harsher tribunal of our own twentieth-century **consciences**. They are hard, challenging questions— and questions that only a small proportion of the generations that pass through this earth have ever faced, or will face.

JUPITER
The Cycle of Opportunity
Orbital Period: 11.88 years

Jupiter is the largest and most massive body in the solar system, apart from the Sun. Of the slow, life-shaping planets, it is the closest to Earth by a wide margin. Intuition suggests that such a heavyweight working from so close a range would have a marked impact upon our affairs. And Jupiter does that—its effects can rattle our rafters. But the giant planet has a tragic flaw, robbing it of some of the depth we find in the transits of Pluto and the others. That flaw is speed. By the standards of the Teachers and Tricksters, Jupiter whips around the birthchart, covering the entire circuit in just twelve years. That sounds like a long time, but it only leaves about five months within the orbs of each aspect. Real meaning can develop in such a period, as we will soon see, but compared to the ponderous pace of the other outer planets, Jupiter rarely has long enough to turn anyone's inner life around.

The Jupiter return—the conjunction, in other words—is the only aspect we need consider. The others certainly have significance, but in this chapter our purpose is to grasp the human life cycle, and our strategy demands that we select carefully from the overwhelming quantity of information astrology generates. Even limiting ourselves to returns to its natal position, Jupiter typically highlights seven turning points in the course of a normal lifetime. Adding squares and opposi- tions, as we did with Uranus, would flood us and defeat our aims.

Traditionally, Jupiter is seen as "the Greater Benefic," a symbol of luck. Jupiter the Trickster, as we learned in chapter three, has a different face. He can snare us in our own pride, laziness, and overconfidence. This is the planet that rules the Cycle of Opportunity— but opportunity must be seized, and sometimes it proves slippery.

No need to be negative about Jupiter; it can bring us wonderful possibilities. The idea is to recognize that no planet does anything **to** us. We work **with** the planets, and just as in any other Ping-Pong game, the outcome depends on **both** players.

"Luck" is a concept that often breaks down under close scrutiny. Every now and then someone hits the Irish Sweepstakes, but more commonly, when we see "luck," we also see a history of hard work, vision, and persistence leading the "lucky" person to the right place at the right time. Jupiter is connected with both stories: it is often prominently configured by transit when the goose lays a golden egg, but it also signals the time when we are ready to **reap the harvests of effort**, and to prepare the way for more satisfying patterns of self-expression. The trick is to learn to wring every ounce of opportunity out of the Jupiter return without letting the planet amplify our own shortcomings to the point that we snatch defeat from the jaws of victory.

At the Jupiter return, the stage is set for good fortune. Opportunity is there, ready to be grabbed. Better not think of it as a gift, though. It is more like an audition. We have a **chance**, not a guarantee. The aspiring actress who gets a screen test with a big producer—and spends the previous night "celebrating her victory"—may very well flub the test. Exuberance must be directed now, and tempered with judgment and humility. Unrealistically high standards can also snag us. We must learn to recognize **doorways to opportunity**—and leap through them while they are open. Once through the door, other paths appear.

Francis Ford Coppola was given his first movie directorship—for an obscure film entitled *Dementia 13*—at his Jupiter return. He took advantage of the doorway to opportunity, and his persistence was rewarded. He was established as a director. By the time his next Jupiter return rolled around, he had *The Godfather* and an Oscar behind him. Leonard Nimoy, then an obscure actor, experienced a Jupiter return in June 1966. Several weeks later, in September, the first episode of **Star Trek** was broadcast and his uncannily plausible portrayal of the Vulcan science officer, Mr. Spock, assured him a place in history. A Jupiter doorway had opened for him in an unexpected quarter. Nimoy was flexible enough to leap through it. His successful navigation of the Jupiter return has continued to bring him prosperity and opportunity two decades later. William Shatner, playing Captain Kirk to Nimoy's Mr. Spock, is only four days older. Thus, their natal Jupiters are conjunct—and Shatner also experienced a Jupiter return just before the airing of the first episode of *Star Trek*; he too seized a chance that changed his life. Sir Francis Chichester demonstrates the sheer exuberance of the Jupiter return perhaps better than anyone. In 1960, while that aspect was operating, he bet a friend a half crown (about 35 cents) that he could beat him across the Atlantic in a small sailboat. The friend accepted. They left a few months later, and Chichester won the race—and the half crown.

What about the Trickster? Jupiter is usually seen as a benign influence, but I suspect that many people have made stupid, fatal driving errors with this planet on a trigger point. Foolishness in an automobile is a good example: with cars and with Jupiter, the stakes are commonly higher than they seem at the moment. Exuberance is heady and leads to feelings of invincibility. To reap the benefits of the Jupiter return, we need to extend ourselves outwardly into life, taking calculated risks, but never unnecessary ones. Above all, we must guard against the tendency to overestimate ourselves, leading to hubris and usually to embarrassment, or worse. Henry David Thoreau, under a Jupiter return in November 1840, proposed marriage to one Ellen Sewall—and was rejected.

THE SCHEME OF LIFE

This is Everyman's life, the basic biopsychic script imprinted in the cell of our bodies and the synapases of our brains. What does it tell us? That life itself is a cycle with predictable phases. That each of us faces a series of foreseeable crises and turning points on the mental level, just as certainly as we face similar milestones in our physical aging. That no one is immune. That, short of premature death, there is no way either to avoid any of the steps, or to hasten their arrival. That the cycle is as old as humanity, and that it describes in a single eternal story the individual biographies of every man or woman who has ever lived—or who will ever live until the first child awakens in the alien air of an other world.

What happened to our freedom? Are we doomed forever to play out the scenes of this ancient drama? The biopsychic script tells us a lot, but it is what it does **not** tell us that inserts vitality into the cold calculus of Everyman's life. Each of these existential steps is a **question**, not an answer. Each of us responds differently. For example, as we discovered a few pages back, Cesar Chavez responded to transiting Pluto sextiling its natal position by leading farm workers in their strike for fair working conditions. The excitation of the sextile gave him not only the charisma, but also the sense of mission that successfully controlled and directed the awesome Plutonian energies. Precisely the same charismatic aspect was in force in Charles Manson's birthchart when his followers committed the gruesome Tate-LaBianca murders. We also see it activated in Adolph Hitler's birthchart throughout World War Two. What makes the difference? The answer does not lie within the scope of astrology. It lies in our own hands. "Everyman" does not exist, except as an abstraction. Only people exist, making their own choices.

How do we use the biopsychic script in the concrete practice of predictive astrology? Once again, actual interpretive strategies are a subject for later on. Right now, we are learning vocabulary. Still, there are two interacting principles we must keep in mind if a knowledge of Everyman's life is going to help us rather than confuse us.

☆ The meaning of **any** transit is partly determined by the timing of its occurrence in relation to the fixed phases of the life cycle.

☆ Superimposed on the fixed phases of the life cycle is a web of transits unique to each individual, which profoundly affects the meaning of the fixed phases.

Take, for example, the passage of Uranus through the opposition to a woman's natal Mercury. After looking carefully at the "root prediction" (the birthchart), there are certain procedures to follow in unraveling the transit—procedures we covered in detail in chapter three. During this period of her life, an explosive element of Uranian individuality is placing tension (opposition) on her intelligence and her style of self-expression (Mercury). Social pressure is pushing her one way; her inner voice is pushing her the other way. That much is true whether she is seventeen or ninety-three.

Understanding her place in the life cycle helps us carry the woman's story further. The Uranian transit is occurring when she is nearly twenty-nine, just entering her first Saturn return. That knowledge ups the ante, she has reached a critical turning point, and therefore every astrological detail stands out vividly. Why? Because that Uranian transit, although normally not such a pivotal one, is flavoring a decision that will shape the next three decades of her life. The biopsychic script, in other words, affects our reading of that Uranus-Mercury interaction. She is making the transition from adolescence to maturity—everything else must be understood in that light. What does the Uranian-Mercurial element add to her experience?

Certain habits of self-expression (Mercury) connected with her youth are ripe to be dropped (Uranus)—but people around her have become accustomed to those habits and insist that she maintain them. This battle for her right to express herself becomes one of the **rites of passage** connected with her entry into adulthood. Deeply affected by the Uranian overtones, her Saturn return takes on a rebellious (Uranus) flavor—and if she is to navigate it successfully she must be especially wary of conventional answers to the questions she is facing. Normally, such rebelliousness is not inherently a major dimension of the Saturn return, but in her case, that free-spirited Uranian element unlocks her logjam.

The woman's name, by the way, is Diana Ross and the astrological drama materialized as her acting debut in *Lady Sings the Blues*. Abandoning her glittery teenage public persona, she took the Uranian step of portraying blues singer Billie Holiday, communicating (Mercury) her adult identity in a way that surprised and shocked (Uranus) all those who would have had her remain a caricature of her adolescent self. Thus, **a transit whose timing was linked to her individual birthchart interacted with the universal biopsychic script to produce a unique rite of passage.** Neither could be understood without the other. In fact, separating the two is only a learning device. In practice, the theme and its variations are one.

□ □ □

This completes our survey of planetary transits. If you feel confused, please don't worry or feel that you should go back and review anything you might have forgotten. Just keep on reading. Later, when we get to the last part of the book, we will talk about how to meld all this material into a coherent whole. At this point, it is best to think of predictive astrology as a jigsaw puzzle. Our first step is to empty the box and survey the pieces, separating sky blue from forest green. Only then do we begin actual construction. Right now, we are still in that early phase of our puzzle-building process; we are just having a look at the pieces.

What have those pieces taught us? Although we have explored many details, the essence of the past few chapters has been simple. First, we learned that the birthchart itself is the **root prediction**. We need to understand it thoroughly before we even begin to think about transits. Second, we learned that transits don't "do anything **to** anybody"; people are **free to respond to them creatively**. Third, we learned that transits fall into two major categories: fast ones and slow ones. The slow ones are the "Teachers" and "Tricksters" that shape the

big themes of life; the fast ones are the "triggers" that create the day-by-day situations through which we actually experience those big themes. Finally, we learned that certain specific slow transits always occur at specific ages. The themes these special transits create are universal ones, happening to all of us at certain predictible times. This underlying **biopsychic script** affects how we respond to other transits, and what they mean to us.

If you can remember all that, you are doing fine.

PART THREE

PROGRESSIONS

CHAPTER SEVEN

PROGRESSIONS I:
WHAT ARE PROGRESSIONS?

Plant an acorn. Give it water and rich soil and sunlight. Throw in a bit of luck. What happens? An oak tree springs up. A century later, it towers over the forest. Now paint a picture of that oak as it will look in a hundred years, but paint it **today** while there is nothing present but a germinating acorn. Well, it's not that hard a predictive challenge. We know the look of oaks in general. We know the shape of the leaves, the texture of the bark. We can guess the appearance of that tree in a century, but our painting is nothing but an **extrapolation into the future** of generalized facts we know today. Perhaps twenty years from now the tree is struck by a bolt of lightning. It survives, but now with a gash running down its trunk. Or maybe the prevailing west wind bows it, forcing all the branches to one side. Or it is stunted by drought or denuded by acid rain. None of these influences can be foreseen as we look at the acorn. They arise later, as the acorn **interacts with its environment**. Sitting at our easel before the newborn oak, paintbrushes in hand, we can only fantasize about such environmental factors—and yet our painting of the oak's future is largely accurate. Details might vary from reality, but no one is likely to mistake our portrait of the tree for a zebra or a chrysanthemum. Why? Because the nature of the seed determines the nature of the blossom. Understand the first and you have at least a rough outline of the second.

This is the essence of the astrological technique known as **progressions**, a separate predictive system that stands alongside transits, but works differently. Progressions furnish a tool that penetrates the developmental logic of the seed itself—in this case, the individual birthchart. They contrast sharply with transits, which are **environmental factors**. If transits are life's lightning bolts, its west winds, its droughts and floods, then progressions are the **genetic code** of each individual human "acorn." They tell us when to spread our branches, when to flower, and when to seed.

Isn't this more "life cycle" material, such as we covered in the previous chapter? Not exactly—although we do find that certain progressions, just like certain transits, are universal in their timing and therefore mark more turning points for Everyman. Most progressions are more personal. Again, they are like the genetic code—but the seed they allow us to understand is not the universal human one; it is unique. Not the genetic code of Everyman, but that of a "third house Aquarian" or a "seventh house Sagittarian with the moon in Taurus in the twelfth house." Just as one person has genes for early balding and another has genes for a flowing mane of snow-white hair, one is programmed astrologically to grow naturally into a time of intensive career activity at age forty-five while another is pushed by his inner developmental logic to retreat from the world at that age. How? Not by transits but by the uncoiling evolutionary rhythm of his birthchart, a rhythm we measure through progressions. Just as with transits, we can use progressions to analyze any period in a person's life—past, present, or future. They work the same in practice; it's just that they measure something deeper inside us than transits do.

> ☆ Progressions reveal the "genetic code" of growth
> inherent in the internal developmental logic of each
> individual birthchart, independent of its larger
> environment.

Once we understand them, progressions complete our predictive system. We have the acorn itself. That is the birthchart. In Part Two, we learned how transits predict the "cosmic weather" to which that acorn is subjected. Now, with progressions, we unravel that acorn's own hidden agenda, deciphering its internal developmental code.

Predictive astrology, as you are doubtless surmising, can become a confusing labyrinth of symbols. It is trickier than the analysis of a birthchart, just as college is trickier than kindergarten. An orderly approach is essential. That is why the last part of this book focuses exclusively on creating effective interpretive strategies. But with progressions we do have an ace in the hole: Almost everything we have already learned about transits also applies to progressions. Having grasped one, we are halfway to grasping the other. In both systems, planets trace paths around the birthchart, stimulating potentials built into the "root prediction," hitting aspectual trigger points, focusing attention first on self-confidence, then on responsibilities, then on sexual issues. There is no rule we learned in the previous six chapters that does not continue to apply. Only the slow-fast distinction is of diminished importance, and that is only because **all** progressions are slow. So slow, in fact, that only the faster ones engage our attention. The rest mean no more to us than a receding glacier means to a mayfly.

> ☆ Once we allow for differences in speed, all
> fundamental laws of transits theory apply also
> to progressions.

SYMBOLIC TIME

Transits are real events. When you experience transiting Uranus crossing your Sagittarian Ascendant, the planet **actually, physically** occupies the part of the sky that was rising when you were born. Once we accept the basic astrological premise that there are parallels between celestial occurrences and earthly ones, there is a certain logic to transits. To grasp progressions, we must abandon that logic. Transits are **observed**; progressions are **calculated**. No progression refers to a **real astronomical event** in the same way that a transit does. With progressions we enter an inner universe governed not by **real time**, but by **symbolic time**.

Perhaps surprisingly, **symbolic time** progressions are just as effective as **real time** transits in helping to answer the questions we face as we move through experience. However symbolic they might be, they correspond to something quite real in the life of the mind.

How are they derived? There are actually several kinds of progressions, each calculated in a different way. All share one common denominator: a short period of time is made to **represent** a longer one. The existential events occurring ten "long units" after birth are reflected in the astronomical events occurring ten "short units" after birth. For example, in **secondary progressions** the long unit is the **year** while the short unit is the **day**. If you want to calculate a man's secondary progressions on his thirty-fifth birthday, look in the ephemeris and find out where the planets were thirty-five days after his birth: those are his current secondary progressions. In this case, one **natural planetary rhythm**—Earth's rotation on its axis—is set equal to another kind of natural planetary rhythm—Earth's revolution in its orbit. The day, in other words, is set equal, symbolically, to the year.

Although we will briefly introduce other systems, these **secondaries**, or "day-for-year" progressions, along with transits, are the workhorses of predictive astrology as I, at least, practice it. Let's take a closer look at them.

SECONDARY PROGRESSIONS

The day equals the year! Taken literally, the idea is absurd. But astrologers don't intend that it be taken literally. The statement is purely symbolic, and at that level it makes sense. All of us use the same kind of reasoning in our everyday lives. We might, for example, say that, "in human terms, Rover is seventy years old." Everyone knows immediately that the dog is not really so ancient, but that in proportion to the human life cycle, he has used up that much of his lifespan. We have set one long unit of time (the human life cycle) equal to one short unit of time (the canine life cycle). The **phases** of one are reflected in the **phases** of the other, even though the lengths of the cycles are quite different. In a sense, we have "progressed" the dog's life. On an even simpler level, we might announce that, "Joe is going through a personal renaissance." That's progression too—we have drawn a parallel between Joe's life and the lives of civilizations, seeing the phases of one reflected in the phases of the other. This is **symbolic logic** and there is nothing uniquely astrological about it.

Extending the same reasoning brings us to secondary progressions. When astrologers say that the day equals the year, all they are really saying is that parallels exist between these two natural planetary rhythms. Once again, the phases of one cycle are reflected in the phases of the other. The final link in the chain is to realize that celestial cycles parallel personal ones—which of course is the basis of all astrological theory. Once we have accepted that, then progressions begin to make sense—in a very abstract way.

The proof of the pudding lies in actually testing the theory against reality. Do progressions **work**? Soon you will be able to determine that for yourself. My own experience suggests that even though transits have the attraction of being a more "natural" system, based on real astronomical events, progressions are equally powerful. To attempt predictive astrology without them would be like flying through fog without radar. You might very well notice an oak tree here and a herd of sheep there—but craggy mountains might skim past your wingtips unnoticed.

Days equal years. The locations of the transiting planets a week after your birth correspond to their progressed positions on your seventh birthday; where they were after forty days corresponds to their progressed positions on your fortieth birthday, and so on. In this way, the **progressions** of an entire lifetime are compressed into the **transits** of the first two or three months of infancy. The primary implication of all this is that progressions unfold at a snail's pace. The slow planets— the "Teachers and Tricksters" of transits theory—might only move a degree or two in several weeks and that could represent their progressed motion over decades. Since all predictive astrological work is ultimately founded upon **changes** in planetary positions, these super-slow progressions do not tell us very much. Whether they have a very subtle order of significance or they have no meaning at all is a moot point. In practical astrology, we ignore them except in a few very specialized circumstances, such as when your progressed Jupiter, say, makes a Station, switching from retrograde to direct motion, for example.

There go the Teachers and Tricksters, out the window. The very quality that gave them such overwhelming power in transits—their slow pace—now robs them of any important role in our understanding of progressions. We are left with the inner planets—Mercury, Venus, and Mars, plus the Sun and the Moon. These move quickly enough in the course of weeks to show clear changes in their aspects and sign and house positions. It is they, along with two more points—the progressed Ascendant and the progressed Midheaven—that form the bulwark of progression theory.

Exactly what do they signify?

The quick planets retain the same fundamental meanings we encountered in *The Inner Sky*. In chapter three of this book we saw them operating as **triggers** for the dramas set up by Jupiter and Saturn and the other slow planets. Now, with progressions, they transcend their role as mere triggers. Now, with progressions, the quick planets become Teachers and Tricksters in their own right.

☆ The fast inner planets are the Teachers and
Tricksters in progressions theory. The motions of the
slow ones are too slight to be of any consequence.

In response to their new level of dignity, we must now write these
former "trigger planets" a more central role in our life script. Mercury
remains the symbol of intellect and information transfer, but now it
goes beyond playing the part of secretary or research assistant to the
ponderous outer planets. In progressions, it symbolizes a person's
evolving mental picture of the world. In other words, it represents the
very basis of all his or her decision-making processes **as that basis
changes over a lifetime.** Similarly, progressed Venus symbolizes one's
**evolving attitudes, needs, and challenges in the relationship
department**—again, a far more significant role than we awarded to
transiting Venus. The basic concepts for each planet remain unchanged,
but now, due to the slowness of their progressed motion, they have
time to build the depth and complexity of meaning characteristic of
true Teachers and Tricksters.

A useful rule of thumb in understanding the meanings of progressed
planets is to remember the general function they represent in a
birthchart, then simply place the word "evolving" in front of it. The
natal Sun, for example, represents **identity.** The progressed Sun
becomes one's **evolving identity.** It works the same way for all
progressed planets.

As we learned in birthchart astrology, knowing that a person's
Venus lies in Virgo and the sixth house tells us a lot about what he
needs in a relationship and what pitfalls lie before him if he is selfish,
stubborn, or unwary. Now, with progressions, our understanding of
that configuration deepens. We know that eventually such a Venus will
progress into Libra and into the seventh house. The birthchart remains
the birthchart, but in the natural course of experience, that individual
evolves into a confrontation with Libran seventh house needs and
issues—just as certainly as a sprouting acorn sooner or later must
figure out how to make oak leaves. Why? Because Libran seventh
house developments are part of the **genetic code** built into an **evolving**
sixth house Venus in Virgo—regardless of what kind of transiting
"weather" rains down on the process.

Similarly, progressing planets move into **aspects** with various
trigger points around the birthchart, just as transiting planets do.
A person might, for example, be born with the Sun situated so that it
eventually progresses into a conjunction with the planet Uranus.

(Not all birthcharts are configured in a manner that allows this to happen. Owing to the progressed Sun's slowness, only about one in five of us ever experiences that particular Solar-Uranian aspect.) Should it occur, we know that the person's **evolving identity** is colliding with a set of distinctly Uranian issues. He or she is challenged to make a radical break with the past, especially with those conservative inner forces that lock people into habitual, self-limiting "tribal" patterns. During the period when the progressed Sun is within the orbs of the conjunction, usually four or five years, we can reliably predict that existential events take a dramatic turn, and that the pattern of opportunity that surrounds the man or woman will be permanently altered. "Wild cards" are played now—improbable Uranian events arise that reveal colorful, unpredictable, unusual escape routes from entrenched but outworn styles of living. In chapter three, we saw how Sally Ride was blasted into orbit aboard the space shuttle while **transiting** Uranus opposed her Sun. Now we can add one more looming piece to her jigsaw puzzle. Not only was she undergoing an explosive Uranian transit, but simultaneously her **progressed** Sun was conjuncting her natal Uranus—a classic astrological "double whammy." Her evolving identity was ready to make a Uranian break with the past. Interestingly, the same progressed aspect was operative in astronaut Eugene Cernan's chart when Gemini 9 orbited the earth.

Once again, our rules for interpreting progressions are essentially the same as our rules for reading transits. First, we grasp the **root prediction** itself. What part of the birthchart is being stimulated by the progression? What potentials are there in the first place? Water won't burn, in other words, no matter what kind of flame is played on it. Second, we understand the **nature of the progressed influence**. Are we talking about evolving assertiveness (progressed Mars)? His evolving outward mask (progressed Ascendant)? Her evolving relationship needs (progressed Venus)? Third, we consider the aspect forming between the progressed planet and the natal one. What is the **nature of the process** unfolding between these two dimensions of the individuality? The astrological symbolism is so rich and diverse that there are no limits to what we might find at this point—no limits, that is, other than the borders of our own empathy, compassion, and imagination. Has a young man's happy-go-lucky outward mask (progressed Ascendant in Sagittarius) now evolved into a state of **friction** (square aspect) with his inwardly mystical nature (a fourth house Neptune in Pisces)? Has the natural development of a woman's courage and assertiveness (progressed Mars) now unfolded to the point where it can **enhance** (trine) her determination to have a meaningful career (natal Saturn on the Midheaven)? Such is the power of progressions, that we can discern these elemental crises and opportunities built into the developmental genetic code of each individual birthchart, predicting when each of us, like the acorn, is ready to spread our boughs—or slow down our life processes in preparation for a long winter.

RETROGRADE PROGRESSIONS

Often it happens that a person is born while one of the inner planets is retrograde—moving backward through the signs. Then that planet also initially **progresses** in a retrograde fashion. Other times, a transiting planet turns retrograde two weeks after a person is born. Then when she is fourteen years old (days equal years!), that **progressed** planet **makes a station** and turns retrograde, perhaps remaining retrograde for the rest of her life or at least a big chunk of it.

Mars usually **transits** through about three quarters of a degree **each day**. As a result, it normally **progresses** that distance **each year**. However, as transiting Mars moves towards a station, it slows down gradually over many days until it finally grinds to a halt—then very slowly gathers momentum in the opposite direction. In the sky, such a transition occurs over a week or two. Translated into the ponderous rhythm of progressions, that transition might occupy a **decade**— resulting in a "stalled" progressed Mars. Should that Mars stall on a trigger point, **evolving courage** must make a stand, preparing to withstand a long siege.

Even if a progressed planet's station does not occur on a trigger point, still the mere fact of its turning retrograde or direct remains significant. Invariably there is a "turning of the tide" in the department of life that the planet symbolizes. Moving into retrograde motion, progressed Venus suggests a relative quieting of the social nature, perhaps a withdrawal from active relating—if the **root prediction** suggests such possibilities. Turning direct, that progressed Venus implies the opposite development—an opening and stretching of the social circle, a renewed ease in intimate settings, perhaps urbanity and poise arising in what had been a more socially awkward character. Once again, much depends upon the promise of the root prediction itself. We must also remember that transitions such as these occupy **years**. To grasp the effects of progressed stations, we must stand back from life, training ourselves to think in terms of decades rather than months. Like continental drift, their effects are profound—but mean very little to the owls and mice who inhabit that continent's forests.

THE ORBS OF PROGRESSED ASPECTS

How precise does a progressed aspect have to be before we begin to feel it? This is an exceedingly complex question. As always with the issue of aspectual orbs, dogmatic answers are invariably wrong answers. The real issue is this: When does an aspect's significance become so subtle that we can safely ignore it? Given the extreme slowness of all progressed planets except the Moon, their force builds gradually over a span of years, peaking when the aspect is precise, then gradually fading over many more years. Personally, I choose to allow an orb of about a degree-and-a-half on either side of the exact trigger point. With the progressed Sun, I extend that by another degree. Never would I claim that there is anything magical about those numbers. Nothing "turns on" or "turns off" at that point. I have no doubt that progressions are felt over a wider range of space and time than these relatively narrow orbs would suggest. It is just that their symbolism outside these orbs is more subtle, and usually other astrological events overwhelm them, claiming center stage.

> ☆ An aspectual orb of one and a half degrees (two
> and a half for the Sun) isolates, for practical purposes,
> the most dynamic period in a planet's progression
> over a trigger point.

Limiting ourselves to these orbs still gives a progressed planet plenty of time to operate. The progressed Sun, for example, moves about one degree per year. Add two and a half degrees on either side, and that gives it about five years of energetic action as it crosses a trigger point, with a particularly vigorous peak during the middle year. Progressed Mars remains active for roughly the same length of time—its orbs are narrower, but its speed is slower. Venus and Mercury progress more quickly, remaining within sensitive orbs for a couple of years. The progressed Ascendant and Midheaven have similar periods of dynamic activity, although the Ascendant, for reasons we investigate in the next chapter, is more variable. For planets that can turn retrograde—Mercury, Venus, and Mars—these active phases can at times be extended over many years. And that is perhaps the most convincing argument against wider aspectual orbs: Our attention spans are such that we can conceive of "periods of life" running over a few years but when we begin to speak of decades, the "period of life" begins to blur into "life in general." The prediction loses its emotional impact. Once again, owls and mice couldn't care less about continental drift.

OTHER PROGRESSIVE TECHNIQUES

Techniques for moving the horoscope through time come in a baffling array of forms. So far, we have introduced only secondary progressions. This day-for-year technique is perhaps the most widely used of all types, and throughout the rest of the book we limit our attention to it. From now on, when we say "progressions," we mean "secondary progressions." Although other techniques are worthy of your attention, I would suggest that you avoid vexing yourself by trying to apply more than one system at a time. As you will discover below, it is possible by using many forecasting systems at once to create a situation in which seven shades of Hades are breaking loose on every trigger point simultaneously—and for the astrologer, confusion quickly replaces understanding

Each style of looking forward has its adherents. Each seems to work, at least some of the time. Each starts from a slightly different premise and answers a slightly different set of questions. Personally, I find the secondaries to be the most broadly effective of all techniques. Since my intention in writing this book is to offer a practical, workable system of predictive astrology, I plan to develop only those techniques that I use every day in my own astrological practice—transits and secondary progressions. What follows is not an exhaustive study of all other progressive systems, but rather a menu from which you might want to order dessert once you have digested the main course.

Among the methods for projecting into the future are two major divisions: **progressions** and **directions**. With progressions, everything in the horoscope moves at its individual speed. The Moon's movement is different from Mercury's and different from Jupiter's, etc. Also, the positions used in progressions **did actually appear in the sky** at some time. (Secondary progressions appeared in the sky a few weeks or months after one's birth, for example.) Transits, by contrast, consider the current planetary positions in the sky in comparison to the birthchart.

With **directions**, everything in the entire horoscope is "directed" (moved) at a specific rate. When using directions, the motions of the Moon, Mercury, Sun, etc. are all the same. For example, solar arc directions move everything forward at the rate of the Sun's arc of motion in secondary progressions (or about one degree per year). In directions, the patterns created when looking ahead generally did **not** ever appear in the sky." Imagine the planets "frozen" to a wheel in their birthplace positions and then rotating that entire wheel at a specific rate. That is the image of directions. All of the different systems of directions and progressions have their proponents.

Primary Progressions (usually called "directions"): A century ago, this was a popular system, but now it has gone out of vogue. Mathematically, primaries are complicated. One year of life is equal to approximately one degree of change in the Midheaven degree and other house cusps. Planets move very little. Probably the main reason primaries are still mentioned in astrology texts is because people always want to know why secondaries are called secondaries. Obsolete.

Tertiary Progressions: The actual positions of the planets **one day** after birth correspond to their progressed positions at the age of **one lunar month**. The lunar month here, by the way, is not the time between two new moons, but rather the average length of time between successive conjunctions of the transiting moon with its own natal position, about 27.32 days. That cycle is called the "tropical month." Where are your progressed planets 243 lunar months (about twenty years) after your birth? Count 243 **days** forward from your birth in the ephemeris—the planetary positions you read there represent your tertiary progressions. Compared to secondaries, tertiaries move rapidly, which means they are very active progressions, full of fireworks and color. Some astrologers swear by them. I haven't had much experience with them myself.

Minor Progressions: Again, these are based on the tropical month. This time, the actual positions of the planets **twenty tropical months** after birth are the progressed positions for age twenty. The month, rather than the day, is said to equal the year, in other words. Minor progressions, like tertiaries, move quite rapidly compared to the glacial pace of the secondaries. I find them uncannily accurate, yet speed robs the minors of their ability to measure the patient, almost symphonic development of life as a **whole**—something secondary progressions do superbly. I recommend them, once you've gotten your feet wet.

Solar Arc Directions: "Solar arcs" are quite popular and powerful. Many people forget that they are basically a variation on the theme of secondary progressions. Each planet is "directed" (moved) the same distance **as the Sun has moved by secondary progression**. If the Sun has progressed 32 degrees, then so have Mercury, Venus, Mars, and the others. In this system, even outer planets are directed. You have a "solar arc Pluto," for example. This is a great advantage, in that many more moving points are created. Even though the system is "slow," a lot is happening most of the time since so many planets are involved. In my opinion, Solar Arcs, being Sun-based, address Sun-based questions. They tell us a lot about the ego and the self-image, in other words. That's fine, but it leaves out many dimensions of our humanity.

Although I am aware of no traditions that actually use this notion, I think one could measure **emotional development** through "lunar arcs," **relationship development** through "Venus arcs," and so on, each calculated based on the motion of that planet by secondary progression and then adding that arc to the position of **every** natal planet.

Degree-for-Year Directions: A degree is added to the position of each planet for every year of life. For example, if you were born with Mercury in one degree of Gemini, on your twentieth birthday, your directed Mercury would be in 21 degrees of Gemini. This is a popular system, but I am suspicious of it personally. The "degree" is a human artifact; there is nothing natural about it. I think degree-for-year directions work because they mimic solar arcs—the Sun's daily arc is slightly less than one degree, so the two systems are almost exactly the same, especially in the progressions of relatively young people. The main advantage of degree-for-year directions is that no calculation is necessary. Think of them as "quick and dirty" solar arcs and they might be helpful to you.

Duodenary Directions: These are similar to "degree-for-year" directions, but they have a more natural basis. The zodiac is divided into twelve signs; in duodenaries, we take that division a step farther— each **sign** is divided into twelve units, each comprising two and a half degrees. Planets are directed one unit for each year of life.

There are other progressive systems, but these are the common ones. Each can be used as described here—and also **backwards**! Counting days or months or degrees or whatever **before** the birth, progressing planets into **earlier** zodiacal degrees is also a recognized technique. These are called **converse progressions**, and they too have their adherents.

Is your head spinning? So is mine. A hunger arises almost automatically at this point to find which system is "right"—and to dismiss the others. It won't work. Each kind of progression gives accurate and dramatic results at least some of the time. I like secondaries because they seem consistently reliable, and because they seem deeply attuned to the inner laws of the human spirit. Study the others if you like. They are part of the picture, too. Perhaps nowhere else in astrology has the human intellect been given such scope for experimentation. The basic birthchart and the transits—these are **empirical**; we don't calculate them, we **observe** them. That link to the fundamental structure of nature has helped keep astrology grounded in reality. Progressions, on the other hand, are **synthetic** techniques, inventions of the mind. And like most of humanity's inventions, they are powerful. The question is, are we ourselves powerful enough to control **them**? Use progressions, but be careful. Don't let them run away with you. **Theoretically**, all these techniques are of interest, but **practically**, the best advice I can give you is to suggest that you begin by limiting yourself to secondary progressions. Along with transits, they arm us with a system of self-understanding that leaves no nuance of experience, no riddle, no paradox of life without a manageable set of symbols to illuminate it.

CHAPTER EIGHT

PROGRESSIONS II: MORE TEACHERS AND TRICKSTERS

Astrologer **(mysteriously)**: Your progressed Neptune is making a quincunx aspect to your natal Venus in the House of Troubles...

Client **(apprehensively)**: Is that...bad?

The preceding dialogue has been acted out for centuries. The astrologer peers cryptically into the birthchart, then makes an incomprehensible pronouncement while the helpless client looks on, nervously awaiting the verdict. Who gains? Only sadists and masochists. Only those who are irreversibly committed to being sheep—and those who feel compelled to play the role of the wolves. Although that brand of astrology unfortunately still exists today, it is dying out. People are no longer so content to have impersonal planetary forces map out their fates. The modern astrologer is no prophet; he or she is more akin to the weatherman who might call for a day of rain and bluster. Most of the time, that weatherman is reasonably accurate—but you can choose to wear a raincoat or to run naked and catch pneumonia, as you please.

In chapter four, we introduced the idea of Teachers and Tricksters—the "good" and "bad" side of each transiting outer planet. Now we are ready to do the same with progressions, seeing each planetary symbol as a force to be understood and used creatively—lest we stumble over our own feet, fail to learn the lesson, and contrive trouble and embarrassment for ourselves. Each progression, just like each transit, creates a certain kind of personal "weather." That much is predictable. Beyond that, we enter the realm of freedom—and therefore of uncertainty. If the forecast is for rain and wind, then the Teacher would have us dress accordingly, while the Trickster would send us out smiling and unprepared—or leave us cringing under our bed as if the report called for tornadoes and a 35 percent chance of nuclear holocaust.

Teachers and Tricksters. Exactly what are we talking about here? The mind likes myths; heroes and villains always hold our attention. To speak of "Mercury the Trickster" or "Venus the Teacher" is evocative. It excites the spirit and alerts the mind. For those reasons, speaking of Teachers and Tricksters enlivens our approach to astrology, making it interesting and effective. Still, we must be careful not to be deceived by the power of our own mythology. Teachers and Tricksters are not forces of Light and Darkness "out there" in space. They are internal. You are your own Trickster and your own Teacher. Transits and progressions signal developmental steps happening inside you. They can be ridden like perfect, cresting waves or tripped over like misplaced furniture—all according to choices and commitments you make.

The Teacher inside you has no message, no doctrine. He or she speaks only the language of life, of endless change. Your inner Teacher counsels flexibility and growth, openness to constructive criticism and to experimentation. The Teacher wants you to trust the natural rhythms of your experience. He delights in releasing old patterns of behavior, old articles of faith, worn-out beliefs and attitudes. She glories in inconsistency—the inconsistency of past with future, of death with life, of childhood with maturity. To the Teacher, nothing is sacred except Truth—and Truth is something we always approach, but never fully attain. He is the part of you that believes so deeply in life that every experience is embraced gladly and willingly, taken as both lesson and gift. If she has a motto, it is this: "Whatever you see, it is more than that."

The adversary is the Trickster, the part of your spirit that **hates to change**. You please it when you cling defensively to the past, making it a point of personal honor not to learn anything, never to be more than you are right now. The Trickster is cunning—but also lazy. It can be outsmarted, if you are not its co-conspirator. To defeat it, you must actively consider the possibility that you are **wrong**. You must leap beyond the picture of the world that your ego has painted for you, a picture in which you are often a hapless victim caught in a web of circumstances beyond your control. You must let the inner Teacher show you a new picture, a clearer one. That picture might humiliate you for a moment, but it also points past the dead ends, toward ever-expanding paths of authentic, vibrant living.

With progressions we add a new set of Teachers and Tricksters. Powerful alliances can be forged here, if you get to know these forces and to accept their fierce friendship. Otherwise, you antagonize a ragtag mafia of internal con artists and thieves, each one more treacherous than the last, each armed with a perfect understanding of your vices and your vulnerabilities, and each one hell-bent on stealing the fire and joy from your trusting spirit.

Scary stuff.

Don't close the book yet—these Tricksters are there anyway. Astrology can only help. Get acquainted with them, and with the Teachers' help, you can be happier than you are today. This is not simply astrology we are talking about; this is life. Walk down the street. Momentarily meet the eyes of strangers chosen at random. Open your heart to what you see. Who are they? Every tone in the human symphony is out there, but some are sad ones. Some move mechanically, while others move with the spirit and dignity of wild animals. Some look back listlessly, fearfully. Some won't look back at all. Others shine at you as if they had the whole cosmos between their ears. To talk about "winners" and "losers" is to reduce the symphony to an advertising jingle. Our aim is not to pigeon-hole anyone. Quite the opposite. **The idea that people are mutable, capable of changing themselves, is the cornerstone of evolutionary astrology.** Those happy faces and magical eyes you meet on the street belong to the people of the Teacher; the dark ones are the victims of the Trickster. Perhaps the deepest mystery of all is that at any moment one might turn into the other. Is a knowledge of astrology the difference between the two? Of course not. The difference is commitment to flowing and growing, to facing squarely the legitimate, inescapable **hurt** of living—and to seizing the Teachers' gifts of regeneration and redefinition. If astrology does anything helpful, it is to serve as a guide, to offer us introductions to life's Teachers—and mugshots of the Tricksters. The rest is up to us.

Please note that **Part Four** of the book is devoted to a "cookbook" interpretation of each of the progressed planets in terms of their contacts with each individual sensitive point in the birthchart. For now, let's meet them as individuals, outside the drama of any particular, specific astrological configuration.

SUN THE TEACHER

Glyph: ☉

The Gift: The ability to alter basic values and priorities, thereby allowing one's actual behavior to reflect developments in his or her evolving inner life.

The Challenge: Are you strong enough to change the very basis of your identity, allowing yourself the freedom to become what you have never been before?

A friend phones you. His wife has just left him. The next day his boss laid him off. Just as he was reaching for the liquor bottle, he got a call from an old college friend in Dublin, offering him a new job—in Ireland. He accepted. He is dazed and wants you to meet him for a cup of coffee. He says that he is going through "heavy changes." You agree. But is he, really? Let's follow the tale a little further.

Two years later, he is back in the States on vacation. Again you meet him for coffee. His life is back on track. He loves his new job. He has remarried. You leave the restaurant with a warm feeling, thinking fondly to yourself, "He hasn't changed." And you are right. He really hasn't changed. He still tells the same jokes, wears the same kind of clothes. His relationship with his new wife bears a striking resemblance to the relationship he had with the woman who left him. Despite the fireworks, his **essence** has barely been touched.

Such events can be understood astrologically—a weaker response to the transiting Uranus might trigger them—but they have little to do with the progressed Sun. Here, the **very basis of identity** is changing. The shy little mouse quits her secretarial job and moves to Italy as a ski instructor. The gung-ho businessman becomes a yogi. The alcoholic stops drinking. These are "events"—but they point to far more profound developments occurring in the foundations of the character, just as earthquakes reflect deeper motions in the earth's core.

The only trouble with the progressed Sun as a predictive tool is that we might wait a long time for it to do anything. Years go by in which the solar presence is all underground. At about 1 degree per year, even in a long life it covers only one quarter of the birthchart—and touches only one quarter of the chart's trigger points. We must be alert to its movements, because when this sleeping giant awakens, more than mere events are occurring—the very rules by which the game is played are changing.

Evolving identity—that is the progressed Sun's significance. The "personal myth" is never static. It is always affected by the experiences it seeks. The process is gradual, but inexorable. When the progressed Sun crosses a trigger point, **realizations arise that rock the roots of the self-image**. Almost invariably, these realizations are accompanied by colorful outer events. Remembering that the progressed Sun remains within the orbs of a trigger point for four or five years, it is easy to understand how the process can become quite complex. A glimmer of realization arises, precipitating certain events that in turn deepen the initial realization and lead to further outward developments, all building toward a momentous crescendo during the year when the progressed solar aspect is most precise. Afterward, there is a period of settling, as the identity integrates and stabilizes the new insights. Superimposed on the process, other transits and progressions play their hands, enriching the fundamental solar event, just as crosscurrents of choppy whitecaps slice over the deeper, slower, vaster swell of true oceanic waves.

The progression of the Sun through the signs and houses of the birthchart is perhaps the deepest astrological life rhythm. One can map a person's general developmental drama simply by following this single indicator. Link it to the **biopsychic script** we introduced in chapter six, and you have outlined at least skeletally a whole biography. By noting when the progressed Sun crosses into a new house or sign, you are not dividing life into mere chapters. "Volumes" is a better word. In a typical lifetime, the progressed Sun contacts only three signs and three houses, so slow is its motion. When it shifts from one sign to another, the **underlying values and motivations** that mold a person's choices undergo basic alteration. When the progressed Sun crosses the cusp of a new house, the **circumstances and characteristic behaviors** of the individual shift into a fresh arena. In either case, the new patterns remain active for about three decades.

A man, for example, was born with the natal Sun in 6 degrees of Virgo. Knowing that the progressed Sun moves a little less than 1 degree each year, we realize that in his middle twenties, the Sun would progress into Libra—and that to remain centered and happy, he would have to give up some of his self-questioning Virgo-ness and add some Libran motivations and values to his self-image. "People like me." "I am creative." "Beauty, at some level, is part of my essence." If he is able to make that transition, his life opens up in a very new direction. If not, he misses the boat—and probably falls prey to some Libran shadow material, such as indecisiveness, commitment phobia, and dissipation. The choice is his. The man, in this case, is singer Michael Jackson, and the entry of the progressed Sun into Libra coincided with the phenomenal success of his *Thriller* album and with his sweeping of the 1984 Grammy Awards.

Jane Fonda's progressed Sun left the conservative domain of Capricorn and entered rebellious Aquarius in late 1967. She was soon swept up by the currents of the time, becoming a symbol of protest against the Vietnam War. In 1970, during the Cambodian invasion and the murder of protesting students by the National Guard at Kent State University, her progressed Sun had moved a couple of degrees into Aquarius—and made a precise square with her Midheaven. Her evolving self-image (progressed Sun) moved into a relationship of **friction** (square) with her established role as a brainless Hollywood sex symbol (her natal Midheaven, then). She had to choose. The Midheaven square had been brewing since the Sun progressed into Aquarius, but now, during the peak year, Fonda reached her crossroads. Which would dominate—her evolving identity or the pressures of society?

While changes in the house or sign position of the progressed Sun represent critical fresh starts, we must also be alert to the Sun's contact with natal planets through aspectual trigger points. Always proceed by understanding the nature of the natal placement first, then realize that the evolving identity must now integrate that birth motif in a new way. A slow, penetrating **beam of self-awareness** is illuminating that part of the birthchart, intensifying it, demanding that it **evolve rapidly** to catch up with the needs of the matured personality.

Stephen Hawking is a brilliant British astrophysicist. In 1963, at the age of twenty-one, he was stricken with the slow, wasting muscular disorder known as "Lou Gehrig's disease." He descended into despair, ceasing work on his doctorate. A couple of years later, with his progressed Sun approaching a perfect trine with buoyant Jupiter, he met and married Jane Wilde—and returned to his studies. His evolving identity (progressed Sun) was supported and enhanced (trine) as it triggered his latent capacity to recognize opportunity (natal Jupiter). His faith in life (Jupiter again) was restored.

When Elisabeth Kubler-Ross published her influential book *On Death and Dying*, her progressed Sun **opposed** her natal Jupiter. Unlike Stephen Hawking's, her evolving identity came to a point where it existed in a state of tension (opposition) with the happier, more jovial dimensions of her character. Here we have a fine example of the danger of thinking of any planet as "good" or "bad." Jupiter, so often viewed as a positive influence by traditional astrologers, often gets us into trouble by whitewashing life, denying its bleaker side. Kubler-Ross apparently came to a point in her growth where, to maintain her sense of personal integrity (progressed Sun), she had to move in a taboo direction, taking a hard look at the process of dying—a distinctly un-Jupiterian activity. She trusted her path, which is the essence of working with the progressed Sun, and thereby opened doors for herself and helped thousands of other people in the process.

The progressed Sun's contacts with Saturn have always suffered under a bad name among fortune-tellers. No need to be so negative. Saturn is challenging—but if we rise to the challenge, such aspects can help us build **great works** that support our self-respect and dignity. Saturn demands **excellence** and utmost **discipline**. If we respond well to the contacts of the progressed Sun with the ringed planet, our persistence, muscle, and concentration invariably bear fruit. We create outward structures (Saturn!) that allow people to see what we have accomplished inwardly. Under the conjunction, George Lucas released his epic film *Star Wars*. His evolving identity (progressed Sun) fused (conjunction) with a new level of maturity, confidence, and authority by throwing itself body and soul into the creation of a great work—the classic Saturn strategy.

SUN THE TRICKSTER

The Trap: The pitfall of overcentralizing ego in one's self-image, ignoring the needs of the larger psyche, infringing on the rights of others, and flattering one's self into foolish overextension.

The Lie: You are the center of the universe.

Take all the planets and roll them up into a huge "megaplanet." Put that megaplanet on one platform of a gargantuan set of scales. Put the Sun on the other platform. The scale tips toward the Sun. Add another megaplanet, and another, and another. Altogether, you need to add over **seven hundred** megaplanets before the scales are balanced, so much more massive is the Sun than the solar system that orbits it. If it were not for their momentum each of the planets would hurtle inward toward the heart of the solar system, torn from the sky by the Sun's overwhelming gravity—and the Sun would swallow them as nonchalantly as you might swallow a peanut.

The mind works the same way. The solar identity is the all-powerful **center** of the psyche. Its "gravity" organizes all the disparate planetary functions into a **coherent whole**. And yet the danger always exists of the Sun murdering the system, collapsing it in on itself like a deflating balloon. Mental equilibrium—happiness, that is—depends upon each individual planet maintaining its independent momentum, thereby allowing personality to experience its innate **wholeness**. We are much more, in other words, than our egos.

When we let the progressed Sun become the Trickster, the balance between ego and the larger self is lost. Mere selfishness takes over. Initially, the feelings this imbalance creates are giddy ones. We feel "perfectly centered," sure of ourselves, energetic, dynamic, as if nothing could stop us. This cockiness is usually short-lived. Either we create disasters, living out "pride goeth before a fall" scenarios—**or we get exactly what we think we want**, and illustrate the idea that "when God is mad at us, He answers our prayers." The challenge during a solar progression is to move the **wholeness of one's self** forward in life, creating new identity patterns that reflect heightened levels of maturity. The Trickster's strategy is simply to allow **ego to move forward, independent of feelings, basic values, and spiritual sensibilities**. Such advances soon fall apart, much like an army that has extended itself too far into enemy territory. Winter comes and starvation proves a more thorough and relentless enemy than any direct confrontation with a physical foe.

Stephen King, the best-selling horror fiction author, wrote for many years with little success. With the progressed Sun approaching a square to his natal Mars, he was working on a particularly violent novel. The writing appears to have reflected the state of inner tension characteristic of this astrological aspect, for it described the destruction of a town by an outcast teenage girl with supernatural powers—Mars stuff, to be sure. King's inner pressures exploded one day and he threw the incomplete manuscript in the trash. His wife retrieved the pages and urged him to persist. He finished the book—and *Carrie*, as he titled it, sold over 4 million copies, setting him on the road to becoming one of the richest authors in history. His evolving identity (progressed Sun) clashed (square) with the issue of the right use of willpower (Mars). Apparently, the Trickster nearly won. How? **By filling his ego with a sense of impossibility, futile anger, and defeat**, while blinding him temporarily to **non-solar** (non-ego-oriented) issues connected with the larger meaning of his experiences, issues such as the fact that he enjoys writing and has a vivid imagination. Would he have pulled the manuscript out of the trash himself? We have no way of knowing, but the story illustrates how pitched the battles between our inner Teachers and Tricksters sometimes become.

MERCURY THE TEACHER

Glyph:	☿
The Gift:	The capacity to replace familiar but outdated pictures of the world with new ideas and points of view.
The Challenge:	Can you grant yourself permission to see more clearly tomorrow than you do today?

In his wonderfully lucid introduction to the "new physics," *The Dancing Wu Li Masters*, Gary Zukav describes an atom as a sphere the size of a fourteen-story building with a grain of salt in the center and a dustmote out near the edge. The rest is empty space. You and I, in other words, are almost completely insubstantial. Only ghosts. A century or two ago, scientists realized that the colors we see around us are only one tiny fragment of the spectrum of energy that rains in on us invisibly—if our eyes were tuned differently, we would "see" the heat in the wings of a hawk, but never notice the rainbow past which he flew. Later, Albert Einstein painted a picture of the universe for us in which time itself slows down and shapes shift and mass increases as we accelerate to very high speeds. None of this makes any common sense. It has little to do with the world we actually experience. Why? Because the world we actually experience is a mental construction—not the whole truth, just a version that works for us. When we talk about "reality," what we are really talking about is a set of attitudes we carry around in our heads. "Reality" is little more than a lie agreed upon.

Individually, our minds work the same way. We stretch outward with our curiosity, testing the world, feeling it, gathering impressions. Then we organize those impressions into a pattern that makes some kind of sense for us. That pattern, or **model of the world**, forms the basis for more experiments, more extensions of our curiosity. Those experiments sometimes support the model, sometimes challenge it. And right there is where the process gets sticky. We **like** those old models. We are attached to them. To let them go embarrasses and confuses us. It is easier to ignore jarring new input, pretending that our old model still works perfectly—and supporting that position by screening the world selectively, seeing only what we expect to see, denying everything else. As the people of India put it, "When a pickpocket meets a saint, he sees pockets"—only in this case we ourselves are the pickpockets and the pockets belong to the universe.

In *The Inner Sky*, we introduced Mercury as the symbol of our capacity to construct a model of the world that works for us as individuals. It is the mental planet, the speaker and the listener, the asker of questions. As we expand our horizons into predictive astrology, we see world modeling as an endless process of trial and error. **Progressed Mercury symbolizes our evolving mental picture of life as that picture is gradually deepened by experience.**

It symbolizes the pockets we **expect** to see—and the possibility that someday we will notice the saint who is wearing them.

The knack in grasping progressions of Mercury is to recognize that when the planet crosses a trigger point, you are ready to see more clearly. Some **fundamentally new concept** is trying to break through, but to absorb it, you are going to have to question ideas which you have long assumed to be proven truths. Mercury the Teacher suggests that you must **doubt everything**, most especially yourself. Like medieval astronomers who thought Earth was the center of the universe, you have been wasting time constructing "spheres within spheres" to account for your perceptions. Like those old astronomers, you need a Copernicus to offer you an **utterly simple, utterly unexpected** new concept that puts everything into place. The only difference is that you have to locate that Copernicus within yourself.

Where will the breakthrough arise? The answer is another question: What part of the birthchart is that progressed Mercury triggering? If it is Venus, then the new model of the world is connected with relationship attitudes or creative inspirations. Triggering a tenth house Mars, progressed Mercury suggests new strategic career insights. Grasp the root prediction, in other words. As always, that is our first step. Can we go farther? Yes—often the sign and house through which Mercury is progressing clarify the nature of the breakthrough. Is Mercury passing through Aquarius and the seventh house? Then insights are likely to come through partners and close friends, especially ones of an "Aquarian nature"—people who are innovative and independent, willing to break with established assumptions. Recognize them and make an effort to be open to their perspectives on the issue in question for **two or three years**—that's how long Mercury is likely to remain within the orbs of the triggering aspect, although fast transits will pinpoint specific moments within those years in which the action is most probable. In any case, those friends are the Teacher's ambassadors. Whether they know it or not, they hold the key to the treasure chest you are trying to open. What if Mercury is progressing through Virgo and the first house? Then don't expect ambassadors; those insights must arise from within you alone (first house) and to discern them you must undertake a painstaking, self-disciplined analysis of the situation (Virgo).

Actor Ben Kingsley was born with Mercury stationary retrograde in late Capricorn. For the first half of his life, progressed Mercury continued to move in a retrograde fashion. When he was twenty, the planet made another station and turned direct, gradually heading back toward the place it occupied at his birth. Only a minority of people ever experience such an event—a progressed "Mercury return." It signals a time when the ability to absorb new concepts and skills operates at a remarkable pitch, similar to the openness of the mind during the first year of infancy. How did Kingsley respond? He startled and inspired us with his preternaturally convincing portrayal of Mohandas Gandhi in the Columbia Pictures release *Gandhi*. His Mercurial inventiveness and intelligence shone like a lighthouse.

In 1923, a twenty-one-year-old illustrator named Walt Disney left Kansas City for Hollywood with nothing but forty dollars and some sketches for an animated film he called "Alice in Cartoonland." Progressed Mercury stood opposed to his natal Neptune. A short-sighted astrologer might have told him that his mind (progressed Mercury) was cracking under tension (opposition), filling him with unreality and glamorous delusions (Neptune). Another astrologer might have prophesied that Disney was inspired by a vision (Neptune) and that even though it seemed to clash with common sense (opposition), he needed to trust it, because the whole evolutionary thrust of his intellectual life (progressed Mercury) now depended upon him demonstrating confidence in his own creative inspiration (Neptune again).

Which astrologer would have been right? In retrospect, we know that the second one would have spoken the truth. That shouldn't blind us to the fact that the first one could have been right just as easily. Progressed Mercury opposing Neptune **can** indicated an unbalanced mind, leading a person to take crazy, unrealistic steps that quickly blow up in his or her face. A modern astrologer would describe both possibilities and counsel a modern Walt Disney to recognize that his imagination was now at an inspirational peak and that he should use his own common sense to weed out the unreality, irrational enthusiasms and hype that always accompany such an inward blossoming. The astrologer, in other words, would say, "Walt, here's your weather report. Now dress as you please."

MERCURY THE TRICKSTER

The Trap: The temptation to misdirect energy needed for learning
and clarifying into rationalization, defensiveness, and
intransigence.

The Lie: You've seen it all.

In the healthy mind, models of the world are merely stops along the
way. We construct a theory. It fits the reality we have experienced
reasonably well. We employ it until a better theory comes along—often
as a result of absorbing new facts that point out weaknesses in the old
picture. The process goes on and on. Theory after theory guides us,
and is then discarded like last week's newspapers. This, at least, is the
way of Mercury the Teacher. Instinctively, he knows that "you can
prove anything with the facts," and so he distrusts all theories as the
speculative work of the human intellect, valuable perhaps, but always
dangerous if we believe them too thoroughly.

Mercury the Trickster plays on our fear of abandoning those
worn-out pictures. He plays on our **natural hesitation to trade
certainty for uncertainty, confidence for doubt**. He is the part of us
that prefers the old theories. He attempts to throw a monkey wrench
into the healthy Mercurial process of observation and experiment by
convincing us that we are **already wise enough**. His lie is "you've seen
it all," and his deceit is to convince us that attitudinal consistency is a
virtue. Few human foibles delight him more than our affinity for
harboring passionate opinions.

If the Trickster's ally is our rigidity, then the Teacher's greatest
friend is reality itself. **Experience** usually proves us wrong if we have
gotten ourselves stuck in a limited viewpoint. White racists sooner or
later meet black people demonstrably more intelligent, moral, and
responsible than themselves. Black racists live in a world containing
more than a few nonjudgmental, trustworthy Caucasians with fair
senses of rhythm. Truth survives scrutiny; lies don't. So how does the
Trickster survive? He **rationalizes**! He reasons, and argues, and
threatens, and begs—and when those tactics fail, he simply jabbers. He
jabbers until he believes his own obvious lies. He jabbers until those
who argue against him are so tired or confused or despairing of ever
making real contact with him that they give up—and then he interprets
their surrender as agreement. And what does he gain? Only the right
to remain just as stupid tomorrow as he was yesterday—that, and his
precious consistency.

An unsavory character, this Mercury the Trickster—but remember
that he is a part of you and me and everyone else who has ever lived.

When you have progressed Mercury on a trigger point, monitor yourself. Are you talking too much? Do your arguments sound empty when you hear them on "instant replay?" What is it that you don't want to know? Your birthchart can help you unravel the answer. Apply the techniques we outlined under "Mercury the Teacher." What part of your chart is progressed Mercury affecting? Where does it actually lie in terms of sign and house? Open yourself to the message of the symbolism, and if you are brave, you will see something that you could not have understood before, even if it hit you over the head. Why? **Because you were not ready then to be that clear.** Don't let the Trickster's stubbornness rob you of this opportunity. He steals wisdom and leaves you with nothing but a mouthful of words.

The Ayatollah Khoumeni declared the Islamic Republic of Iran while his progressed Mercury was trining Jupiter. His evolving mental picture of the world (progressed Mercury) enhanced (trine) his faith and optimism (natal Jupiter). That sounds good on the surface, but we must always read beneath the words of these formulas. Jupiter can overextend us, filling us with delusions of grandeur. That is its darker side. With his evolving worldview pumped up by Jupiter's certainty and fervor, the Ayatollah, not unlike Walt Disney in our previous example, was in a risky spot. Opportunity was clearly there, but so was the possibility of a vainglorious pratfall. An evolutionary astrologer would not predict the outcome of the progression, but only issue the weather forecast: "Your mind is inspired and energized now, but perhaps not quite so inspired as you think. Be careful."

VENUS THE TEACHER
Glyph: ♀
The Gift: The capacity to achieve balance within the psyche through the establishment of relationships, the creation of "art," and the deliberate release of tension.
The Challenge: Can you open your heart, allowing love in and creative or emotional expression out?

Zen Buddhist masters startle their students by asking, "What is the sound of one hand clapping?" The mind boggles; like a drawing done out of perspective, such a question breaks the laws by which this world operates. Medieval scholars argued over whether God was almighty enough to create two mountains without an intervening valley. Once again, the question boggles us; it breaks the rules. In each of these conundrums, we are asked to conceive of a universe without reference to relationship. And we can't do it. **Two** hands are needed for clapping. The mere existence of a pair of mountains must of necessity create a valley, which is the **relationship** between them. The truth is that an awareness of relationships is the foundation of human consciousness. Without that awareness, the very fabric of the universe we experience would unravel.

In the birthchart, Venus symbolizes the part of human awareness that **discerns and establishes relationships**—although we must remember that these "relationships" can exist between colors and shapes and sounds as well as between people. This is the planet of **harmony**. Venus, in the birthchart, symbolizes what kinds of experiences best serve to **calm** us by helping us feel like **part of the whole**, woven into the tapestry of life like a colored thread. Much of that feeling comes from establishing ourselves in a network of satisfying **human** relationships. Venus, in other words, is the romantic planet and symbolizes bonds of friendship and partnership at all levels—but to understand it fully, we must go farther. Open your heart to a perfect sunset. React inwardly to the beauty. Let yourself be hypnotized by the swirling wisps of red and orange against the background of deepening blue. What's going on? Your Venus is humming. Your spirit is extended outward, open to the larger tapestry of life. What you are sensing is not simply the sunset, but rather **your relationship** to the sunset. That's where all the emotion comes from. You are experiencing the single fabric of which both you and those shifting colors are individual threads. What effect does this process have upon consciousness? As we experience ourselves in relationship to the world beyond us, we feel **serenity**—the mark of Venus the Teacher.

The Venusian need to feel linked to other parts of life remains with us throughout life, but the form of that linkage changes with the years. A woman might be a social butterfly in her teens, but choose to live alone in the backwoods of Vermont in her forties. Her Venusian needs are now satisfied by sunsets and ladyslippers and a few good friends who live down the road. What has happened? Her relationship motivations have grown different with the passage of time and the accumulation of experience. To put it astrologically, **her Venus has progressed**. Perhaps it has moved from the busy third house into the reclusive fourth, or from experience-hungry Sagittarius into solitary Capricorn. Either way, what once nourished her now seems empty; what before was incomprehensible now feels rich and multidimensional.

Always, while considering the progressions of Venus, remember that when you fall in love, you often write poetry. In the circuitry of the human mind, the same force that motivates us to form bonds with other people also motivates us to create beauty. Energizing those same mental circuits also inclines us to sit back and allow beauty to soothe and inspire our spirits. After showing off our new poem to our new love, we might sit together and gaze at the rising moon.

Harmony is the keynote here. Whether we are enjoying the flow of awareness and attention between ourselves and someone we love, or experiencing a similar flow between ourselves and that yellow moon, or sitting at our canvas painting imaginary landscapes, we link our attention to that which lies beyond our own personality—and we are guided by Venus the Teacher.

To nourish ourselves like that, we must soften our defenses. Ego must melt. We must intentionally relax. Remember the last time you fought with your mate or your best friend? Remember how good it felt the first time your eyes really met and held after the fight was over? That's Venus. Granting us the wisdom to recognize that need for openness and peace in ourselves is the work of the Teacher.

As Venus progresses into a new house, our relationship-forming **behavior** needs to change radically, moving into new **arenas** and **styles of expression**. There is a new ocean to cross; old navigational methods fail us now. Walt Disney was born with Venus in his natal fifth house. His self-expressive behavior (fifth house) has a Venusian tone— creativity of some form was essential to his well-being. In 1928, at the age of twenty-six, his progressed Venus crossed into his sixth house— and his creativity was at a turning point. If he responded vigorously, we know that this new chapter would have a sixth house quality—an emphasis upon hard work, professionalism, increasing responsibilities, improved techniques. We also know that even though Venus would remain in his sixth house for many years, such transitions usually begin with a dramatic event that **foreshadows** all that is to come. In Disney's case, the event was the screening of a cartoon entitled "Steamboat Willy"—and the birth of Mickey Mouse.

Aspects formed by progressed Venus are briefer in duration than the planet's passage though signs or houses, usually remaining in effect for two or three years. These periods represent times of **adjustment** in our relationship life. Here is a helpful way to think about them: a relationship must exist between the **totality** of one person and the **totality** of another. We cannot, in other words, realistically isolate a person's "love nature" or "creativity" from the larger processes of his or her individuality.

To put it astrologically, you don't just love or create through your Venus or through your fifth or seventh houses—you love or create through the totality of your birthchart. This is vast subject, and it's covered in a lot more detail in *Skymates*, the third book of this "Sky" trilogy which I wrote with my wife, Jodie Forrest. Suffice to say that when Venus contacts a trigger point, the part of your psyche to which that trigger point is linked is now ready to learn how to exchange love and how to be integrated into your creative processes, enriching both. Saint Francis of Assisi, for example, began his public ministry with progressed Venus conjuncting Mars. His evolving capacity to love (progressed Venus) now fused (conjunction) with his courage and initiative (Mars). He had always known love, he had always known fire—but a wall had existed between the two. With this progressed aspect, that wall broke down, catalysis occurred, and his ability to express his particular brand of love took on a fervor and dynamism impossible earlier.

It is a common observation that the experience of love deepens over the years. A fifty-year-old man loving his wife of thirty years feels differently than a teenage boy on his first date. The word "maturity" is usually invoked here; astrologically, we would say instead that the progressed Venus in the older man has contacted many more trigger points than that of the youth. The man now loves not only with his romantic sensibilities alone (Venus), but also perhaps with his intellect (Mercury), his individuality (Uranus), his solitude and self-discipline (Saturn), and so on, depending upon which progressed aspects Venus has made. Usually, by the end of life, Venus has progressed through a wide enough arc to have made at least one major aspect to every planet. The whole birthchart is eventually called into the service of love.

Similar Venusian processes affect creative life. Bursts of inspiration can occur at any age, usually when strong Venusian transits or progressions are in play. But often an artist's greatest works come later in life, when progressed Venus has accumulated passages over many trigger points, allowing creative expression to arise from the totality of the individual's vision.

□ □ □

VENUS THE TRICKSTER

The Trap: The pitfalls of manipulation and hypocrisy, which establish
temporarily harmonious but inauthentic relationships.

The Lie: Sincerity is everything—if you can fake that,
you have it made.

The lie I quote above is from comedian George Burns. It epitomizes
the deceptions of Venus the Trickster. To some extent, each of us has a
natural Venusian ability to come to terms with another person. Each of
us can **see** another, establishing with that individual a common
language and some degree of interactive trust. In that process,
sincerity is essential. We must make an effort to be real, helping the
other person to grasp who we are, what we might offer, and what we
want. We share something of our inner life, detailing whatever gifts we
bear—and also, perhaps unconsciously, warning the person regarding
what's dangerous about us. If sincerity dominates the process both
people gain, and the inevitable hurt of human interaction is minimized.
That is the way of Venus the Teacher.

The Trickster has other plans. He (or She!) seeks to pervert the
natural processes of forming relationships, undermining them,
twisting them to the service of lower ends. He grasps the nature of the
other person—and then uses that information to create an illusory
picture of himself in that individual's mind. Why? To get what he
wants! By appearing to suit the other's needs, the Trickster ingratiates
himself and manipulates the other into supporting his ravenous ego.

What is the nature of the Trickster's hunger? That depends upon
what kind of trigger point progressed Venus is touching. A woman
has a fifth house Neptune. Progressed Venus triggers it through a
sextile, and she succumbs to the Trickster. Her evolving need for love
(progressed Venus) stimulates (sextile) her urge for glamorous
(Neptune) love affairs (fifth house). She becomes the femme fatale,
leaves a trail of broken hearts behind her—and gets little satisfaction
herself. Why? Because those lovers weren't allowed to see her any more
clearly than she saw them. Just shadows dancing with shadows,
exploiting and manipulating each other.

What about the planet's creative dimensions? The Trickster can work
here, too, tempting us to play to the crowd, betraying our natural voice
and replacing it with one that merely profits us. This sickness is not
reserved for professional artists, either. Anyone can succumb to it. Even
our clothes are creative—the Trickster would have us dress to impress,
seeking only selfish ends. The Teacher, by contrast, might delight in

changing our style of clothing so that it reflects what we have become inwardly—thereby attracting like-minded people, and giving a clear "go away" signal to those with whom we have no legitimate business. Every aspect of life, from how we decorate our home to the jokes we tell, is creative and self-expressive—and can collapse into manipulativeness under the pressures of the Trickster. We "fake sincerity," people buy the lie—and we miss the deeper satisfaction of true creativity and authentic relating.

A chilling vision of the Trickster's impact can be seen in the birthchart of Peter William Sutcliffe, the infamous "Yorkshire Ripper." Allegedly believing himself to be on a "divine mission to kill prostitutes," Sutcliffe from 1975 until his arrest in early 1981 gained the confidence of thirteen women—eight of them prostitutes—and then brutally murdered and mutilated them. Never can we offer a complete astrological analysis of a situation by considering only a single progressed factor, but in the "Ripper's" case, we see the unmistakable hand of Venus the Trickster. When the awful killings began, progressed Venus was sextiling his natal Mercury. As the years of his rampage went by, Venus moved into another sextile, this time with his antisocial Uranus. In his birthchart, Mercury, Uranus, and the Sun form a triple conjunction in Gemini in his seventh house. Under these progressed Venusian sextiles, Sutcliffe's innate hunger for human contact (strong seventh house) was stimulated and excited (sextile) by his evolving capacity to form relationships—in a sick way. Trickster work. Throughout the period of his murders, yet another Venusian force was in operation, this time a far more critical one—his evolving identity (progressed Sun) was fusing (conjunction) with his personal magnetism and relationship-forming drive (natal Venus). None of these factors signify murder—fortune-tellers, in fact, would have called for romance—but the Trickster within him twisted the forces, and Peter William Sutcliffe became a symbol of human depravity, and of the black abyss into which an unbridled, misdirected Venus can hurl us.

□ □ □

MARS THE TEACHER

Glyph: ♂

The Gift: The ability to act decisively, moving onto the offensive, defending our rightful territory, and claiming what is legitimately our own.

The Challenge: Are you brave enough to live like a "spiritual warrior"— or will you sit back and let life steamroller you?

The "spiritual warrior"—unlock that notion and you have unlocked the riddles of progressed Mars. To misfortune-tellers, the progressions of the red planet spell trouble, suggesting conflict, injury, and pain. True enough sometimes, but we must take it farther. This is a planet of **challenge**, and the terms of the challenge are straightforward: In this sometimes cruel, always competitive world, can you take **responsibility for your own survival**?

Initiative, strategy, confrontation—those are certainly paramount words in the Martial vocabulary, but to Mars the Teacher, they are secondary. Far more central is achieving the **attitude** of a spiritual warrior: inner transformation, not outward fireworks. To the spiritual warrior, the "enemy" we must face first is always within, never outside. That enemy is our fear, our inattention, our self-importance, anything that blurs the power of our will, leaving us open to avoidable injury. With the inner enemy conquered, the outer one shrinks. The real battle—the battle with our own spirit—has been won. All that remains is to express that inner victory behaviorally. When progressed Mars contacts a trigger point, the time has come to **act**, and to act **decisively, confidently**, and **with authority**. Above all, that action must be rooted in crystal clear self-appraisal and reflect single-minded, unambiguous intent. What if we fail in our outward efforts? No matter. Victory is still ours. We may lose the battle, but even in losing, our spirits gain strength. That is the warrior's secret, and the key to his equanimity in the face of both gains and reversals.

A drizzly Sunday afternoon. You oversleep. You wake up bored, headachy, unfocused, and flat. You had planned to clean the house, but your energy level dims that prospect. You have breakfast. You halfheartedly scan the paper. You bounce from wall to wall, feeling guilty about the mess but still refusing to face it. You settle down with a novel, read forty pages, close the book. You drink a glass of wine, then wish you hadn't. Walk uptown? No. Catch up on that correspondence? No again. Almost against your will, you are drawn back to the newspaper. Finally, in desperation, you get out the vacuum cleaner, crank up the radio, and get to work. Ten minutes later your emotional funk has dissipated. You feel happier, stronger, less crazy. You have found a direction—and your Mars is cooking.

Pump up the scale of that scenario to the level of major **existential housecleaning** and you have grasped the impact of progressed Mars. Whenever this planet contacts a trigger point, you must intentionally elevate your level of engagement with life. That takes energy. If you muster enough juice, a Mars period can be exciting and rewarding. Projects are undertaken. Obstacles are surmounted. Your intentions crystallize. If instead you choose to stay in bed, that energy backs up inside you, turning to poison. Sigmund Freud once observed that depression is internalized anger. Astrologically, we can make a more general observation: Depression often stems from internalized, unfocused Will—Mars problems, in other words. If you fail to grasp this Teacher's message and do not act, then you endure a depressing, disjointed Sunday afternoon—only it lasts for years and years while Mars gradually progresses over the trigger point.

Examples of bravery associated with progressed Mars abound. With Mars conjuncting his natal Jupiter, Neil Armstrong became the first man to set foot on the moon. His evolving courage (progressed Mars) fused (conjunction) with his sense of personal confidence, faith, and triumph (natal Jupiter). With progressed Mars conjuncting his Midheaven, lone explorer Tristan Jones set sail from Reykjavik, Iceland, on his epic two-year arctic journey—and returned to become a symbol of the far boundaries of human willpower. His evolving courage entered public awareness (Midheaven; tenth house). Seven hundred days of frozen solitude honed him inwardly—and the books he subsequently wrote about his adventures added the public (Midheaven) dimension.

Martial courage does not always take such an outwardly adventure- some form, although many of us do respond to the red planet with physical action and exercise. At the age of thirty-seven, with progressed Mars conjuncting her natal Venus, artist Georgia O'Keefe married photographer Alfred Stieglitz. Her evolving courage was ready to face the challenges of committed love. Sir Francis Chichester faced a fatal lung cancer diagnosis—and survived—under the guidance of Mars the Teacher. His evolving courage (progressed Mars) **opposed** his awareness of forces beyond personal control (natal Pluto). He refused to die, entering a "nature cure" hospital in Britain and subsequently living many more years—with enough vigor to race singlehandedly across the North Atlantic three years later while progressed Mars squared his Sun!

MARS THE TRICKSTER

The Trap: The temptation to "kick the dog," while collapsing into fear, denial, and feelings of victimization.

The Lie: Screw them before they screw you.

When Johnny is thirteen, he has his wallet stolen by bullies in the junior high school bathroom. He goes home, invents a provocation, and slugs his younger brother. Billy storms out of the house, slamming the door. The glass shatters. Billy flees, ignoring his mother's angry demands that he return immediately. Johnny lies low. Mom phones Dad at work, tells the story—and scores a few digs about the strain replacing that glass is going to put on his scrimpy paycheck. On the way home, Dad stops at the bar to get braced, and winds up in a fender-bender an hour later. Is all this the fault of those bullies in the boys' room? Well, maybe. But three of them have abusive, alcoholic fathers, who were abused by **their** fathers, who had been abused by **their** fathers.

Violence breeds violence, fear breeds fear, victims victimize more victims, until our analysis disappears backward into the Big Bang. The ancient madness. The Achilles' heel of the human spirit. It puts venom in marriage, poison in friendship, hatred in human diversity. If our world ends up as an irradiated desert, if instead of reaching together for the stars the nations of Earth reach for each other's throats, lay it at the door of Mars the Trickster. That lifeless gray Earth stumbled upon a billion years from now by some creature whose species was peaceful enough to survive—that is the Trickster's goal and his prize.

When progressed Mars contacts a trigger point, you have a chance to break that endless chain. You can be the weak link, save yourself and withhold destruction from those around you—and most important, not allow the madness to be transmitted any farther into the human future. How? By holding back your anger? No—anger is rarely transcended. Usually "transcended" anger is simply delayed and later released on some hapless target—we kick the dog or we give ourselves an ulcer. The secret with the progressions of Mars is first to **recognize precisely what we are angry about**, and second, to **move efficiently and strategically to eliminate the problem**. Fail in either regard and the Trickster wreaks havoc.

Remember the spiritual warrior. The real enemy is always within us.

When Johnny turns fifteen, he dyes an orange streak in his hair and pierces his ear. Mom, who has progressed Mars squaring her Sun, hits the ceiling. If the Teacher wins, she soon calms down, recognizing that her enemy is not the boy's style, but her own illegitimate desire to control him. Her evolving sense of her own power (progressed Mars) is applying friction (square aspect) to her ego (natal Sun)—and both sides of her character need to mature. If the Trickster has his way, she misapplies her power, attempting to force Johnny to change. He rebels, and their relationship is scarred.

If Mars the Teacher comes out on top, Johnny's mother doesn't fall into a guilty depression and silence—but she actively works on the problem, talking to Johnny, listening to him, and gathering support from other "warriors." Instead of usurping Johnny's right to present himself as he chooses, she lets him know that although she respects his freedom, she fears that stylistic differences might create a painful gap between them—and she asks him for reassurance. She has discerned her real enemy. The rest was only the Trickster's spiderweb.

On the other hand, we sometimes realize after honest self-scrutiny that a problem is not entirely within ourselves. If that is the case, then we must **act upon the world**. This is always the spiritual warrior's last resort, for such action is inherently perilous. It reveals ego, and opens us to injury. The warrior undertakes such action decisively, but never lightly. The Trickster's ploy here is to fill our awareness with **self-righteous anger, passionate opinions, and bravado**—hoping to trip us into sending in the marines when an ambassador would suffice.

As the mother of a fifteen-year-old son, Johnny's mom still has a degree of legitimate responsibility for his well-being. When she learns that not only has he dyed his hair, but he is also part of a ring of bicycle thieves, and that he is buying cocaine with the money, she knows she has to do something.

Three different problems, three different responses. She realizes that his hair is his own business, so she keeps quiet about it, despite the fact that she doesn't like orange hair. But stealing bikes and fooling with a potentially risky drug cross the line into her own legitimate territory of action as a mother. What does she do? The Trickster whispers an easy answer in her ear: "Shave his head and pack him off to military school." The Teacher moves more cautiously, always aware of the distorting effects of fear and desire. The woman responds well to the pressures of progressed Mars squaring her Sun. She **confronts** her son. She **explains her feelings** to him. She lets him know that while she understands that he is old enough to start making his own decisions, she still feels

personal responsibility for him. Her own conscience will not allow her to keep silent while he steals other kids' bikes. Perhaps she quietly but clearly announces her intention to call the police if the thievery continues.

But regarding her son's experimentations with cocaine, Johnny's mother recognizes her inability to strike a decisive blow. She is a spiritual warrior, and as such, she recognizes her own limits. She never makes an idle threat nor overextends herself. She tells him his use of the drug worries her and she tells him exactly why. She **asks** him to stop using it, knowing that a demand would be futile. She asks him also for **his** side of the story, for any perspectives she might be missing. Listening, in other words, becomes part of her warrior's strategy. If the bicycle thievery continues, Johnny's mother probably calls the police. If his cocaine use continues, too, she only makes an effort to keep the lines of communication open. Is that all? Why nothing more? **Because she understands the limits of her power.** Johnny himself must choose.

Actress Sharon Tate and the LaBiancas were murdered while Charles Manson was experiencing progressed Mars trine his natal Aquarian tenth house Moon. Such a lunar configuration in the birthchart suggests feelings of exile, of standing outside society looking in. Placed in the tenth house, Manson felt the need to express that lunar energy in the forum of the community. Had he made a healthy response to his birthchart, then he would likely have found a role as a social reformer of some sort. As it was, with his evolving rage (progressed Mars the Trickster) enhancing (trine) those feelings of alienation (Aquarian Moon), he appears to have inspired others to murder people who were symbols of success in society. The Trickster won, and another link was forged in the chain of the ancient madness.

THE PROGRESSED ASCENDANT

The Ascendant in the birthchart represents our **style**—the self-portrait we create, often unwittingly, in the minds of others. It is our **mask**, although no phoniness or hypocrisy is implied. We have to present ourselves somehow—and that presentation can never reflect all the subtleties of our personality. When we are in harmony with our Ascendant, we feel comfortable. Our style works for us. We feel centered and at ease. The old cliché about the farmboy nervously asking the girl for a date, shuffling his feet, looking at his shoes—that's a sick Ascendant. It makes us feel goofy. Slickness without substance, style without heart—that's another possible distortion of the natal Ascendant. Instead the awkward farmboy, we find the "lounge lizard," radiating smooth manipulativeness, smacking of emptiness. We sense that we are in Tombstone, Arizona, 1869, Hollywood style: a perfect facade, with nothing behind it.

In mastering the **progressed** Ascendant, everything depends upon whether we are flexible enough to avoid letting our style slip into rigidity. The aging college professor with his memorized jokes, his "position papers" on every subject, and his 1957 sportcoat—he is the victim of the Trickster. Why? Because he still acts the way he did a quarter century ago. He is stuck in an old pattern, at least outwardly, and as a result he probably feels like something of a joke—but instead of changing, he retreats into defensiveness. To entrench and defend our style **as if it were important**—that is the Trickster's game. The Teacher would have us bend and flow, changing with the times, but even more so with the changing seasons of our own spirit.

When the progressed Ascendant moves from one sign to another, our evolving style has entered a period of profound alteration—and of profound crisis. For the vast majority of us, this happens only two or three times in the course of our lifetime. What does it mean? A set of memorized behavioral routines (old progressed Ascendant) are no longer appropriate to the circumstances we have created. They need to be dropped and replaced with new ones. But we are so accustomed to those old routines! They feel as natural as a favorite old shirt—one that is now so moth-eaten it threatens to fall off our back. We need a new style. The sign the progressed Ascendant has just entered illuminates the nature of that style.

When Marie Curie was doing the quiet research that led to the discovery of radium, her Ascendant was still progressing through Cancer, the sign it was in at her birth. In her early thirties, she received the Nobel Prize—and her Ascendant progressed into Leo. Her evolving style needed to adjust to the public prominence she unintentionally created by doing what came naturally to her Cancerian Ascendant— quiet research. One evolved naturally out of the other. Elisabeth Kübler-Ross's Ascendant progressed into Gemini the year she published her monumental work *On Death and Dying*. Her style had to evolve into that of the lecturer, the teacher, the leader of workshops— all Gemini material.

The progressed Ascendant moves into the second house and then the third in the course of a normal lifespan. Owing to differences in the sizes of houses and variations in the Ascendant's speed, we cannot time these events by any rule of thumb. Each represents a turning point in Everyman's life, but unlike the predictable transits we traced in chapter six, their timing can float around within the otherwise relatively rigid framework of the biopsychic script.

When the progressed Ascendant enters the second house, a disquieting period of self-appraisal ensues. We suddenly become hyper-aware of our mask, and strangely detached from it. Who am I? What am I really worth? Who am I kidding? These are the questions that well up from the heart of the self. Pete Townshend, the brilliant rock composer who shaped The Who, had lived close to the limits of what the body can endure due to his drug habits. With his progressed Ascendant just into the second house, he contacted the Scottish surgeon, Dr. Meg Peterson, and was "saved from chemical self-destruction" through her revolutionary neuroelectric therapy. The crisis of self-doubt so characteristic of the second house helped him change his personal style for the better. He lost his sense of invulnerability—and moved away from a self-destructive style of living.

As the Ascendant progresses into the third house, we are typically maturing past middle age. Often this transition corresponds to a "second wind." We experience a renewed **curiosity** (third house). We want to explore, to move around, to learn—and perhaps to teach. Elisabeth Kubler-Ross's Ascendant progressed not only into Gemini upon publication of her landmark book, but it simultaneously progressed into the third house, doubling the power of the passage—and marking a decisive new beginning in her life.

Scattered through the first, second, and third houses, most of us have a great number of sensitive trigger points linked to planets through various aspects. When the progressed Ascendant contacts any of these, we must integrate that planetary function into our evolving personal style. Much like the progressed Sun, the progressed Ascendant focuses a **beam of self-awareness** on each planet, helping to weave it more tightly into our daily experience. The differences between the Sun and the Ascendant often blur in practice, but theoretically a solar progression involves integrating some new factor into our **essence**, while, with the progressed Ascendant, the integration has more to do with outward issues—**appearance and behavior**. Either way we are altering the foundations of **identity**, and such a progression cannot be overlooked if we are to grasp the developmental significance of a chapter in a person's life.

When Diana Ross made her film debut in *Lady Sings the Blues*, her evolving style (progressed Ascendant) clashed (square aspect) with her glamorous aesthetic sensibilities (natal Venus in Pisces). She had come to a place in the existential terrain of her life where her style had to change. That style did not reflect who she was any longer. Her Piscean

Venus needed to be checked (square) before it ran away with her. She recognized the need for adjustment in her personal style, responded strongly, shocked a few people—and got on with her life in a more mature way.

Bruce Springsteen experienced a similar astrological situation, but with one important difference: Progressed Ascendant and natal Venus were linked by a **trine** rather than a **square**. Instead of clashing and friction, we expect enhancement and harmonization—and the risk of sleeping through the opportunity. The year was 1972. Springsteen was strictly "local talent," playing in bars. During this progression, he was discovered, supported, and offered a recording contract by Columbia Records. His evolving style (progressed Ascendant) came to a point where it enhanced (trine) the brooding intensity of his early compositions (natal Venus in Scorpio). Suddenly, as a result, he seemed more convincing as an artist. His personal style now harmoniously integrated his Venusian sensibilities—and that integration showed in his personal carriage. People now took him seriously, and his meteoric career began in earnest.

THE PROGRESSED MIDHEAVEN

The Midheaven itself represents our **public identity**. It differs from the Ascendant primarily in that it is far less personal. The Midheaven indicates the **symbolic function we serve in our community**. Often that function is closely linked to our profession—especially if the profession gives us joy. Profession, however, is too small a bucket to hold all the water of the Midheaven. This point represents not only how the Internal Revenue Service views us, but also embraces statements such as "I am going to vote for Jones" or "I support a nuclear freeze." Anything that serves to define us in the minds of people who do not know us is related to the Midheaven. Our job is a big piece of it, but don't be misled by traditional astrology books into thinking that how you make your money is the whole Midheaven story. The issues here are much broader.

Naturally, our relationship with society **evolves** as we get older. Measuring that evolution and timing its various turning points is the province of the progressed Midheaven. It symbolizes our **evolving public identity**. Like the progressed Ascendant, the progressed Midheaven moves slowly, passing through two or three signs and houses in the course of a normal life, and making contact with a number of aspectual trigger points. If we allow the progressed Midheaven to be our Teacher, our evolving public identity reflects ongoing changes in our nature and values. If the Trickster within us has his way, then we get stuck in a public role that we have inwardly **outgrown**. Boredom sets in, numbing us to our daily routine, usually filling us with a sense of aimlessness.

Boredom is not the only problem the Trickster creates when he twists our progressed Midheaven—as anyone who has ever worked a rotten job for too long is quick to attest. Anyone who has ever felt trapped in such a role knows how demoralizing it can be. If, on the other hand, we continue to adjust our public role to the changing patterns of our inner life, then we maintain harmony between **who we are** and **how we look to people who don't know us**—and the Teacher rewards us. Our work is then the blossom; our individuality itself is the roots and branches. And the Trickster within us goes to bed hungry.

When the progressed Midheaven entered mystical Pisces, George Lucas released *Star Wars* and became a **public symbol** (progressed Midheaven) of **fantasy, creativity, and imagination** (Pisces stuff). Under the same pattern, Carlos Casteneda met don Juan and began his apprenticeship in the ways of sorcery. He became a **public symbol** (progressed Midheaven again), representing to his many readers a distinctly Piscean universe of magic and seeming impossibility. Tristan Jones set sail alone for his arctic expedition with his progressed Midheaven entering Aries—his evolving public role now became an embodiment of courage and the love of adventure (Aries).

House changes in the progressed Midheaven's position are significant, too. During roughly the first third of life, the Midheaven is slowly moving through the tenth house. Typically during this period, our public role is largely defined by the culture into which we were born. We are the generic "student," the "laborer," the generic "office worker." Don't let glamour fool you here: it is also possible to be the generic "rock star," "movie heartthrob," or "athlete." The point is that **society is still calling the shots,** whether we know it or not. As the Midheaven progresses toward the eleventh house cusp, fundamental attitudinal changes are brewing. The eleventh is the house of **personal goals**—and at this point a convergence occurs between our goals and our personality. We are ready to get recognized publicly for being **who we really are**.

Most astrological events have one element in common: a response. We respond either well or poorly, but we **always** respond. Either the Teacher or the Trickster rules the day. In my experience, the progression of the Midheaven into the eleventh house follows the same rule, but subtly; we either respond well or we seemingly do not respond at all.

It is a release of **potential**—the potential to find what we might call our **destiny**. If your **root prediction** contains many references to destiny—a strong tenth house, much Capricorn emphasis, Pluto a key focalizer—then this progression represents a critical "make it or break it" time. If your birthchart is quieter, then this period might pass almost unnoticed, showing up mostly as a vague feeling of having "grown up." But when a person succumbs to the Trickster here, then there is a quiet surrendering of any hope that one might might ever do anything important or make a difference in the world. The whimper of a dream dying is very faint.

Jerry Brown became governor of California while his progressed Midheaven was crossing his eleventh house cusp—his public identity began to reflect his personal goals in a big way. One of my favorite stories regarding this transition dates from over a thousand years ago. If the birthchart we have for Charlemagne is accurate, then as his Midheaven was entering the eleventh house, he was filled with a sense of his own inadequacy. He sought a teacher, and found a scholar-priest named Alcuin. This Merlinlike figure seems to have played a profound role in shaping Charlemagne's consciousness, and creating his sense of personal destiny. The king's contact with the old wizard aligned his evolving public identity (progressed Midheaven) with his sense of personal direction and priorities (eleventh house).

The entry of the progressed Midheaven into the twelfth house generally comes at the close of midlife. There is often a gradual withdrawal of life energy from public activity now. Retirement is one possible keynote of this transition, although the entry of the progressed Midheaven into this house does not imply sleepiness and dotage. Much like entering the third Saturn cycle (see chapter six), this Midheaven progression suggests a "passing on of the torch." The time has come to disperse what we have accumulated, materially or inwardly, sharing it with those who come after us. Again, Elisabeth Kubler-Ross provides an example. Along with her progressed Ascendant changing both sign and house, her progressed Midheaven was also undergoing transition into the twelfth house at the time she shared her wisdom with us all by publishing *On Death and Dying*.

Throughout the tenth, eleventh, and twelfth houses, we find "hot spots"—trigger points where any transiting or progressing planet ignites the fires of growth by interacting powerfully with some fundamental structure in our character. Sometimes that process occurs almost without effort—we just **flow** into the new role, supported by trines and sextiles. Other times, the addition is **grafted on to us** through tension and challenge, as suggested by squares and oppositions. When Bruce Springsteen got his recording contract, his progressed Ascendant was trining Venus, as we just learned. Now we can add another level to our understanding of that period in his life—his progressed Midheaven was simultaneously sextiling Jupiter. His evolving public identity was stimulating and supported by his own natural exuberance and confidence (natal Jupiter).

One more Teacher remains, shadowed by one more Trickster. The progressed Moon: Luna—symbol of change. So elemental is the Moon's role in predictive astrology that we deal with it separately in the following chapter. And then we devote a whole section to the specific exploration of each progressed planet with each natal planet as well as the natal Ascendent and Midheaven.

CHAPTER NINE

PROGRESSIONS III: THE PROGRESSED MOON

The Moon is the mother of astrology. Thousands upon thousands of years ago, when human intelligence first peered upward into the blackness of night, the Moon was there, hypnotizing, tantalizing, fascinating. Shape shifter, surpriser, illuminator of darkness, Luna quickly became the goddess of mystery, standing beside the solar god of light. Unraveling the messages of her phases became priestcraft, and those priests soon discovered there was more to her motion than phases. First she would appear as a crescent in the constellation of the Archer. During her next cycle a month later, that same crescent would appear in the sign of the Sea-Goat, then among the stars of the Water-Bearer. Moon phases fell on starfields, always following the same ancient path, yet always renewing and recombining, endlessly creating.

The Moon's phases held our forebears' attention, but her simple speed against the starry background revealed something more fundamental: Luna was predictable. She always followed the same path through the starfields: the zodiac. Much later we realized that the slower "wandering stars" also limited their wandering to the zodiac, and even later, we figured out that the Sun followed it too.

Every four weeks the Moon makes one complete tour of your

birthchart, hitting every trigger point and passing through each house. Every two or three days it enters a new sign. In about a day, it forms an aspect, perfects it, then passes out of orbs. In transits, the Moon's speed robs it of significance. It never has **time** to build the great beehives of meaning characteristic of slower-moving planets. The Moon's transits do have significance, as we discussed at the end of chapter three, but that significance is never profound enough to shape a life, serving only to help create the ever-varying **moods** through which the unconscious mind keeps in touch with consciousness on a daily basis; necessary, but not the work of a Teacher or a Trickster.

What happens when we **progress** the Moon instead of plotting its quick transits? Like the other planets, it slows down dramatically. Days become years, and a new predictive giant is born. In the sky, the Moon's cycle unfolds in about four weeks; in progression, that cycle expands to almost **three decades**. (Remember: in progressions, days become years.) The twenty-seven days of the Moon's visible cycle is translated into twenty-seven years of progressed time. Two or three **years** are spent in each sign or house. An aspect develops over a period of **months**. Plenty of time for contemplation—and choice.

Even crawling along at the pace of progressions, the Moon is still fast—by progressed standards. It cruises along at about six times the best speed of its nearest competitor, Mercury. One very practical bit of fallout for the astrologer is that the progressed Moon is nearly always doing **something**. It is difficult to imagine an interpretation that would fail to make some mention of its activities. A more important effect of the progressed Moon's speed is that it often serves as a **trigger**, precipitating events suggested by other progressed or transiting factors, much as we observed fast planets interacting with slow ones in transits theory.

> ☆ The progressed Moon triggers the effects of slowly
> evolving astrological configurations, just as transiting
> Mercury (fast) might trigger the potential of transiting
> Uranus or Saturn (slow).

As we see in Part Five, the line between transits and progressions often becomes fuzzy in practical predictive astrology. The progressed Moon might very well trigger the effects of an outer planet **transit**. The two systems work together.

The progressed Moon is quick enough to function as a trigger, and slow enough to operate as a Teacher or a Trickster. It is also the last of the astrological factors we need to explore before melding all that we have learned into a true predictive system—our goal in Part Five.

THE SIGNIFICANCE OF THE PROGRESSED MOON

In the birthchart, the Moon symbolizes **feelings**. It represents the **heart**—that is, the **emotional, subjective** substratum of personality. Traditional astrologers are quick to call Luna "feminine" since it displays some of the qualities that were traditionally associated with women—nurturance, sensitivity, timidity. (The Sun, with its ego orientation and active nature is of course viewed as "masculine" by those same astrologers.) Use such language if you are comfortable with it—but never forget that **every birthchart contains both Sun and Moon**. Each of us has what we might call a "masculine" and a "feminine" dimension, and I personally am highly suspicious of astrology texts that emphasize distinctions such as "in a man's chart" or "in a woman's chart." Every woman must develop her Sun; every man must develop his Moon. Cultural pressures may complicate the process, but in a healthy human being, both functions are operative and in balance.

Progressions always imply **evolution**. In the previous chapter, we learned a useful trick for defining the significance of progressed planets. We simply take a short definition of their function in the natal chart and precede it with the word "evolving." Thus, Mercury represents, among other things, our intelligence. Progressed Mercury then becomes our **evolving intelligence**. The Sun is identity. The progressed Sun is **evolving identity**. One-liners like these are helpful, but they can never tell the whole story. To acquire that level of knowledge, you need to absorb more complicated ideas about each progressed factor, and most important, you need to scrutinize their impact upon your own life. Still, rules of thumb like this one often help us focus our thoughts, thereby triggering our own creative and intuitive processes.

What do we learn when we apply our trick to the progressed Moon? "Evolving feelings." "Evolving heart." These ideas are sound, but they don't evoke very much. The progressed Moon is certainly connected with emotions, and its passages through sensitive zones are often accompanied by laughter and tears. Whatever part of life the progressed Moon is touching **engages our heart**. For a while, those issues excite us, baffle us, annoy us, perhaps thrill us.

A powerful undercurrent of emotion underlies most human decisions. Left to our own devices, we do what we **feel** like doing, then use logic only to establish strategies. We follow where our hearts lead, and even if they lead to the study of mathematics or bookkeeping, we must not lose sight of the fact that the decision to follow that road was probably not based upon raw, disembodied logic. For the individual concerned, it was an affair of the heart.

The Moon in the birthchart represents a kind of emotional input for which we have a perpetual craving. As astrologer Stephen Arroyo has observed, the Moon shows where we feel **comfortable**. Astrologer Noel Tyl describes it as a "**reigning need**." With the natal Moon in Taurus, for example, we feel **comfortable** in a secure, stable, natural environment. We have a **reigning need** to establish ourselves in that kind of situation. With the Moon in Aries everything is different. Now we see a person who is only comfortable in what Taurus would call distinctly uncomfortable environments—in the midst of adventure, friendly competition, achieving success against long odds. That is the kind of emotional input he or she needs in order to feel content.

Parallel reasoning applies to the progressed Moon, but unlike the natal Moon, the reigning needs to which it refers are transitory. We might call them **passing whims**—provided we recognize that these whims are intimately linked to fundamental psychological and spiritual processes within us. As the Moon progresses over a trigger point, we experience a mood which temporarily heightens our emotional involvement with whatever issues that trigger point symbolizes. When the progressed Moon contacts Venus, for example, our heart is with the Venusian dimensions of life—friendship, marriage, creativity. When it contacts Saturn, our reigning need focuses for a while on practical concerns. We are in the mood to "get it together"—that, or we temporarily expand the dark side of Saturn, filling our heart with feelings of impossibility and frustration. With the progressed Moon contacting Uranus, we feel **whims** of rebellion. On Neptune, our heart seeks quiet and contemplation—or we zone out with the television set for a couple of months. The progressed Moon, in other words, **tells us what we feel like doing**. In predictive astrology, it serves as the **emotional weathervane**, always pointing in the same direction as the winds of the heart.

> ☆ The progressed Moon indicates, at any given
> moment, where our heart is.

Once we let the progressed Moon show us where our heart is, we also know that our **attention** is likely to be in the same place, and that the area is being stirred up with developments and activity. Often the progressed Moon brings a number of predictive factors to a **focus** in the astrologer's mind, pointing out our current area of **greatest emotional emphasis**. Grasp that, and you have grasped the heart of the matter. Miss it, and even if your interpretations are otherwise theoretically sound, they feel empty and beside the point. The Moon, the mother of astrology, is the final link in our chain of symbols. By adding that link— the human heart—she turns the key in the locked door, revealing the treasures we have been approaching for so long.

PROGRESSED MOON THROUGH THE HOUSES

When we are young, we tend to measure the "chapters" of our experience according to the school year: "When I was in fourth grade" "When I was a sophomore . . ." As we mature, years seem shorter and shorter—and the chapters of our lives expand accordingly. The year isn't long enough anymore to contain a complete cycle of experience. We need more time. Often, we find ourselves sorting our memories naturally into chapters of two and three years. Such a unit seems to represent a basic "quantum" of personal history, long enough to get our business finished, short enough to encompass in our imagination. That length of time—two or three years—corresponds to the period it takes the progressed Moon to move through a complete sign or house of the birthchart. The progressed Moon, in other words, establishes the framework of personal experiential history. Other planetary cycles are superimposed on the lunar cycle, and often produce more dramatic turning points, but the progressed Moon's cycle is the one we feel most deeply and the one through which we mentally organize our emotional history.

> ☆ As it passes through the signs and houses of the
> birthchart, the progressed Moon establishes life's
> experiential chapters.

The cycle of signs, the cycle of houses: sometimes the line separating them blurs, as **events** (house material) are spawned by **realizations** (sign material), or as realizations lead inevitably to events. Remember that signs and houses each represent a fundamentally different locus of experience—signs are **psychological**; they are in your head, while houses are **experiential**; they are places you enter. When analyzing the passage of the progressed Moon through a sign, keep in mind that events are secondary. The person needs to learn something.

With the Moon progressing through a house, the emphasis is on action. The individual needs to adjust his or her circumstances. Knowledge grows and awareness changes, just as with signs—but now those developments arise because of **events**, rather than the other way around.

Monitor the Moon's passage through either cycle, signs or houses, and you arm yourself with one of the most vigorous and reliable of all the predictive tools in astrology. It is simple, clear—and powerful.

Let's briefly review the passage of the Moon through each of the twelve houses, fleshing out our understanding with some examples from real life. For a detailed exploration of the cycle of houses, refer back to chapter four. Although that chapter was written as a general introduction to the use of house symbolism in predictive astrology, it is tailor-made for helping you grasp the feel of the Moon as it moves around the birthchart. In fact, most of what I wrote there I learned from watching the progressed Moon course through the houses of my own chart, helping me to really feel (Moon!) what each one meant. Later I generalized that emotional knowledge into a theoretical understanding of the cycles of the other planets.

Progressed Moon in the First House: We are beginning a new cycle of experience, laying down the foundation of our next three decades of life. Everything we undertake now—all new habits, new commitments, new attitudes—plants the seeds of the next three decades. The first house is like that; it's always a new beginning. Every breath we take now is important. With each step we bind ourselves to a new future. And yet we have no idea what we are doing! Emotionally, that **uncertainty** is really the point we must understand. In the first house, we are improvising a new personality. An old cycle of experience has finished in the twelfth house. We must begin anew.

If the Moon is progressing through your first house, you need to become a master of **enlightened selfishness**, learning to listen to your intuition about what **feels** like the right path—and then follow that path no matter how much upset you create in the people around you. Don't let anything or anyone hold you back in the past you have outgrown. You are ready for something new. Feel your way and then **go for it**, wary of ego's excesses but warier still of letting opportunity slip away. In the immortal words of Joseph Campbell, it is now time to "follow your bliss."

With the Moon progressing through his first house, Walt Disney launched Mickey Mouse, and thereby launched himself on a roller coaster of experience that carried him through to the end of his life. Marie Curie won her first Nobel Prize under the same lunar placement, with similar results. On a darker note, Charles Manson also initiated a new cycle with the Moon progressing through his first house— the Tate-LaBianca murders occurred, and his long prison term began.

Progressed Moon in the Second House: Can you finish what you have started? That is the question life is asking you now. During this phase, you are three or four years into a new cycle. Some of the giddiness has worn off. You have time to get scared, to question whether you are really good enough to carry out the projects you have undertaken. Everything depends upon finding the courage to **follow through** on the new beginning you have made. You must **prove yourself to yourself.** You desperately need some victories now, to reaffirm your confidence and to dispel the feeling of being an imposter in your role, which is so characteristic of this phase in the lunar progression. Create those victories for yourself. Take on further commitments, deeper challenges. You are probably better and stronger than you think you are. Take a risk. Convince yourself. If you lack anything, it most likely takes the form of concrete resources: money perhaps, but it could just as easily be a human connection or a tool you need to acquire. You are in a new cycle. Accept it. Prepare yourself for the long haul by creating a resource base that can sustain your new pattern of development. Financial affairs can be an issue now, but so can other resources such as specific skills, supportive relationships, a car or a boat or a flashy green parrot to stand on your shoulder—anything which invigorates your faith in the new personality you have created.

With his Moon progressing through the second house of his birthchart, Muhammad Ali proved himself to himself by defeating Sonny Liston for the heavyweight boxing championship of the world. He was notorious for his "float like a butterfly, sting like a bee" bravado, but this lunar configuration suggests he was inwardly far less confident than he made himself out to be. He had won the Olympics— but could he really make it in the pros? Under the same configuration, Marlon Brando came out of retirement to undertake his epic portrayal of Vito Corleone in *The Godfather*. He was widely perceived to be "washed up." Could he again generate the intensity and magic of his earlier years?

Progressed Moon in the Third House: You have more confidence now. You are ready to expand your horizons and flex the muscles of your newly developed character. What you seek is **information**. Your heart is filled with **curiosity** and **restlessness**. Less awkward, less cut off from other people by your own self-doubt and insecurity, you begin to **establish relationships**, seeking knowledge and understanding through conversations with others. Often, the progression of the Moon through the third house is a time of study and learning. Many times, it initiates a period of geographical mobility. You might travel, making connections with new environments and different kinds of people. In an effort to help my clients understand the significance of this progression, I have often used the metaphor of "buying a new car"— only to have them gasp and say that they just did exactly that. Whether or not you buy a new car, the point is the same: Now is the time to banish laziness and reserve. The time has come for you to jump headlong into life and learn from the world around you.

Explorer Robert Peary made a radical response to his Moon's progression through the third house—he led an expedition by dogsled to the North Pole. Under the same placement, Pete Townshend of The Who began to hunger for an answer to his drug dependency. He found his curiosity stimulated by the neuroelectric therapy techniques practiced by the Scottish surgeon Dr. Meg Peterson. He later said that she helped save him from "self-destruction." She was his answer, but he himself had to initiate the seeking—and under the pressure of his third house lunar progression, that initiation occurred.

Progressed Moon in the Fourth House: Running around gets tiring and unproductive after a while. With your progressed Moon entering the fourth house, the time has come for you to sit back and quietly **take stock of yourself**. Houses vary in size, so we can't make precise, generalized statements about timing, but roughly seven years have now elapsed since you launched your new lunar cycle. Your "mini-reincarnation" is stretching toward maturity, and to find the maturity it seeks, that new character must confront the **roots** of its own behavior. You are probably overextended. Cut back on the extraneous. Turn the volume down on your life. Have a long talk with yourself. Settle down—that talk will take two or three years. You are ready for an encounter with your own **personal myth**. What are your ideals? What do you really want out of life? How have you been fooling yourself or letting yourself be fooled by others? You might find yourself drawn closer to your family now—or closer to that modern version of family, the circle of special friends. Either way, the establishment and reaffirmation of personal roots is the issue. Oftentimes, people move to new homes now, or somehow reenergize their old ones. The "nesting instinct" is strong with us—and the egg we are hatching is a matured and chastened version of the personality we recreated when the progressed Moon was in the first house.

Muhammad Ali was drafted while the Moon progressed through his fourth house. He confronted himself, and found that he could not in good conscience fight in Vietnam. The decision cost him his heavyweight title and thrust him for a while out of the extreme activity of his life. Three years later, the same astrological position developed in Jane Fonda's birthchart. It was during the time of the invasion of Cambodia and the Kent State debacle. Like Muhammad Ali, she, too, confronted her own conscience and made a stand.

Progressed Moon in the Fifth House: Deepened, intensified, sharpened by your quiet confrontation with the self in the previous house, you are now ready to **express yourself** in a far more sophisticated way than ever before. The time has come to **create symbols of yourself.** Paint, write, sing, dance—if you are artistic in temperament, those outlets strengthen and gladden you now. Not all of us are artists, but each one of us can express himself or herself, and that is the point in this phase of the lunar cycle. If you are an athlete, put energy into your sport. If your nature is domestic, decorate your house. If you are in business, then trust your imagination now—it will never be stronger. You must recover your ability to **play.** That sounds easy, but often proves challenging. If you lack anything now, it is probably joy. Find it and seize it!

With the progressed Moon passing through the fifth house of his birthchart, Michaelangelo executed what many consider to be his greatest masterpiece—the paintings adorning the upper reaches of the Sistine Chapel in the Vatican. After the progression of the Moon through his fourth house, he was ready to **express his soul** to the world—the essence of the fifth house terrain.

Progressed Moon in the Sixth House: Nose to the grindstone now. This is a time of hard work, responsibility, and relentless effort. Traditional astrologers speak of the sixth house Moon progression in terms of outward labor. That idea is accurate enough so far as it goes, but often our inner labors dwarf our outer ones now. This is frequently a humbling period. The time has come for you to **assess your weaknesses**—always an edifying process, but rarely a cheerful one. You are learning **humility**—don't learn **humiliation** by mistake. You are not stuck. You are no one's slave. You can change whatever behaviors and circumstances limit you, but wishing for such change is not the same as accomplishing it. Self-discipline and persistence are what's needed. Accept your responsibilities to others, but more importantly, to yourself. Be true to your word, and **do what is right**. Support yourself with new techniques and skills. Build a foundation of focused energy, honesty, and willingness to accept rightful criticism. Echoing the second house, you must once again prove yourself to yourself. **Effectiveness** is the keynote. You are experiencing a "darkness before the dawn."

Astronaut Eugene Cernan demonstrated his mastery of the sixth house lunar progression by piloting Apollo 10 to the Moon. Certainly the flight required long hours of intensive preparation along with absolute self-discipline and perfect concentration during the voyage itself—all sixth house lessons to be sure. Perhaps more poignant is the fact that it was the **next** Apollo mission that actually landed on the lunar surface. Neil Armstrong will go down in history next to Christopher Columbus and Leif Erikson, while Eugene Cernan might be relegated to the role of a Vasco da Gama (who?). Still, he played his role perfectly and did not let ego get in the way of the execution of his mission, and that is the point in this phase of the progressed Moon's cycle through the houses.

Progressed Moon in the Seventh House: Often a dramatic time, you are now ready to bring your restructured personality to bear upon intimate relationships. This progression is notoriously hard on marriages, but to say that it "signifies separation" would be destructive and inaccurate. A relationship, whether sexual or otherwise, exists between two fluxing human totalities. If one partner changes, then the relationship changes, too. With your Moon progressing into the seventh house, **you must refresh and restructure** the lines of communication with your partner or your closest friends. Be honest. Weed out ritual and habit, and concentrate on **renewing** the relationship. Unless your intimates are extraordinarily psychic, they have no way of knowing what you have become. So speak up. Declare yourself. Hang in there with the process. If that process fails and a relationship cannot survive the changes, then at least the failure is a clean one. New people arrive in your life now, often helping, sometimes complicating the situation. Open up to them—they have something to tell you, and once you grasp it, it will change your life.

With his progressed Moon in the seventh house, Ram Dass, then known as Richard Alpert, emerged publicly as Timothy Leary's ally in their radical work with hallucinogenic drugs. Together, they were fired from their positions in Harvard University's psychology department, and for a while, stood together as rebellious symbols (progressed Moon in Aquarius!) in the collective awareness of America in the middle 1960s.

Progressed Moon in the Eighth House: The dungeon gates fly open. Out fly wraiths and warlocks, demons and deceivers. Among them are fierce angels, eager to lift you into new realms of inner strength, but **impatient with your madness**. With the progressed Moon in this house, you confront some of the less attractive aspects of your own character. It is not a pleasant process or a breezy one, but **if you open yourself, it heals you**. Half-perceived hungers and fears have been accumulating in the garbage cans of your psyche while you rightly concerned yourself with other issues. Without any clear awareness on your part, those hungers and fears have been exerting an influence in your life, making their shadowy presence felt, distorting your behaviors. This lunar progression tells you that those psychic garbage cans are brimming over and that it is time to carry out the trash. Quiet yourself now. Withdraw. A pattern I have found in myself and in my clients during this cycle is that a mood of depression quickly turns into a mood that is simply quiet as soon as the individual is left alone. We do often feel a deep need for intimacy and bonding with another at this time. Meet that need, but don't overdo it. At least half the answer must be your own. Learning to trust the "mating instinct" and to flow with it is a big part of the eighth house, but above all else, you need to face yourself.

Henry David Thoreau began his long sojourn at Walden Pond with the progressed Moon in the eighth house. Jerry Brown, the former governor of California, entered the Jesuit monastery under the same pattern. Both men reflect the urge for quiet self-scrutiny so characteristic of this progression.

Progressed Moon in the Ninth House: Stretch yourself! With the Moon entering your ninth house, if your heart could speak, it would pound on its pulpit and tell you that life is for the living, and that the only thing wrong with you is that you are bored stiff with yourself. To the medievals, this was the house of "Long Journeys over Water." The progression doesn't always signify literal travel, but travel is a perfect metaphor. You need to break up old routines and patterns. You are more interesting than your circumstances would suggest. Do something about that. Take chances. Study something that fascinates you. Buy those tickets to Macchu Pichu you've been dreaming about for so long. Philosophize! Speculate about the meaning of life! In the film *Harold and Maude*, Ruth Gordon delivers a speech much like the preceding one, and ends it with the observation that if you live otherwise, "then you won't have anything to talk about in the locker room." If your Moon is progressing through this house, the best advice I can offer is to go find that old movie and sit through it twice.

With his Moon progressing through the ninth house of his birthchart, Jimmy Carter campaigned successfully for the governorship of Georgia. He broke up the old routines of his life, daring to enter unknown and alien existential territory. Whether you "break into politics" or "break into backpacking" doesn't matter; the point remains the same: **you need to trust yourself enough to undertake some activity you have never attempted before.** For you, at this point in your lunar cycle, boredom is the ultimate foolishness.

Progressed Moon in the Tenth House: We humans are social creatures. A million years ago, that and our intelligence were the only virtues we had, and the only barriers separating us from the saber tooth tigers. Nature rewarded sociability, and long ago most of the true human hermits were weeded out of our gene pool, appearing as entrées on the menus of those tigers. Nowadays, for the vast majority of us, to be fully sane means to be **integrated into the community**. We might not always be part of the social mainstream—some of us are integrated into various subcultures. But that's still integration. It still gives us a **role to play** and a sense of **belonging**. With the progressed Moon entering your tenth house, the time has come to **scrutinize and restructure your relationship to the community**. You might need a new job, or to revamp the old one. You might become more involved in some "good cause." You might marry or divorce or announce that you are gay or Republican or Christian or communist. The point is that you need to redefine and clarify your standing in the eyes of all those other social creatures out there to whom you are not so much a friend as a symbol. Then pick up your roses, or take the heat. Given the diversity of human culture, there will likely be some of both.

Journalist Jack Anderson appeared on the cover of *Time* magazine and received the Pulitzer Prize in the spring of 1972 in connection with his work on the Watergate scandal—all with the Moon progressing through his tenth house. Jerry Brown, working under the same lunar placement, made the decision to leave the Jesuit monastery after several years there. The reason? He felt like becoming more involved with the issues of society.

Progressed Moon in the Eleventh House: This is the "fullness of time." The harvest. The cycle of character development that began over twenty years ago is now stretching toward culmination. Claim what is yours, and most centrally, insist upon your **right to be recognized for what you have done**. As the British Lords and Ladies might put it, you are now ready to be "raised to Peerage." You can take your place now within whatever social stratum you have chosen to make your mark. Expand your circles. Share what you have and what you are with others who are following similar roads through life. The eleventh house Moon progression is no time for shyness or for "hiding your light beneath a bushel." Set goals. Establish priorities. Think strategically. What is really important to you? Figure that out, because there is a good chance you are surrounded by opportunities now and you don't have time to pursue all of them. You have become what you set out to be so long ago. Experience has deepened you and collisions with reality have left their scars, but the old dim dream of the first house has at last solidified. What was a **feeling** then is a **reality** now. Deuces or aces, your cards are on the table, face up.

Earlier, I mentioned Elisabeth Kubler-Ross's *On Death and Dying* which was published when her Moon was progressing through her eleventh house. Such a "tour de force" is not an uncommon expression of the **maturation** this configuration symbolizes. A darker example of a character coming into its own and expressing that development with a tour de force is provided by James Oliver Huberty. With the progressed Moon in his eleventh house, the hatred and madness that had been quietly brewing in his almost frighteningly indrawn birthchart suddenly burst out. He entered a McDonald's in San Ysidro, California, and murdered almost two dozen strangers. His twisted process of growth reached its culmination, and his life was ended by a policeman's bullet. His "dream came true."

Progressed moon in the Twelfth House: Let go. You have come to the end of a cycle. Accept that. Something within you is failing now, but don't worry—once it fails utterly, you will he happier, wiser, and stronger. In two or three years, you are going to go through a rebirth. In fact, you are going through one right now, but it's very private and internal. Your main task currently is to clear away everything that stands between you and that new beginning. What was once opportunity now enslaves you. What once tasted sweet has now turned bitter and dry. Recognize those transformations and **release the past** or you fight a losing battle for your right to retain your slavery and your bitterness. In the previous house, you were asked to **clarify your priorities**, deciding what was truly important to you. If you accomplished that and were not blinded by glitter or praise or peer pressure, then you move into your twelfth house progression streamlined and simplified. If, on the other hand, you are retaining attachments and identifications that are too **childish** to be carried forward into the next cycle, then those structures are torn from you now. Again, we experience a time of **withdrawal**. Find the deep center around which the merry-go-round of life orbits. Find it and stay there, where it is safe. Meditate, pray, relax, stare into candle flames—and **trust the process that is happening within you**. Trust it, even though it is beyond your control. Trust it, if for no other reason than that **you have no other choice**.

Charlemagne, the great warrior-king of a millennium ago, felt a surge of discontent in his character, a sense of his own inadequacy— feelings typical of the twelfth house Moon progression he was undergoing. He sought counsel, and in the spring or summer of 781 he found Alcuin, the mysterious Celtic deacon who taught him astronomy, mathematics, medicine, rhetoric, music—the knowledge of the classical world. Nineteen years later, the vision that was beyond his understanding at the time blossomed: He was crowned Holy Roman Emperor, bringing Europe closer to unity than it has ever been until now. We of course must be cautious about the birthtimes of historical figures, but in this case, the chart seems to be working quite well.

PROGRESSED MOON THROUGH THE SIGNS

Signs are **processes in the mind**. As the Moon progresses into a new sign, we end a chapter of life dominated by one constellation of emotions and begin one characterized by another constellation of emotions. Our mood, in other words, undergoes a change. Naturally, that mood swing alters our behavior, but the behavioral change is secondary rather than primary as it is with house symbolism

As we learned in *The Inner Sky*, the wheel of signs spins around the earth every twenty-four hours. In the course of a day, each sign rises, passes overhead, sets, passes beneath us, and rises again. In other words, in the course of a day, every sign passes through every house. At birth, that celestial roulette wheel clicks to a stop, at least for astrological purposes. A certain sign was rising at that moment. It becomes the child's Ascendant. Another one was overhead. That is his or her Midheaven. For that individual, a **fixed relationship** is established between certain signs and certain houses. As long as he lives, that child has Sagittarius on his Midheaven, Capricorn on the cusp of his eleventh house, and so on. It helps to understand this idea thoroughly, because the linkage of certain houses and signs in the individual birthchart offers a fundamental insight about the Moon's progression, and in fact about transits and progressions in general.

☆ For each one of us, a particular set of attitudes and motivations (signs) are forever associated with a particular kind of behavior or circumstance (houses).

There is plenty of room for growth and maturation, but if you have Aries (the **process** of attaining courage) on your seventh house cusp (the **behavior** of forming relationships), then throughout your life, your various partnerships always bring out Arian qualities in you. At first, you might let yourself be **tyrannized** by a domineering mate, wearing yourself down with an ulcer or chronic headaches. Once you figure that problem out, you might begin to **assert yourself**—but perhaps by slamming doors and throwing plates. Later, you might begin to learn the **constructive** use of just conflict. It's all Aries material, but there is a wide spectrum for choice. To use the language of *The Inner Sky*, you can get stuck in the sign's **shadow**, achieve its **endpoint**, or enjoy the scenery in between. It's up to you, and your choices cannot be predicted astrologically.

As the Moon progresses around your birthchart, it **stimulates into action** your basic house/sign combinations. For purposes of clear presentation, we separate the two symbol systems, but in practical predictive astrology, you should never think of either a house or a sign in isolation. In each individual chart, a certain sign and a certain house are an inseparable package. One cannot be understood without reference to the other.

What follows are some specific insights and examples about the progressed Moon's passage through the twelve signs. For a more thorough understanding of each one, have a look at *The Inner Sky* and remember that what is presented there as the work of a lifetime (birthchart astrology) now emerges in lunar progressions as the emotional focus of a period of two or three years.

Progressed Moon in Aries: You are learning courage. This is no time for passivity. Defend your territory. Expand your territory, too, if you can do so in a way that is consistent with your principles. You might feel surges of anger. Trust them—carefully. They represent the energy you need to accomplish your inward task, but since we are talking about a force arising from a **sign**, that energy is purely psychological. In other words, it might not be very closely related to outer reality— yet. Be cautious about foolish, misdirected outbursts. You are the "spiritual warrior" now. Think: What do I want to **do** with this new, raw, unfocused **power** I feel rising up in me? Check the **house** the Moon is in; there's your battlefield. Now swallow whatever fear you feel, and **claim what is yours**.

After being punished for refusing the draft with the loss of his heavyweight boxing title, Muhammad Ali fought his way back up the standings. Finally, with his Moon progressing through the sign of the Ram, he regained the championship. On a softer note, Eubie Blake claimed what was his by publishing his first musical composition, breaking out of the racist patterns in the music industry of World War I America.

Progressed Moon in Taurus: Your mood shifts away from the affairs of ego now, moving closer to the affairs of the heart. You need to alter your consciousness in the direction of peace and tranquility. The battles of the last two or three years are over. Relax. Go sit in the woods on a rock by a brook. Calm down. Tend to your body—it's tired and full of the strain of battle. Release tension. Exercise. Let your hair down. Learn to take off your shoes at the end of the working day. Eat well. You might gain a few pounds. Go easy on yourself about that. You'll lose them quickly enough when the Moon progresses into frenetic Gemini in a couple of years.

Many times, the Moon's progression through Taurus suggests a time of **solidification**. Projects come together. Effort is rewarded. After playing in a variety of bands, Pete Townshend finally found the right musicians to express his musical vision. With his progressed Moon in the sign of the Bull, he formed The Who.

Progressed Moon in Gemini: Flexibility is the point now. You have gotten too stiff, too sleepy, too predictable. Open yourself up. Recover your capacity to feel **amazement**. Speak, read, listen, write—these are your "yogas." Undertake them with spirit and verve. Aim your mental antennas at the world. If an idea or experience **feels interesting** to you, go investigate. Don't worry if you appear to be running around in circles. Keep it up and you are bound to run into something fascinating. You are gathering material now, and that is all you really need to consider. No master plans are necessary at this point in the lunar cycle. No matter how old you are, accept the idea that you have returned temporarily to **childhood**—and let that notion fill you with **exuberance** and **curiosity**.

This was precisely the astrological mood that filled Charlemagne when he encountered Alcuin, as we discussed a few moments ago. J. R. R. Tolkien's progressed Moon was also in Gemini as he completed his epic *Lord of the Rings*.

Progressed Moon in Cancer: Your imagination and subjectivity are at one of their peaks during this phase of Luna's cycle through the signs. The progressed Moon's entry into Cancer puts you on notice that **your heart needs some attention**. With the Moon passing through other signs, sometimes life gets frantic; sometimes the mental or intellectual dimensions of your personality must be emphasized. Nothing wrong with that, but it does take a toll. Sooner or later, you have to sit down and **listen to your feelings**. Moon in Cancer is a quiet time. Let fantasies bubble up. Take time. Make a cup of tea. Scratch the cat's ears while she purrs in your lap. Cut back on outer stimulation—you've got inner stimulation enough to last you a couple of years. Security is an issue now, mostly because of the way security translates into the freedom to pay no attention to the outer world. Stabilize your circumstances, hush the roar of events, and listen.

Such a mood motivated Henry David Thoreau when he withdrew to Walden Pond. It also inspired trumpeter Miles Davis when he made his first recording—and a jazz legend began to flow up from his introverted soul. John DeLorean was arrested for allegedly dealing in the international cocaine market while his progressed Moon was in the sign of the Crab. Did his urge for security overpower his normal Capricornish ability to test reality?

Progressed Moon in Leo: Celebrate yourself! Your mood is expansive now. You are ready to express yourself more colorfully, to be appreciated, to be noticed. Don't burden yourself with thoughts about "how big your ego has gotten." Just play. Give your poor ego a break. Let it flow. Just try to do everything with good humor. "Hallelujah! I'm ridiculous!" That's the spirit. Avoid being too **solemn** about yourself. A little drama won't hurt, provided part of you retains enough grace to be sitting in the front row eating popcorn while the show goes on. This progression is hard on egomaniacs—the very **expressiveness** of the sign forces their hands. Hopefully, their embarrassment matures into a bit more wisdom about themselves. It is also hard on that other kind of egomaniac—the "spiritual type"—who invariably gets fooled into being somebody's guru when the Moon enters Leo. Again, we can only hope that he or she learns the elemental lesson of the Lion: All egos are inherently absurd, and as long as you are in the world, you are stuck with one, so **laugh**.

Cesar Chavez **expressed himself** under the Leo-Moon progression. He became the figurehead and leader of the historic grape strike against the commercial growers in California. Actor Ben Kingsley offered us his stunning portrayal of Mohandas Gandhi in the film *Gandhi* under the same lunar placement.

Progressed Moon in Virgo: Your mood shifts gears now. Instead of the self-celebration characteristic of Leo, you now move into an attitude of hyperawareness regarding your faults and shortcomings. However, don't waste time being hard on yourself. That is not the point of this lunar progression. Instead of tearing yourself down, use that energy to build yourself up. Of course you are crazy. Of course you are neurotic, greedy, power-hungry, untrustworthy, insincere. Welcome aboard! That's the human condition, and cataloguing your glitches won't change anything. Pick one of them and start working on it. That's the thrust of Virgo. Roll up your sleeves and change a few bad habits. Acquire some better skills. If the energy of this mood is not squandered in pointless self-criticism, it can be directed into an extremely fertile period of **preparation, self-improvement, and methodical growth**.

Eubie Blake honed his compositional skills under this progression—while playing piano in a bordello. It is not always the most glorious of times, but a successful navigation of Virgo's tricky corridors can **set the stage** for exciting developments later on.

Progressed Moon in Libra: This is a **friendly** Moon. You are in the mood to meet some new people, to share some of your insights and experiences, to compare notes. Nature designed us in such a way that the **relationship** circuit in our head is also the circuit of **personal grace**. To learn about relationships, we must attract others, and to attract others, we must be attractive. You are ready to present yourself more appealingly, more gracefully. Issues of clothing and grooming arise now. If you are already very concerned with such things, beware of vanity. There is more to be groomed than the body. If you have always prided yourself on taking a slap-dash attitude toward personal grooming, be careful you aren't making **that** into a kind of vanity. Try to be more aware of other people. What kind of impact are you having upon them? How can you make it easier for them to be open and comfortable with you? In Spanish, the word **gracia** has a double meaning—"grace" and "humor." Live with gracia while your Moon progresses through Libra. Enjoy the aesthetic side of life—beauty, art, social interaction, **quality**—but do it with lightness and an inward sense of life's grand comedy.

Cesar Chavez drew the grape strike to an end while his progressed Moon was in Libra, the sign of the peacemaker. Leonard Nimoy, much to the surprise of his producers, engaged us all with his emotionless and yet irresistibly attractive portrayal of *Star Trek's* Vulcan science officer.

Progressed Moon in Scorpio: Rarely an easy progression, never a light-hearted one, the entry of the Moon into the sign of the Scorpion signals a period of intense inner confrontation. The "moodiest of the Moon's moods," Scorpio drives you very deeply into yourself, into the mystery of life, and sometimes into its horror. There is no dodging the truth now. The curtain is raised on your most personal psychological processes. Sexuality in the broadest, most human sense of the word, is intensified. You feel hungry, although it often seems that no human touch could ever still the hunger. An awareness of death arises. Oftentimes, this progression suggests an actual confrontation with the death of someone close. You are **integrating the unconscious mind into your personality**—and the reason that part of the mind became unconscious in the first place is that it was too hard to face. But you are stronger now and ready to see more clearly. Be careful of losing perspective, though. A powerful telescope might let you count the hairs on a squirrel's back a mile off—but you might miss the rainbow above him.

Sir Francis Chichester was diagnosed with lung cancer while his Moon was progressing through Scorpio. He survived, but still he had to confront the reality of his own death. Geraldine Ferraro experienced her father's death under the same lunar placement. Peter Sutcliffe, the infamous "Yorkshire Ripper," committed the last murders of his killing spree and was caught and sentenced while his Moon was in Scorpio—his inner demons translated all too clearly into the world of behavior.

Progressed Moon in Sagittarius: An expansive, exuberant, devil-may-care mood arises now, and lasts for two or three years. You are reacting against the inward intensity of the Scorpio Moon chapter you just finished. Suddenly the universe takes on a third dimension. Everything seems more vivid, more real. Senses tingling, you are ready to stretch out into life, **seizing opportunities**. The **exotic** in all its forms fascinates you now. Trust that feeling. You need a breath of fresh air in your life. Dare to change. Risk an adventure. Ride a hot air balloon. You are learning to break up routines of thought and feeling. You have memorized a mood. Shatter that memory. Flood yourself with impressions. Make yourself new.

Novelist Ursula K. LeGuin wrote much of her prizewinning *Earthsea Trilogy* while her progressed Moon was in Sagittarius. She stretched her imagination into an adventuresome new environment full of magic and the possibility of surprise. The wizard world she created for us reflects the mood we must strive to attain while our own Moon is progressing through the Archer's sign. If you are not feeling **inspiration**, you need to stretch a little farther.

Progressed Moon in Capricorn: Time to get serious. Not heavy, not miserable, not melodramatic—just serious. Look clearly at yourself and the world you've created. Capricorn and Cancer are opposite signs. The Crab symbolizes pure feeling. In Capricorn, we see the other end of the spectrum: **self-discipline**, that which **balances feeling**. This is the nearest the progressed Moon ever gets to reality itself. And Luna doesn't like reality much. You are in the mood to accomplish something. You feel a need to be recognized for your accomplishments and for your effectiveness. It is an ambitious time, although that ambition needs to be linked irrevocably to your inner life. Operate with absolute integrity during this period. Once ambition loosens the bonds of the inner voice, you have unleashed a monster. Make a point of talking about your feelings. Too often we create unnecessary loneliness for ourselves during this cycle—and with this kind of power available, that's not only painful, it's dangerous.

Jim Jones shocked the world with the horrible Jonestown massacre-suicide while his progressed Moon was in Capricorn. He had become increasingly maddened over the years by his craving for authority and respect. The Capricorn-lunar progression was enough to push him over the brink. More positively, under the precise discipline of this progressed placement, Peggy Fleming awed us with her flawless figure skating at the 1968 Olympics.

Progressed Moon in Aquarius: Break the rules! With the progressed Moon in Aquarius, your mood needs to be rebellious and free-spirited. Other people have been too successful at telling you what to feel. This is a time to defend and explore your **individuality**. Experiment. Think anything. Don't be afraid of anyone's disapproval. Something deep within you, something irremediably irrational, something explosive, is crying out for freedom That voice is trying to inspire you to make your life your own. Listen to it. If you silence the voice for fear that someone to whom you have given too much power will hear it, you are setting yourself up for trouble. Sooner or later, the walls crack and all your stored up anger, rebelliousness, and iconoclasm come pouring out at once, beyond control. If you let that happen, you feel crazy and unbalanced—and you unnecessarily hurt the people around you. Better a lot of little tremors than one horrendous earthquake.

Michael Jackson's innovative individuality was stimulated by his Aquarian Moon progression—and in early 1984 the music industry recognized him for it by awarding him more Grammy awards than anyone in history. John Belushi shows the other side of the same lunar progression. His rebelliousness proved self-destructive, as he unintentionally killed himself with a drug injection.

Progressed Moon in Pisces: Relax, and trust this often surrealistic feeling. Laugh with it, because it will ask you to laugh—but the object of the humor is not your favorite one. It is yourself. Life begins to look like a cartoon now, two-dimensional, stylized—and funny. The cosmic joke. Pisces has the reputation of being the "mystical" sign, and in a sense that is true. It is here that consciousness confronts its true nature: that vast space between your ears. But so often we take "mystical" to be synonymous with "reverent" or "introverted"—and those moods have little to do with the Fishes. Here we are asked to experience the essential **unity of life**. We stare pie-eyed at the world, full of wonder. The progression of the Moon through this sign is often a friendly time, but a vague one. By taking ourselves less seriously—and by seeing our own pretenses mirrored in the crystal-clear pretenses of others—we prepare ourselves for the new emotional beginning in Aries. It is as if our deeper self sends us a simple but rather startling message: Erase the blackboard of your personality. Everything you know—and everything everybody else knows—is delightfully, hysterically **wrong**.

With his progressed Moon in Pisces, Jerry Brown heard the inner call and entered the Jesuit monastery. Such spiritual undertakings are quite appropriate to the Fishes, provided we recognize that the essential spiritual process lies in creating a vantage point within consciousness that is **external to ego**. Pumping ego up with self-important illusions has precisely the opposite effect. I once heard a Tibetan lama say that to ego, "enlightenment is the ultimate disappointment." He understood Pisces very well.

Fidel Castro began his long invasion of Cuba under a Piscean-progressed Moon. He landed at Oriente in December 1956 with eighty-two men, all but twelve of whom were soon killed. He was successful in the end, but he illustrates a very basic insight into this progressed lunar configuration: Our "reality testing" is too weak now to support vigorous commitments in the world of circumstance. Pisces represents a time of **reflection**, not action. Save the fireworks for Aries in a year or two.

PART FOUR

THE PROGRESSED PLANETS

CHAPTER TEN

PROGRESSIONS IV: THE PROGRESSED PLANETS AND ANGLES

The single most magical word in astrological interpretation is **integration**. Behind every aspect that ever forms in your chart, that's the key point: two elemental drives in the psyche are striving toward integration.

Maybe the planets are inherently compatible, such as the emotional Moon meeting mystical Neptune. Maybe they're natural antagonists: consider warm-spirited Venus and cool, rebellious Uranus. And then there's the aspect itself: perhaps the angle through which they are joining is a harmonious trine or sextile. Maybe it's an edgier, more explosive square or opposition.

No matter what the combination, never forget the magic word: integration.

Your aim, whether you're using astrology to help yourself or to help someone else, is to think of ways that these two forces can be made to enhance each other and come together in some greater wholeness. At the same time, again no matter what planets or aspects are operating, you deepen your understanding when you remember that there's nothing so sweet in symbolism that enough foolishness can't turn it into something destructive.

In the previous chapter, we went into detail about the progressed

Moon. In the pages that follow, we explore the other major progressed points in a similar way: the Sun, Mercury, Venus, Mars, and the Ascendant and Midheaven. As we learned earlier, we don't really need to pay attention to Jupiter, Saturn, Uranus, Neptune and Pluto in terms of their progressions. They just move too slowly to be of much use.

What follows is a "cookbook" approach. If you are experiencing, say, a progression of Mercury through a sextile to your natal Pluto, you can simply look it up here. What you'll read will describe the essential psychospiritual integration that is trying to happen in your life. You'll learn about the inner drama, and in most cases, about the kinds of events that generally ride this "synchronistic wave" into your life. In other words, since Mercury is about communication, its inner meaning always has something to do with "finding your voice," but that process usually brings in its wake lots of concrete Mercury stuff as well: books, letters, email, educational opportunities, and stimulating new experiences in general. That's the **synchronistic** element: the way the seemingly random pieces of our outer lives always seem weirdly connected to our inner lives. As always, astrology provides an uncannily accurate Rosetta Stone for deciphering all that.

You'll also read about the darker possibilities connected with each progressed combination. Those cautionary words are not predictions; they're simply warnings about what you'll feel like and what you'll experience if you fail in the integrative process. With progressed Mercury, that basically means running around in circles, feeling nervous and scattered, and probably talking too much.

In the pages that follow, the actual aspect that's forming between your progressed planet and your natal one isn't named specifically. In other words we don't deal with each possible sextile or opposition individually. You'll see a section for "Progressed Mercury/Natal Pluto," but not one for "Progressed Mercury **sextile** (or trine, opposition, whatever) natal Pluto." We've done it that way for a couple of reasons. The first is that what's really important is the **nature of the integration itself**, which really comes down to the personalities of the two planets involved, not the aspect that's joining them. If you understand that integration, you've really grasped about ninety percent of what's helpful to know. At the risk of oversimplifying the question a bit, knowing whether the aspect is square or a trine or a sextile basically just tells you if you are likely to **enjoy** the process or not, and a little about whether "luck" is running with you or against you.

The second reason we leave out detailed analysis of each specific aspect in the thoughts that follow is purely practical. It would fill up too many pages. We're about to explore the interactions of the six major progressed points (other than the Moon) with all the other planets, plus the Ascendant and Midheaven. That's seventy-two combinations. If we multiply that again by the five major aspects, we'd have three hundred sixty of them—a book in itself, unless we reduced each one to the intellectual level of a bumper sticker. And this is the evolution of your soul we're talking about, so no "bumper sticker" insight is adequate for the task.

In the following pages, you'll often run into phrases such as "under easy aspects" or "under hard aspects." The easy aspects are the trine and the sextile; the hard ones are the square and opposition. If you're into using any of the minor aspects, go for it! They're powerful and fascinating, especially the 150 degree quincunx. Probably you'll benefit most from treating them as "hard" aspects, although each has its own personality. Conjunctions are unique, and we'll say a few special words about how to handle them below. But the critical point with any aspect always lies in understanding the nature of the integration itself; the aspect just gives us some details about the mechanics of the process.

There's a third reason for my not going separately into each possible aspect: I really believe that "cookbook" interpretations can become a terrible crutch. My intention in this book is really to help you learn how to **think like an astrologer** rather than to encourage you to depend on me or anyone else to do your thinking for you. That isn't just some kind of empty moralism either—it's pure practicality. Here's why: even if we did explore each of those three hundred sixty possibilities, it would still leave out a tremendous amount of detail. In our earlier example we imagined that you were experiencing a progressed sextile of Mercury to Pluto. But what if your natal Pluto lies in Libra and in the Third House? And what if the progressed Mercury is sixty degrees ahead, in the Fifth House and Sagittarius? The specific "flavors" of that progressed Mercury and that natal Pluto bear deeply on the interpretation. And then on top of it all there's the larger astrological context: what if six months after sextiling Pluto your progressed Mercury is going to move into a square with your Piscean Second House Venus? The first event fades into the second, and tells a very particular story.

You get the picture. The real richness and startling detail that astrology is capable of providing simply can't ever be put in "cookbook" form, unless the world's most patient astrologer computerized it somehow...and by the time that pitiable soul was halfway through the project, he or she would be so full-blown bat-headed crazy that the interpretations wouldn't be very helpful anyway.

There is a better way. Learn the symbols, and practice a bit. Learn to perform the synthesis and symbolic thinking yourself. It's like riding a bicycle: hard at first, then suddenly it's second nature. My hope is that the following little sketches help trigger creative astrological thinking in you rather than dulling your natural ability to do the integrative magic. Always, as your facility with this language deepens, try not to think just about "your progressed Mercury." Try to think about your "progressed Mercury in Sagittarius in the Fifth House." Bring in those Gypsy-flavors (Sagittarius) and those creative and romantic outward expressions (Fifth House) as you meditate on what's happening with your "Evolving Voice" (progressed Mercury.) That's how you really do it. The material that follows is just a seed.

CONJUNCTIONS

As we mentioned earlier, conjunctions present special problems. Let's consider them before we go any further. Basically, they just don't fit the "easy versus hard" categorizations that work reasonably well for the other major aspects. The essential action with a conjunction is **fusion**, and some planetary factors **like** to be fused, while others do not. Our task is to figure out which conjunctions we should view as "harmonious," and which ones we need to frame in more "challenging" terms. Here's a way to do that:

Some planets naturally fall together as "soft." They are the Moon, Venus, Jupiter, and Neptune. Other planets feel "hard." They are the Sun, Mars, Saturn, Uranus, and Pluto. Mercury seems to be in a category by itself, able to take on the qualities of either type.

When two "hard" planets come together in a conjunction, they see eye to eye. There may be fireworks, but the **planets themselves get along**, and we should treat the conjunction as harmonious or easy. Similarly, when two "soft" planets align, there's also a natural harmony between them. Thus, in the following pages, you should pay particular attention to the "under easy aspects" references if you are experiencing a conjunction of "hard" progressed Mars with "hard" natal Uranus. Same for a conjunction of "soft" progressed Venus with the "soft" Moon. **And please immediately note that "easy" doesn't in any sense mean "good!"** It just means that the two planetary energies "marry" without much fuss! Under that Mars-Uranus interaction, you may be hell on wheels. Under that Venus-Neptune combination, maybe you'll flop in front of the TV for six months eating bon bons. All we're saying is that the **planets themselves** don't clash. Neither did Adolph Hitler and Heinrich Himmler.

When a "soft" and a "hard" planet combine, there's more tension—and maybe a deeper perspective as well. Focus especially on the "under difficult aspects" areas below if, for example, your "hard" progressed Sun is approaching a conjunction with the "soft" natal Moon.

If either of the planets is Mercury, treat it like an "easy" aspect.

All of these ideas about conjunctions need to be placed in the context of the critical point we made when we kicked off this chapter: The single most magical word in astrological interpretation is **integration**. The specific aspect itself is far less important than a deep understanding of the actual integrative process that is trying to happen. That's why most of what you read below about any planetary combination is in the "one size fits all" category, quite independent of the specific aspect that's connecting the two bodies.

A FEW DETAILS

What you'll read below has been fine-tuned to the realities represented by Secondary Progressions, which is the technique I've personally found most valuable over the years in my own astrological practice. The other major forms of forecasting—minor and tertiary progressions, and solar arc directions—are quite powerful as well, and each has passionate partisans. If you are interested in any of those techniques, the following seed-concepts should serve you well as a beginning point.

The **duration** of a progression is always difficult to pin down specifically. Knowing the time of the exact aspect is a straightforward mathematical question, and that provides us with a sense of when the integrative process will peak. In general, I find it helpful to frame the timing of the progressed process as follows: I allow an orb of two and a half degrees on either side of exactitude, defining a sensitive zone five degrees wide centered on the exact aspect. I think of that zone as a "bell curve," with most of the power concentrated in the middle degree. How long a given progressed aspect will last depends of course on how quickly the planet progresses through that five-degree zone. With the Moon, it's about five months. With the Sun, about five years. The rest of the progressed planets speed up and slow down so much that the only rule of thumb is to check out the ephemerides—or more likely nowadays, boot up the computer.

By the way, that "two and a half degree" figure may seem quite arbitrary, but it's not. It represents **one-twelfth of a sign**, each sign being thirty degrees wide. And twelve is of course astrology's magic number...

Let's meet the progressed planets.

PROGRESSED SUN: YOUR EVOLVING SELF

PROGRESSED SUN/NATAL SUN

Because the Sun progresses only about a degree each year, the major Sun-Sun event for all of us is the progressed sextile at around age sixty, although the semi-square at around age forty-five is a significant experience as well. In either case, the ground upon which your identity itself stands is shifting. To avoid stumbling into a dead-end state of devitalization and entrapment, you need to pass a couple of tests—and don't worry: the circumstances of your life will soon supply them! One test lies in a deepened willingness to claim, boldly and audaciously, what is rightfully yours. That means that you must seize the kinds of experiences and situations that truly feed your spirit, letting all the practical and relational chips fall where they may. This action will certainly be perceived as "egocentric" by many of the people around you. No way can you simultaneously take good care of yourself and keep everybody else happy during this period—it's necessarily more "self"-centered than that! The second critical test you'll face involves making sure that you are truly aware of **who and what you have actually become**, so that you don't put vast quantities of time and energy into claiming something you **used** to want, but which has now become irrelevant to you. Down that road, you wind up damaging others unnecessarily and not really helping yourself very much at all in the bargain. The Solar Ego is a vast reservoir of power, but its Achilles Heel is a kind of blindness and a tendency to treat old habits and attitudes as if they were a religion. You are invested with a tremendous ability to "make things happen" now. **The art lies in knowing what you really want**—and a useful hint is that it's probably not a recitation of old dreams and complaints, but rather a fresh, powerful new Intention that reflects the ways you have grown and deepened over the years.

PROGRESSED SUN/NATAL MOON

Some degree of logic and reasonableness is an essential ingredient of adult life, but a far more interesting—and distinctly "lunar"—observation is that the really important decisions of life can never be made logically! What do I really want from life? What are my priorities? Where should I live? Should I be in this relationship? What color to paint the living room? These are **questions of the heart**, not the intellect—and they are exactly the sorts of issues that are up for you now. In order to navigate wisely in this period, you need to trust your instincts, not your intellect. In Moon-times, you **feel** your way forward. Your soul (or your unconscious mind, if you prefer that metaphor) is stirred up right now, mostly because it's trying to attract your attention and guide you with its transrational understanding of who you are becoming. Watch your dream life; be alert to sudden shifts in your mood; study the omens of your heart. You are *deepening* enormously now, getting in touch with core psychological issues and fundamental needs. "Moon" issues—home, fertility, nourishment, creativity—are likely to emerge very centrally in the shaping of your biographical life right now. Perhaps you've come to a crossroads where you physically need to move to a new house. Maybe deep "nesting" issues are up for you right now: pregnancy, the care of the old, milestones in primary relationship, working on your health and self-care. As always, if the aspect connecting the progressed Sun to the Moon is a square or an opposition, the messages you are receiving remain valid and real—they're just a little more upsetting, and a lot more costly to implement. Trust them anyway: they represent the future of your happiness. Under the trine, sextile or conjunction, the integration is easier—but be careful you don't dream your way through it!

Progressed Sun/Natal Mercury

The buzz of events is as thick as a swarm of mosquitos. Everywhere you turn, you are bombarded with more "data." Conversations, books, telephone calls, letters, web sites...they all press at you. The time has come simply to learn. Learn what? There's too much information. "Everything" might seem like too glib an answer, but it's not far from the truth. Just look at the shape of your life and you'll see the proof of that. The sheer speed of the life-process is blinding now; you're being flooded with experience, new perspectives, and endless information. It may seem random and chaotic, but behind the flying crockery and ringing phones, **you are integrating into your evolving psyche a new level of open-mindedness and curiosity**. Get it right and you'll surely become one of those inspiring eighty-year-olds who shows up at interesting lectures, goes trekking in Nepal, and knows more about the cultural cutting edge than a college junior. Blow it, and you'll become closed-minded and predictable. The universe is a fabric woven of omens for you right now. Watch them! Synchronicities abound. Three people will tell you about the same book in the same week — read it! By "chance" one Friday afternoon you'll see two photos of the same beach. Go there that weekend! That kind of openness, fluidity, and flexibility are the soul of Mercury...that, and conversation: endless, glorious, open-ended chatter, sent and received, and pregnant with the undigested imagery of what you are about to become. You can sleep when you're dead.

PROGRESSED SUN/NATAL VENUS

With the Sun contacting Venus, any fortune-teller would accurately predict "fated" meetings with people who would prove pivotal to you—"tall, dark strangers" and the like. Count on it—but count higher too! Venus is not narrowly romantic or erotic, although those delights may indeed press on you now. The deeper meaning here is that your evolving self has come to a place in its unfolding journey where, in order to go forward, you need some help. You need to surrender to the different perspectives of another soul or two, with whom you feel a magical sense of rapport and a clear sense of equality—a sense of "being in the same boat" together. These people are available to you now. All you need to do in order to connect with them is to take a few risks, reach out a bit, extend yourself socially. That's the active, conscious ingredient in this mix, and you need to supply it. Under hard aspects, you'll feel some resistance to the process. With the softer ones, your spirit agrees, and will "up" your social, affiliative, and sexual drives. You may find yourself buying new clothes, doing your hair differently, going to more gatherings—and these seemingly trivial developments are all pieces of the synchronistic puzzle. The bottom line, from an evolutionary perspective, is that you currently require the **psychospiritual catalyst of deep contact with your "soulmates"** in the broadest sense of that term—dear friends and lovers, rivals who bring out the best or the fiercest in you, and perhaps some less profound relationships that simply serve practical "door-opening" purposes. One more point—these human contacts come in two flavors: brand new relationships and renewed, freshened connections with people whom you've known for a long while.

PROGRESSED SUN/NATAL MARS

The Progressed Sun collides with the War-God! Obviously, this event promises some fireworks. Harmonizing yourself with the "Law of the Jungle"—the eternal dance of Hunter and Prey—is the key here. And that's uncomfortable business for most of us unless we've attended a few too many Arnold Schwarzeneggar films for our own good. Nature teaches us some savage lessons, whether we approve of them philosophically or not. **Which role do you prefer: Hunter or Prey?**

Ferocious circumstances are coalescing around you now, forcing a choice. To navigate them successfully, you will have to accept that you are being given a crash course in assertiveness training. You will attract "petty tyrants" to yourself now—people who would take unfair advantage of you, treat you disrespectfully, intimidate you into submissiveness. Stand up to them! Don't be afraid of your own power and intensity! Mildness and compromise will not be rewarded now. Spiritually, you are learning Mars-lessons: Courage! Know what you want, where your boundaries are, and don't be afraid to speak up. Under easy aspects, "winning" here will be relatively easy—if only you are willing to demand it. Under hard aspects, the costs of victory may be higher and the battle more trenchant. Still, the alternative is too dreadful to contemplate: a mouse's life! If your nature is gentle, this progressed aspect calls forth an unaccustomed fire in your nature, and you may help yourself get into harmony with it by undertaking some physical adventures: backpacking, martial arts, vigorous dance. If your nature is already fiery, be careful of overreacting: you are vulnerable to excesses of self-righteous rage or even paranoia now—particularly under the "easy" aspects. Under the hard ones, your blood is so up that you might also overextend to the point of hurting yourself or doing unnecessary damage to others, so take a breath and think about your long-term aims and values before you launch your photon torpedoes.

PROGRESSED SUN/NATAL JUPITER

How have you been underestimating yourself? How have you been settling for too little? These are the evolutionary questions woven into the underpinning of your circumstances. Real opportunities abound for you now, if only you recognize them. Glitzy, empty possibilities exist too—good roads for others maybe, but not for you. The key in major Jupiter events lies in **knowing clearly what will make you happier than you are today**, and then having the audacity to claim it. Naturally, the world is constantly advising you in that department, exhorting you to buy this car, eat these organic vegetables, prostrate yourself before this or that guru or belief-system, or travel to this "amazing place." And, right now, at least a couple of those doorways are probably right for you! You need a brighter future than the one that seems to lie before you now. You are ready to expand, to take up more space —and if you don't do that in an existential way, there's a good chance you'll "embody the metaphor" by simply eating too much! Jupiter wants to "feast"—on Life, but failing that, it will feast on simple appetites. Paradoxically, it's easier to get into that kind of trouble under the "good" Progressed Sun/Jupiter aspects than the hard ones. The latter tend to be accompanied by uncomfortable pressures that may actually help keep you on track—you need a better job, for example, because you're losing your old job and your car just gave up the ghost. As always, though, under squares or oppositions there's more of a price tag on the improvements—but they are still improvements, and improvement is the key concept for you right now. You are better than you look.

PROGRESSED SUN/NATAL SATURN

Somewhere in the history of astrology we made a serious wrong turn. We began to equate "difficult" with "unfortunate," and poor Saturn suffered. And yet common human experience teaches us that when we attempt difficult things in a disciplined, consistent way, we gain self-respect, maturity, and a deepened sense of our natural legitimacy. With your progressed Sun contacting Saturn, you've reached a point in your soul's journey where you need to rise to a challenge. You need to make a tremendous effort, under your own steam and at some considerable personal cost—a greater cost, if the aspect involved is a hard one. Why change? **Because if you think that you feel bored and stuck now, think how those same circumstances will feel to you in ten years!** You have outgrown yourself; you are older and wiser inside yourself than your current situation suggests. So that situation must change—which leads us to the mountain you need to climb. For some people, it may involve biting the bullet and getting that educational credential. It may mean the sober work of leaving a dead-end relationship—or committing to the serious, grown-up effort of building a new one. It might involve disciplining yourself to take better care of your body. It could have to do with moving to the next level in your profession, or changing it entirely. Whatever form it might take, these changes go beyond what they appear to be. They allow a new expression of what you have become to flow into expression: older, wiser, more confident. The toast may land butter-side-down more often than chance would predict for a while, but trust your path anyway, even if you have to walk it alone.

PROGRESSED SUN/NATAL URANUS

Remember how you looked in your junior high school annual? Embarrassing, huh? Back then, you had little idea who you really were—and so the appearance you presented to the world was an amalgam of your real self and whoever your heroes happened to be at the time. That layer of "cultural artifacts" which still lies like sediment over the core of your soul is getting thinner now—which is why people around you think that you are behaving strangely! In truth, what you've really been all these years is starting to shine forth in a far more uninhibited way. Your spirit seems to be saying, "it's about time I did something for myself for a change!" Just turn "myself" to "my Self" and you have the picture: **you are in full-blown rebellion against the need for other people's approval**. What is at stake is nothing less than your ability to be true to who you really are. This is giddy energy, so if the aspect involved is a hard one, be extra careful of going off half-cocked. If it's an easy aspect, be just as wary of too much accommodation, too many "deals." The point is, you've got to shake things up in your life now. Too much of your energy has gone into maintaining a fictional self—that "artifact" of your family, peers, and the social climate. If you are willing to shock a few people, including yourself, you'll find that unpredictable, long-shot events begin to get thick as flies, opening up doors for you now that no sane person would have anticipated. One rule of thumb: if you can't find at least ten people who think you've gone crazy, you probably have!

PROGRESSED SUN/NATAL NEPTUNE

Your progressed Sun is making an aspect to your natal Neptune— what should you do? Here is a pretty good answer, at least for starters: **nothing**. Do nothing. But do nothing the way the Zen master does "nothing." As Henry Miller said, "stand still like the hummingbird." This is a time to cultivate **alertness**—but an alertness to consciousness itself, and to the omens of the outer world. Why? **Because you are now seeking a Vision.** Admit it: you need one. You are lost. You are becoming mechanical, efficient maybe, but uninspired. Life tastes like dust. Sounds terrible, doesn't it? But that humble self-appraisal is the key! The time has come to stand naked before the gods and goddesses (pick your favorite theological coordinate system), and beg them to offer you new inspiration and new direction. This kind of redirection and revitalizing arises only when a person is humble, hungry, and open. It never comes to the cock-sure. The Neptunian synchronistic wave will bring many oracles and omens into your life. It will bring spiritual teachings and teachers. Psychics, meditators, and metaphysicians will be as thick as fleas on a dog. Pick and choose among them, but remember that the real magic only happens when you are alone, open-hearted, and naked of defenses. Under hard aspects, beware particularly of self-deception and of "going off half-cocked" with grand, empty schemes or philosophies. Under easy aspects, be wary of the sort of numbness offered by food, alcohol, money, drugs and the television set. Mainly, remember the ways of your ancestors: go to the "mountain-top" and wait, humbly and patiently, for a Vision.

PROGRESSED SUN/NATAL PLUTO

Your evolving Self is lining up to do battle with the Lord of the Underworld: the "god of Hell," in other words—but keep reading! It's not necessarily as bad as it sounds. Life is full of terrible wear and tear, and we are all wounded somehow. Look at the life-shaping hurts of your childhood, as a psychotherapist would. Look at the karmic wounds on your soul, as a true Seer might. See the bloody tracks left on us all by sexism and all other silly prejudices. See the losses you've endured—the friends you've buried, the love gone bad, all the catastrophes of life...all the things "you've gotten over." Now, what exactly does that last phrase mean? To "get over something" often means to put it away somewhere inside yourself where it doesn't dominate your behavior or attitude anymore. You cry, and then you stop crying, in other words. But it still exerts an unseen "magnetic field," altering your course through life, usually in unfortunate ways. You might doubt yourself more than you should. Maybe you are vaguely angry all the time. Maybe you feel badly about your body. **You are now wise enough, strong enough, supported enough to look at those hurt places**. And, to help you with that honorable work the universe is creating uncomfortable situations in your present life that **resonate with the wounds of the past**. Under hard aspects, these situations are very pressing. Under easier ones, they are less so—and more support is available. But Pluto is still Pluto in either case, and the bottom line remains the same: to go forward meaningfully in life, your evolving self needs truly to release the burden of its history. You need "soul-healing," which is the real meaning of the word "psychothera-py"—and any good shrink will tell you that you must do 90% of that work yourself even if you are drawn to get some help with the process.

PROGRESSED SUN/NATAL MIDHEAVEN

Some deep spiritual changes happen so subtly that the person sitting next to you has no idea that anything happened—profound realizations, for example, can occur very quietly. Then there is the Midheaven, where anything that happens is immediately acted out on life's big stage, where all the neighbors and their relatives can see it. Under this aspect, we can expect **obvious changes in the visible shape of your life**. A new job. A physical move. Changes in relationship status. The birth of the first child—or the last child leaving the nest. Milestones, in other words. Going beyond what the fortune-teller would say, the evolutionary astrologer would realize that **a certain tension has arisen between your evolving Self and its outward, social expression**—that "tension" is more marked if the aspect is a hard one, but it's there even in the case of an easy aspect. You are ready to put more of your Self into the role you are playing in the world's eyes. This calls for your moving boldly forward, claiming more room for self-expression and also announcing your intention of being taken more seriously in your community and very probably in your profession. For modern people, the Midheaven in practice often does boil down to professional questions, but it's important to remember that it embraces other dimensions of our role in the "tribe." Very significantly and authentically, the Midheaven connects to "unprovable" feelings of Destiny...feelings which should certainly be trusted and honored, if the progressed Sun is touching the Midheaven. The time has come for you to bear fruit in your tribe. You are ready, and the world is ready for you. Go for it.

PROGRESSED SUN/NATAL ASCENDANT

The Sun and the Ascendant are often confused with each other in astrological practice. There's a good reason for that: they are very similar, at least when we start translating astrological symbolism into the English language. For both symbols we accurately enough use words such as "self" or "personality." There are differences between the two points, though—and right now, with your progressed Sun contacting your natal Ascendant, it's critical that you make the distinction. In a nutshell, the Sun is **who you really are**, while the Ascendant is **how you present that identity to the world**. Think of the Ascendant as a stained glass window through which the light of your inner Sun shines. Under this aspect, the evolutionary challenge lies in better aligning the colors of the two. What you have actually become— symbolized by your progressed Sun—is currently distorted and constrained by your old "mask." Your style needs to change. At the risk of trivializing a very serious astrological event, you need some new clothes! This is not just about shopping for vanity's sake. This is about the symbolism of your clothing, and what it says about who you think you are, and how you are presenting that information to the world. It goes far beyond clothing, but that's an effective way to focus the issues. The usual hard aspect/easy aspect distinctions apply. If the aspect is a hard one, then the clash between inner reality and outer expression is sharp and radical, and fixing it will be emotionally costly—although far cheaper than the alternative! If it's an easy aspect, the changes are less dramatic—but beware of sleeping through them. They are no less important for being less pressing.

PROGRESSED MERCURY: YOUR EVOLVING INTELLIGENCE

PROGRESSED MERCURY/NATAL SUN

What's that buzz in your ears? Why is everything suddenly going twice as fast? Why is everyone talking at once? Progressed Mercury has arrived in an aspect with your natal Sun, and the proverbial "Messenger of the Gods" is leaving his synchronistic mark on your existence: an intensification of the "data load" on your senses. We can expect that you'll be offered educational opportunities during this period, some formal, some as simple as an interesting or informative web site, magazine article, or conversation. You will also be offered changes of scenery—chances to travel, for example. Under hard aspects, all these realities may press on you as requirements or necessities. Under easy ones, they take the form of little gifts. The universe simply offers them and puts no pressure on you. Moving to a more penetrating level of analysis, under this progressed Mercury aspect, new perspectives are trying to bash their way through your, er, thick skull...which is a fair metaphor for the natal Sun with all its egocentric focus. The critical information your psyche is trying to absorb during this Mercury event is never what you already expect. **The pivotal data lies outside your current belief-system**—that's the key to understanding this aspect. As my Viking wife, the former Jodie Jensen, points out, the Roman Mercury corresponds to the Norse god, Odin—the Bringer of writing. And to the ancient Norse people, Odin also rules over Omens and synchronicities, as well as much that we would nowadays call "shamanic." This is a critical part of understanding progressed Mercury, and one that is mostly lost in our present Greek and Latin astrological traditions. But watch it work in your life: three people will mention the same obscure book to you in the same week—read it! A crow will fly across the face of the sun the instant you get a new insight—trust the insight! These Omens fly by as quickly as lightning bolts, and that's why you feel you've had too many cups of coffee. Your deep psyche is revving up the pace of your perceptions to a point where you can follow these tiny fluxes in the synchronicity-grid of the universe that surrounds you...fluxes in what some of our ancestors called the "Web of Wyrd."

PROGRESSED MERCURY/NATAL MOON

Mercury's arrival by progression to an aspect with your natal Moon operates on a couple of distinct levels simultaneously. The first involves a chance to improve your capacity to **express your feelings verbally**. The second, which is closely related to the first, involves a deepening of your own intellectual understanding of your emotional life. A good rule of thumb for all of us is that we know what we are talking about before we begin to speak, so understanding needs to come a little ahead of verbalization here. There has never been a better time in your life to keep a journal—or to do the equivalent, which is to write heartfelt letters (or e-mail) to people whom you trust. **As you write, you will find that you are deepening your own understanding of what you are feeling**. You are also finding just the right words to express yourself. This is why we emphasize writing skills here rather than simple conversations. Emotionally-charged conversations will abound for you now, but writing allows you a certain spaciousness of time—and of course the luxury of crossing things out when they don't really capture the emotions in exactly the way that feels most comfortable to you. **The essence of this process lies in translating between two ultimately incompatible symbol-systems: the English language, and the energy-states of the human heart**. That's why it's difficult, and why taking time to settle into just the right words and phrases is so important. Really try to see past the mood of urgency that characterizes this kind of aspect—you need truth more than you need speed right now! If the aspect between progressed Mercury and the Moon is a hard one, then you may receive some emotionally-jarring data from your environment—inescapable messages that clash with your preconceived view of the way things were. If it's easy, then the growth can just flow along naturally, with just the right words and books and moments all lining up in a blessedly easy way...if you remember what you are doing, and don't just slip into mere diversion and entertainment.

PROGRESSED MERCURY/NATAL MERCURY

As always when a planet progresses into an aspect with its own natal position, we are dealing here with the pure, unadulterated article: absolute, quintessential Mercury energy...which means, among other things, that your life has just flipped up to a new quantum level of speed. The sheer density of your perceptions and experiences is unprecedented. You are being flooded with change. Every time you contemplate the "dots" of your life, there is a new way to connect them...a new constellation to form from the stars of your experience. Look again: now there are three or four **new** stars, and process escalates up to another level of complexity. What should you do? When will it all settle down? The answer to the first question is to just keep your eyes open—this period isn't so much about achieving any kind of final understanding of anything; it's more about simply gathering data. The second question—well, nothing will settle down until Mercury progresses out of the aspect. And by then your mind will be vastly enriched. Having trusted your curiosity, having wisely followed your fascinations, having exercised your radically open mind, you will have moved yourself into an entirely new framework of perception. Figuring out "what it all means" comes later, under other planetary aspects. For now, it's really about simply keeping your eyes—and your mind—as open as they can possibly be. If the aspect is a square, then the data you need will clash with your pre-existing theories. You'll be like a devout and rather conventional Catholic nun startled to find Timothy Leary sitting at the left hand of God in her morning meditations. If it's the conjunction or the sextile, the shock will be much less severe and the perceptual adjustments to your existing belief-system that much more subtle.

PROGRESSED MERCURY/NATAL VENUS
Venus is a real sweetie of a planet, until it bites you. And one of the classic ways Venus hurts us involves our own merry collusion in the romantic bonding process. Here's how it works. We fall in love with someone and he or she "seems too good to be true." And of course that's probably a fact: nobody fits us nearly as perfectly as appearances promise at the beginning of the mating process. So what are we really looking at when we imagine ourselves to be gazing into the soul of the Beloved? Well, half of it is our own "projection," to use the psychiatric term—we are looking at something wonderful **inside ourselves!** And this applies to early friendships as well as to romances. It just runs at a higher voltage when sexual energy is involved. Anyway, enter progressed Mercury—the world's most underrated Love God. Why? Because this is the planet of Communication. And when Mercury progresses into an aspect with your natal Venus, the time has come really to **listen** to your partners in life, be they friends or lovers. Try to find out who they really are, how their minds actually work, what

really makes them happy or sad. Ask questions, and slow down and shut up enough to hear the answers. It's a two-way street here as well: you need to strive to express who you are clearly and **in words**. Silent understandings are delicious, but wait for some Neptune/Venus contacts to polish your chops in that department. As usual, the information is easier to hear under trines and sextiles, and correspondingly more challenging to pre-existing assumptions when squares or oppositions are involved. But that doesn't change the heart of the Mercury process at all: it's always about stripping away that numb feeling of predictability, and replacing it with the naked senses. And in this case, those senses are trained on the ultimate human mystery: other human beings.

PROGRESSED MERCURY/NATAL MARS

Imagine (and this won't be hard...) a married couple about two years before their big, messy divorce. They're friends, and you go over to their place for dinner one night. You could cut the tension between them with your butter knife. They don't have a fight in front of you—not precisely. But there is an unstated subtext of rage, criticism, and sabotage in their every interaction. Where did it originate? Sometimes that's a very tough question to answer in a convincing way. There's no "one offense" that underlies each person's negative view of the other one. The devil in the stew is really an accumulation of unexpressed, unresolved frustrations—his snoring, her PMS, his old socks on the bedroom floor, her cosmetics cluttering the bathroom sink. Friction like that is part of life, and not just intimate life. Even at work familiarity sometimes breeds contempt—or at least minor abrasions. Enter progressed Mercury aspecting Mars: the time has come to learn how to better **articulate your frustrations**! You are feeling touchy. More than you realize, you are argumentative now. Prickly. Your nerves are on a hair trigger, and short-circuited straight to your tongue. You could make a mess now with the sarcasm and the unnecessary barbs in your comments—and the sheer lightning-bolt speed of this Mercury/Mars explosiveness is emphasized under hard aspects in particular. You have a right to your boundaries, your real needs, and even to most of your quirks. But beware of self-righteousness in expressing those realities now! The trick, as always with Mercury, lies in translating the raw stuff of human experience—drives, hungers, the heat of the blood, in this case—into the **logic and transparency of clear English**. That translation, never really natural or perfectly satisfactory, is nonetheless the only bridge that binds us to each other sometimes...and the best hedge against the idiocy of unnecessary war.

PROGRESSED MERCURY/NATAL JUPITER

Some of the iconography of cartoons works so perfectly that it has entered the realm of universal recognition. One look and we all know what the cartoonist is saying. A good example of that is the character who suddenly has a light bulb appear over her head. Everywhere, people recognize the sudden flash of inspiration which that image conveys. We've all had the experience: we're stuck, worrying ourselves sick over some concrete problem and getting nowhere. Suddenly, the answer appears: maybe the planets actually revolve around the sun, not the earth! Maybe I should move to Alaska! Maybe I should just kiss the worthless bum good-bye! Sometimes such revelations are very real. Other times, for all their glory, they can't stand the cold light of dawn. In either case, fasten your mental seat belts. With progressed Mercury aspecting your natal Jupiter, **a season of inspiration is upon you**. There's both a joy and caution to convey here. The joy is that you have entered a period in which simple insights can lead to very real breakthroughs: new information, new techniques, and new perspectives can change your life now. Mere ideas are rarely so powerful, but now they truly have existential clout. The only caution is that you are currently somewhat subject to inflated "enthusiasms," and it might pay to wait until next Monday before selling the house and lighting out for Alaska. It would be misleading to imagine, as many astrologers do, that the crazy, inflated, dead-end responses would tend to happen more around the hard aspects, and the wiser ones with the so-called "good" aspects. If anything, it's the opposite—those sextiles and trines can operate like grease for both good ideas and bad ones, while the squares and oppositions carry more inherent checks and balances.

PROGRESSED MERCURY/NATAL SATURN

In generating theories, the mind can move ahead at warp speed. Card-castles of ideas can be erected, only to come crashing down. All it takes is one bad assumption. Start with the idea that God Made Woman As Man's Helper, for example. The rest of your reasoning can be as tight as Einstein's, but you're still going to collide head-on with reality sooner or later. (Witness the last thirty years or so for the proof of that one!) In one of the tunes he wrote for the "Talking Heads," David Byrne has a great line: "Facts don't do what I want them to"—and that number could really be the theme song for progressions of Mercury into aspect with Saturn, especially the harder aspects. Your evolving intelligence, your evolving view of the world and your place in it —progressed Mercury in a nutshell—is colliding with hard, cold reality. And reality will win, as always. You'll win too, if you're willing to let go of some of your favorite opinions and pet theories, and make the effort to go further into the direct experience of the actual truth. The refutation of those erroneous assumptions you carry is very much in your face right now. And something old and wise inside you is actually eager to advance this process. You'll be feeling studious and serious now, eager to get your intellectual teeth into some kind of learning. You'll also be up against any fears or insecurities you may be harboring regarding your level of intellectual prowess, your degree of mental self-discipline, and possibly your education. Nothing for it except hard work—that's always a big part of the picture with Saturn, the planet of blood, sweat, and tears. And it will bring you self-respect, real accomplishment, and the dignity they breed.

PROGRESSED MERCURY/NATAL URANUS

Imagine you look in the mirror one morning and the person staring back at you is six inches taller than you were last night. Imagine he or she is of the opposite gender. Or a different race. The facts are there before you, plain to see—but they clash with what you've always known. Which do you believe—your common sense or the message of your eyes? This is the feeling generated when progressed Mercury contacts Uranus: the rug is pulled out from underneath you. There are many dimensions to this process. Some of them are purely intellectual: you will be exposed to an inordinate amount of shocking, disjunctive information during this period. There is an abundance of the sort of perceptions that lead you to "go back to the old drawing board" or simply to question old articles of faith. Lots of what a shrink would call "cognitive dissonance"—and what a shaman might call **seeing**. The heart of this process has to do with information about who you yourself are in distinction to who you've been trained to be—that's the classic Uranian signature. The underlying notion is that your image of yourself is based partly on the realities of your perceptions and human experiences, but it also rests significantly upon the foundation of your cultural training and socialization. Under the hard aspects, the shocking new perceptions undercut parts of yourself that you hold precious: a silly but cogent example might be a man of thirty dismayed to notice that bald patch on the back of his head for the first time. Under easier aspects, your image of yourself can change radically without it bothering you very much...until you visit some friends you've not seen for a couple of years and they all lament about how "you **used** to be so normal!" In any case, fidelity to your own perceptions and nature is the key.

PROGRESSED MERCURY/NATAL NEPTUNE

Progressed Mercury usefully relates to two semi-connected concepts. One is the mental model of the world that we carry inside ourselves. The planet is thus intellectual, cognitive, and has at least pretenses of logical coherence. The other concept is our **senses themselves** in all their chaos and delight, and all their magnificent illogic—the wild way the world might look to a brilliantly intelligent newborn baby. Ideally, our sensory experiences enrich our model of the universe, which is simply to say that if we keep our eyes open, gradually we get a little smarter. But the senses are inherently immediate and trans-logical, while the mind constantly strives for logical consistency. Thus, we can all easily **visualize** a flying pig, but if we **observed** one, it would seriously unhinge us. Well, with your progressed Mercury contacting mystical Neptune, get ready for some flying pigs! So much in our actual experience is unexplained—and inexplicable. Some greater world overshadows our own, and permeates it. Your mind is naturally drawn to these mystical, spiritual perspectives now. Trust that part of yourself and feed it with perceptions and experiences. This is an excellent time for meditation training, for metaphysical reading, for mind-stretching activities. Open to that larger world and the density of miraculous, visionary perceptions will increase exponentially for you right now. Under easy aspects, you only have to ask for them...lift one finger and all the Angels in the universe will bend over backwards to feed you a diet of Mysteries. Under the hard aspects, the mystical realms will impinge on you unbidden, and sometimes rather disconcertingly. Work with your ability to make peace with the realm of Spirit, or you'll feel spacy and confused, as if you are losing your marbles.

PROGRESSED MERCURY/NATAL PLUTO

It's fashionable in many quarters to lament the failure of "mere words" to invoke the full poignancy of the human condition. But there are words that sink to the bottom of your soul as quickly as a stone hits the bottom of a still pond, by-passing those pious clichés as if they were just the whining of frustrated English majors. Examples: The right "I love you" coming from the right person. The doctor saying, "I've got bad news." Mom saying, "Your father isn't really your father." **There are words that change everything, radically**. They explode like bombs in our lives; they forever alter the inner landscape. The most shocking ones tend to arrive when Mercury progresses into a harsh aspect to natal Pluto. But Pluto is always Pluto, regardless of what planet is making which aspect to it. And Pluto is always about facing the darkness, always about going deeper. Even with an easy aspect between Progressed Mercury and natal Pluto, you are still invited to entertain serious insights, none of them for the faint-hearted. With Mercury involved in the picture, the process is verbal. It may involve uncovering "clues," as a private detective would—finding old letters, having an "illuminating" talk with someone you trust...or manipulating someone whom you do not trust into revealing more than he or she thinks is being revealed. This kind of sleuthing into the truth, ferreting out hidden information, is the soul of Mercury/Pluto contacts—and it carries in its synchronistic tide a current of other Plutonian material: murder mysteries, occult investigations, deep psychological reading or conversations. Ride the wave, and trust it: ignorance is bliss only for the congenitally ignorant.

PROGRESSED MERCURY/NATAL MIDHEAVEN

Change is in the wind—very obvious change, in the most outward and visible parts of your life. What do you look like to people who don't know you? Who don't even really give a damn about you? That's the Midheaven. Some astrologers, in my opinion, get a little too narrowly focussed on mere career with this symbol. It definitely **is** about career, but not everybody is operating on that wavelength. The Midheaven, in a nutshell, represents what you look like from a great social distance—the hats you wear in this world. And with Mercury progressing into an aspect to it, we can expect developments there. Changes in your status and public role in general. Job changes? Sure. If you are a working person, expect new data, messages, and perceptions—Mercury stuff—that alters your sense of what you are doing professionally. The hard aspects tend to bring more unsettling material there, while the easier aspects bring milder news...non-pressing opportunities, for example. The same logic applies outside the domain of career as well. We could, for example, imagine a woman who is focussed on raising her kids while her husband brings home the paycheck. Mercury progresses into an aspect to her Midheaven, and her husband unexpectedly gets transferred to another state. Her "work" remains the same, but she's taken out of her accustomed social context, and must create a new context in a new place—perhaps opening up to a very different public role than she had played in the previous town. In any case, whenever progressed Mercury contacts the Midheaven, there is something you need to **say publicly**...some wisdom that has matured in you and which the "tribe" now needs to hear. So teach that class, write that letter to the editor, speak up at that big public gathering.

PROGRESSED MERCURY/NATAL ASCENDANT

Two parts of yourself have gotten a bit out of kilter. One of them is your outward style—the way you customarily present yourself to the world: your clothing, your humor, the way you carry your body. The other part is your "evolving Voice"— quintessential progressed Mercury symbolism. The evolutionary aim of this event is to create a more harmonious marriage of those two pieces of your puzzle: **you are learning to speak with your true voice**, and to have that skill feel natural and easy to you. What if the aspect is an easy one? Shouldn't that make the process of integration easier too? Definitely—but "easier" doesn't mean automatic. You still need to make some effort. How? Well...talk! And write. There's no substitute for simply logging hours with your mouth open...**meaningfully** open, that is. Jump on any chance to speak publicly, even if it's informal—offer a toast at a wedding, for example. Tell a joke in front of more than two people. More formally, you could join a theater group, or Toastmasters. You could teach an astrology class, or do a reading for a friend. Exactly the same strategies are effective if the aspect connecting progressed Mercury to the natal Ascendant is a hard one. The only difference is that there is a greater natural tension between your true, authentic Voice and the habitual style of your reflexive personality. You may literally feel tongue-tied or experience stuttering as these two tectonic plates in your soul rub up against each other. The cure remains the same: just get yourself out there, telling the rest of us what you see and what you think. Do it until it feels smooth—which is the way your soul reports to your conscious mind that the "mission is accomplished."

PROGRESSED VENUS: YOUR EVOLVING PARTNERSHIPS

PROGRESSED VENUS/NATAL SUN

You are broadcasting on Venusian wavelengths at a billion watts now, calling to yourself everyone with whom you have any kind of evolutionary "business"—lovers, partners, friends, rivals, and mortal enemies alike! You have reached a point in the Big Journey where, in order to move forward, **you require the catalytic, triggering impact of such people upon your consciousness**. To that end, your soul is calling out to very specific individuals, exhorting them to "be in seat 12A on the flight to Chicago tomorrow morning"—which is to say that you will experience a great density of encounters which feel distinctly "fated" during this period. Body, mind and spirit being one great integrated wholeness, your personality and your body are also sending out the same signal in their own fashion, magnetizing into your life the people with whom you must share energy and time. In other words, you are socially, and probably sexually, motivated now, relatively more eager to connect with others than you might typically be. Your body itself is also sending out a message to the world along the lines, "I'm pretty cute, aren't I?" The latter observation requires some clarification. It's not that you are necessarily trying to be alluring; it's just that a kind of aura of pheromones exists around you now, attracting people with whom you do have serious work to do. A few totally irrelevant strangers may sniff those pheromones and try their luck with you as well; if you agree, you may illustrate one of the darker dimensions of this "lucky" planet! Under easy aspects, these more serious relationships tend to get off to a smooth start, but be wary of so much "agreement" and "harmony" that nothing much is really exchanged. It's so easy to fall deeply in love with an image we've projected onto someone! Under the tougher aspects, progressed Venus connecting with the Sun can suggest passionate relationships that are character-ized by sharper tensions and differences between the individuals, or relationships that simply come at a much higher price in terms of dislocations, confusions, and upset in one's existing life.

PROGRESSED VENUS/NATAL MOON

The ancient Moon inside us all remembers a time when humans were scarce and perhaps felt a little more precious to each other because of that. Clan. Kinship. Marriage. Those were the basic heart-connections. People who "smelled right" to us. People at whom we might be angry, but whom we knew would not leave us, or us them. Ever. The bond was indissoluble. When progressed Venus contacts your natal Moon, regardless of the aspect, a primordial drive arises in you to **form permanent bonds** of that nature...or to renew existing ones. The hunger for "family" is powerful...and "family" is one of those words with so many layers of meaning that you can savor it for a long time. Pregnancies are not uncommon during Venus/Moon times. Same with marriages or commitments. The urge to spend more time with parents or distant grown children may make itself felt. Aunts, uncles, third cousins twice removed...sure. But those kinds of kinship bonds are not nearly as compelling to most of us nowadays as they once were, even though our need for "family" in some sense is archetypal and therefore eternal. Many of us have replaced those traditional kinship connections with very special friendships. You will be drawn to spend time with people who play that kind of role in your life now. You need to experience yourself in that simple, unpretentious, natural way that comes from sitting at a kitchen table with someone whom you don't need to impress or to "win," one who knows you inside out, accepts you the way you are, and will love you no matter what happens in your life. Your soul is hungry for that sense of "clan-connection." As always, feeding it will be a little simpler under easy aspects and a little harder under challenging ones. Either way, do it no matter what the cost!

PROGRESSED VENUS/NATAL MERCURY

Imagine there's an author whose work you really admire. Imagine you meet the person at a conference. Imagine she is even more eloquent in person than she is on the printed page. Along with a dozen other people, you sit down to dinner with her at the banquet. There you begin to realize that while she can talk, she can't listen. The thoughtful remarks you make seem irrelevant to her. She just rambles along, eloquent and oblivious. At first maybe you feel badly about yourself, then you start feeling angry at her. There is a huge difference between speaking **at** someone and speaking **to** the person. The latter involves choosing one's language sensitively—not using big words with uneducated people, not using dirty words in front of the proper old lady, and so forth. Far more pivotally, it also involves *listening*. Giving the other person a chance to respond. Acting (at least!) interested in him or her. These are the skills of Venus applied to Mercury, and with your progressed Venus contacting your natal Mercury, you are getting some lessons now in learning to **communicate directly, supportively and effectively with the listener**. Eloquence, articulation, and fluidity with language are certainly part of it—and you'll find yourself drawn "by chance" to poetry and well-written fiction, perhaps to theater and public speeches, as this synchronistic wave breaks in your life. But the essence of it lies in **deepening your attention to the details of people's response to your words**. If the aspect is a hard one, you may learn some painful things about the way your style can lead to misunderstanding. If it's an easy aspect, think of it basically as a chance, not so much to solve a problem, as to further develop a set of intimacy-building skills that will serve you well as long as you live.

PROGRESSED VENUS/NATAL VENUS

Quintessential, unadulterated Venusian energy is running in torrents through you now, and regardless of the aspect, we've got good news and bad news! On the merry side of the equation, we can expect that you are feeling better about yourself than you have felt in a while. You are looking good, feeling attractive on many levels. You may have found just the right colors for yourself. You may be having a "good hair year." You may have made some new friends. There's also a sense of **refinement** in your life now. Elegance. It is reflected in your circle of friends, in your cultural experiences, and perhaps in recent beautifications of your home. So where is the down side? As usual, it's optional—no law, except perhaps the law of averages, says that anyone has to go down the dark road with any astrological symbolism. But when Venus goes dark, it's a mess. We become so **unconsciously seductive**, so good at getting people to like us, that we may mislead them—and ourselves!—into imagining a relationship to be deeper or more important than it actually is. Venus progressing into contact with natal Venus, whether it's the sextile or the square, is notorious for coinciding with passionate romances from which we wake up wondering, "what was **that** about?" It can also draw fair-weather friends to you faster than winning the Publishers' Clearing House contest. Worse, in the midst of that social intensity, there is actually a true soulmate or two trying to get to you through that perpetual "busy signal." The trick here, paradoxically, lies in your being as un-charming as you possibly can, at least with people whom you think you might love. That may sound like strange advice, but you need to give anyone with whom you are spending time a solid reality-test. Give them a raw, unadorned dose of who you really are, with no whipped cream and no little chocolate jimmies, and **see if you still like each other**. It's as simple as that.

PROGRESSED VENUS/NATAL MARS

Here's your bumper sticker: "**Trust Your Lust**." Now all you need is a red sports car, some tight clothes, and the open road. And condoms, of course. Everything else you need, God gave you.

I had fun writing those words, but there's something troubling about them too—something about the way our culture teaches us to materialize and trivialize human sexuality. And, emphatically, this is a sexy aspect: make no mistake about that! When Venus progresses into contact with Mars, your blood runs hotter. And it needs to. **You are being invited to bring your physical sexuality and your tender need for soul-contact into closer step with each other**. When Mars meets Venus, they both get quite excited about it—these are, at least traditionally, the Primal Man and the Primal Woman after all, and they love being "in aspect" with each other, so to speak. You feel the drive to connect passionately with other people. That passion can certainly be sexual, but people can connect "passionately" in other ways too: over art, or personal growth, or even exciting new business ideas. The need here is not centrally for orgasms, although they'll be eminently welcome. It is for the **exchange of strong, direct emotions**. Sheer aliveness. Sheer Eros. Under hard aspects, in your primary relationships, you may find that long-simmering tensions, hidden behind walls of mature "détentes" and "agreements-to-disagree," will come barreling out of the labyrinths like angry Minotaurs. Clear the air—or discover that it can't be cleared. Mars always demands courage, and if you and your closest friends and partners have the courage to face the cobwebs that are deadening you to each other, you'll renew and refresh yourselves. Under easier aspects, you really have a precious opportunity. You can nip those relationship-rending explosions in the bud, catching them early. Stir up trouble with people you love! Strange advice? Not really. The trouble is there, festering. So take advantage of all the "lucky" vibrations around the easy Venus/Mars aspect and do some preventive maintenance. Go after those passion-killing "deals" we all make and root them out. You need the intensity and the realness now, so be brave and strip away anything that numbs them.

PROGRESSED VENUS/NATAL JUPITER

Venus progresses to Jupiter and, provided there's a "good" aspect involved, almost any fortune-teller will predict that you'll soon be sharing bed and board with a generous and devilishly good-looking heir or heiress, swept from the pages of *In Style* magazine straight into your heart. Well, maybe they are right—if that's ever going to happen, it will be now! When the "Goddess of Love" triggers the traditional "Greater Benefic," the merry chemistry between them is powerful. But, as always in serious astrology, there are evolutionary issues hiding behind the Superlatives, and the more lasting sorts of happiness depend on figuring them out and getting them right. Do it, and that heir or heiress might just show up. How? The question with Jupiter is always, "**why have I been settling for so little?**" When Venus comes to Jupiter, recognize that it is time to think positively about your relationships or relationship prospects, and enact that attitude with bold steps. Ask for what you want. Take some chances. Ferret out those places in you that might settle for being taken for granted. Tacky vanity is always a soul-trap, but taking some pride in your appearance and investing in it a bit is quite appropriate now: buy that expensive suit that flatters you, put some money into your hair, join the Spa. These may sound like trivial remarks, but they cut right to the heart of the matter: you need to love yourself before you can expect anyone else to follow suit! Under hard aspects, there are more "bumps" involved— and perhaps complexities that revolve around more than one other person being involved. Under easy aspects, make sure you don't grease along in such a harmonious way that serious, underlying questions are avoided. In either case, be wary of anything—or anyone—that seems too good to be true. Love isn't patient, but wisdom is.

PROGRESSED VENUS/NATAL SATURN

There's a myth, in the low sense of the word, that Saturn and Venus are antithetical. Some of that attitude is truly dumb in its origins—the archaic notion that Saturn is "malefic" and Venus is "benefic." But there is also a real clash between them: Saturn is about solitude and Venus is about love. Definitely some tension there. Take it further, though: Saturn is more than the Lord of Solitude. It's also the planet of **vows**. It's the planet of commitment, maturity, and responsibility. Anyone past junior high school, psychologically speaking, knows that those qualities are profoundly central to any kind of real human bond. When Venus progresses into contact with Saturn, **your evolving capacity to love is invited to integrate those mature Saturnian qualities**. In that department, you are "growing up"—yet again. Whether or not you are in a relationship, your sense of the meaning of intimacy is ready to take a serious maturational step. Under easy aspects, you may be faced with the sobering realities of making a formal commitment to someone. Under hard ones, you may be **looking reality in the eye**, realizing that a given commitment just isn't going to work—or a certain cherished attitude or assumption on your part has got to die if you are going to move forward. In either case, provided that you are in a non-violent relationship, consider staying in it for the duration of this progressed event, even if you are feeling very frustrated or trapped. The problems may stem more from your own side of the court than you imagine, and in any case, Saturn is about vows. Regardless of the future of your present bond, what is happening now inside you from an evolutionary point of view is that you are deepening your own sense of honor, dignity and integrity in the intimate area. Whatever patterns you lock in now, you will carry forward. So make them something of which you are proud.

PROGRESSED VENUS/NATAL URANUS

The interactions of progressed Venus and natal Uranus have an unnecessarily cranky reputation. True, the planet Uranus is freedom-loving, rule-breaking, and volatile. Think of it as a powder-keg of rebellion and explosiveness inside you. When Venus touches it, there can definitely be fireworks. But if you understand the real issues that are at stake and act on them with a mixture of audacity and good judgment, this period can resolve many long-standing frustrations in the intimate sphere of your life. At the most elemental level, what this progression tells us is that, **to maintain stability in love, you have paid too high a price in terms of freedom.** You have lost some of your authenticity, sacrificing it on the altar of "reasonableness" or "sensitivity" to the other people in your life. In order that those who are important to you might approve of you, you have compromised your real individuality. That must change. And remember, as always with Venus, we are not talking about "relationships" in any narrowly romantic or erotic sense; we are talking about the people with whom you are sharing your journey in any meaningful way. One symptom of this present Uranian evolution is that you need some "space" now. More centrally, you need to feel freer to express your own interests, values, and style spontaneously in the presence of those you love. Ask for that liberty. Under easy aspects, you may be surprised to see how readily your partners open up and adjust to the "new deal." Under harder aspects, ask for liberty too—but be prepared to demand it, and to "wheel and deal" aggressively, if simple asking doesn't bring the support you need. Despite its reputation, this aspect isn't necessarily about ending relationships, but one point is sure: no one does very well with it unless he or she is **willing** to end a relationship, if doing so is the road to truth and authenticity.

PROGRESSED VENUS/NATAL NEPTUNE

What's the sexiest part of your body? Kids might giggle at the question, and provide obvious anatomical answers. Sophisticated, grown-up lovers, tempered by the wisdom of years of rich, unabashed erotic experience, would probably say "your eyes"—or cheat the question a little and give the real answer: "your soul." This is Neptunian territory. The mystical, transrational planet. Consciousness itself. The magic in your eyes. And when progressed Venus contacts Neptune, the natural creature-hungers of both the human body and the simple human heart both long for that higher love. **They want to use the body as a gateway for contacting the soul**. Sex must be sacred, or it's empty...and by "sacred" we don't mean pious or constrained or whitewashed: this is the wild, fully adult, passion that starkly shames the shallow pretenses of pornography, Hollywood-style or otherwise. And it comes in through the eyes: that is a simple point, but it is elemental here. You need a deeper, merging, melting kind of eye contact with someone you love now. If your lover is avoiding it, challenge that avoidance. If **you** are avoiding it, challenge the blockage in yourself—or you'll imagine that what you're after now is something other than what you truly need. You might think the need was for psychological talk or shared religion; you might mistake the soul-hunger for a need for a new lover or sexual variety; you might confuse it with simple sexual release. But it is always a need for soul-contact. One caution: we all have beautiful, crystalline souls. Under the Venus-Neptune energies, you are better at seeing that quality in others than ever before—but, in new love, you might miss the "humanness" of the lover...and have it bite you on the behind. That is the source of the common astrological exhortation to "beware of disillusionment" under this aspect, whether the aspect is easy or hard.

PROGRESSED VENUS/NATAL PLUTO

Even the best of us have dark sides—and probably the most dangerous people in the world are the ones who pretend otherwise. In normal social interactions, we usually politely edit the more dreadful parts of ourselves, but just watch the way people behave behind the wheel of a car on a highway. Or the way we treat the people with whom we are truly intimate, especially if the intimacy is physical and has lasted more than a year or two. In either case, we see plenty of what Jung called the "Shadow." Every time you've been touched by another person's Shadow, especially when you were younger and more vulnerable, you've recoiled and learned to defend yourself a bit. **In every contact with the Shadow, your ability to trust has eroded**. When progressed Venus contacts Pluto, the time has come to explore that wounded, untrusting part of yourself. You are potentially ready to love more deeply, with more intensity, emotional nakedness, and honesty— and to demand the same. But first you must heal, and healing means remembering and **really feeling** some places in yourself that have been quietly bleeding for years. Under easy aspects, the support you need for this process is available; a little effort on your part bears sweet fruit. Under the hard aspects, the costs and pressures are greater. Still, the basic issues remain the same. As always with Pluto, **that which you do not explore psychologically is played out existentially.** If you were once abandoned, for example, then you could be drawn to an "abandoner" under this aspect, or you could arrange to "pass on the favor" by abandoning someone who deserves better. And don't be fooled by the notion of "good aspects" here: if a trine or sextile is involved, the slope is just a little more slippery! Insights will save you; not aspects.

PROGRESSED VENUS/NATAL MIDHEAVEN

When Venus progresses into contact with the Midheaven, experience has taught me to bow a little bit more reverently than is my custom in the direction of the traditional "good aspect" and "bad aspect" notions...with a few twists to make room for human freedom, of course! Under the hard aspects, you may very well be faced with some difficult, seemingly "no-win" choices between love and career. These two realities naturally exist in some tension with each other for most of us—working long hours may advance us professionally, but it starves our friendships or relationships, for example. Those kinds of tensions, always simmering on the back burner, tend to come out in full battle-dress now, demanding that you set your priorities consciously and intentionally. The trigger is Venusian, which is to say that what precipitates it is either an evolution in your partner's or friend's attitudes, or developments in the relationship itself. Under conjunctions, trines or sextiles, the picture is often very different. Generally, this configuration does offer delightful openings in terms of one's career or status in the community. As always, the key with "good" astrological weather lies in avoiding passivity and actively taking advantage of opportunities. In this case, these opportunities are presented to you from other people. Look to the advice of partners, associates, and patrons now. Think of yourself as a blind person, benefiting from the vision of others. Let yourself be led and advised. To butcher a proverb, "the lone wolf catches no worm," at least when Venus progresses to an easy aspect with the Midheaven.

PROGRESSED VENUS/NATAL ASCENDANT

A major Venusian event, and this is definitely one of the most dramatic ones, can always be relied upon to bring contact with people whose impact on our lives changes everything. This impact does not, emphatically, always arise through sexual or romantic entanglements, although they are exceedingly common at such times. **The point is that you have reached a point of impasse in your life which can only be resolved through the catalytic impact of another person upon you.** Everything depends on your openness now, and upon your willingness to be touched, influenced, guided, even corrected. Synchronistically, you feel a more compelling social impulse now than you typically do. You are more willing to reach out. It is very common for people experiencing this aspect to make changes in their outward appearance, generally for the better. That too is just part of the synchronistic "come hither" wave. Under hard aspects, this Venusian surge feels uncomfortable. You may feel ill-at-ease in your body or your clothing; your personal style may feel crude or fake to you. It may be hard to establish an equilibrium between your old patterns and beliefs, and the new terrains of life that these new soul-friends are opening up for you. Under easy aspects, the challenges in those areas lend themselves to more serendipitous resolutions, but the risk of superficiality presents itself. Your skill at creating a magnetic, seductive aura around yourself may have never been greater, so be careful you don't trick anyone into falling in love with an illusion you've created. Whenever that happens of course, more than one person is fooled!

PROGRESSED MARS: YOUR EVOLVING COURAGE

PROGRESSED MARS/NATAL SUN

Nature teaches us some hard principles: "Kill or be killed, eat or be eaten, only the strong survive"—that kind of stuff. The Law of the Jungle. The Survival of the Fittest. There are gentler channels on the cosmic television set, but those are the eternal lessons of the War God. And when Mars progresses into contact with your natal Sun, the terrain you are navigating represents one of the two or three most "martial" periods in your entire life. So act accordingly! Show your teeth! Be dangerous! Find your power! Don't just set boundaries—defend them! Expand them! And don't just feel badly about my overuse of explanation points here! Write me a nasty letter about them!!! Well, maybe you do have to pick your battles, but **assertiveness, healthy**

pride, and a sense of what you are really worth are qualities that life will reward in you now. And their opposites—mousey, compromising, conflict-avoiding behaviors—will only get you eaten alive. This is obviously not a progression for the faint-hearted. Even if you're tough, you may need to get in shape for it by doing adventurous things: paddle up the Zambezi, get your pilot's license, take a karate class. You've reached a point in the evolutionary journey where, in order to go forward, you very simply need to be braver. Demon Fear is guarding the gate to the Garden of Enlightenment—**and Fear's job is to ensure that no wimps get in!** Be alert to the ways that "forgiveness" and "tolerance" may sometimes only assist other people in creating "evil karma" for themselves. That aggressive fool who's riding your bumper may not really benefit spiritually from your immediately pulling over behind that slow-moving, smelly truck the way he wants you to. Some astrologers would caution you about accidents, especially if progressed Mars is making a hard aspect to your Sun. The warning is appropriate, but the key is that what could make you accident-prone during this event is an accumulation of suppressed anger and frustration. So get it out! Don't punish yourself for other people's offenses.

PROGRESSED MARS/NATAL MOON

Most of us, unless we are exceedingly mild human beings, occasionally feel the need to "raise a little hell." This explosive release of life's accumulated tensions can take many forms, and some of them are more therapeutic than others. Driving too fast for the sheer joy of it is a good example of both sides of the equation. The behavior may not represent the acme of "good citizenship," but it's probably harmless once in a while if you do it consciously and carefully. Of course, if you are preoccupied with angry thoughts about something else, and you are unwittingly expressing that aggressive energy in the way you are handling your car, you might kill yourself or someone else. This kind of edgy, volatile **mood** is the central earmark of the contacts of progressed Mars with the natal Moon. You are ready to blow it out, and you probably need to do just that. Your body, your attitude, the underlying tone of your thoughts, all of them reflect the fact that you are carrying a big stress-load. There may be good outward reasons for that, reflected in the specific houses and signs involved in the aspect. But the real key doesn't lie there. It lies in the deeper fact that life is always stressful and that sooner or later we all need to bleed off some of that tight energy, or it will hurt our health and put an abrasive edge on our personalities. You've reached such a point. Under easy aspects, the "pressure valve" is relatively easy to turn. Just do something a little wild, something that gets your blood pumping and makes you feel a little dangerous and dashing. Under hard aspects, the formula remains the same, but the pressures—and probably the costs connected with releasing them—are simply higher. Something's got to give; make sure it's you who decides what it is.

PROGRESSED MARS/NATAL MERCURY

When Mars progresses into contact with your Mercury, think of it like this: the God of War has entered your mouth. He's sitting on the tip of your tongue, armed, dangerous, and full of attitude. Just sit with that image for a moment, and you get the picture. Or the pictures, plural, because as always in astrology this event has several layers of meaning, some of them more useful to the growth of your soul than others. At the low end of the spectrum, this Mars/Mercury combination simply puts an unnecessarily nasty edge on your speech and an uncomfortable level of nervous tension in your body. At the high end, it is quite empowering, suggesting a turning-point in your ability to **express yourself with clarity, force, and authority**. In any case, under this configuration, you experience a certain quickening of your wit and a sharpening of your tongue. Your taste for barbed humor increases. You may be drawn to parody, teasing or sarcasm. Deeper down, the real drive here is for **passion** to return to your intellect and your interactions with others. As is typical with the so-called "malefic" planets, Mars does just fine if we give it a job to do. It only gets us in trouble if it's sitting around, unemployed. In this case, there is a need to embark aggressively on some program of learning or self-expression. Study some new astrological technique. Write a book. Teach a class. Above all, express yourself with verve and heat, and if that's hard, then re-frame the problem: you need to **find something that fills your intellect with verve and heat**. Be particularly wary under the hard aspects: you might unwittingly hurt people about whom you care with casual remarks that come out much more sharply than you ever intended!

PROGRESSED MARS/NATAL VENUS

As Mars progresses through an aspect with Venus, Love's two ancient faces—hot passion and sweet tenderness—dance together, contemplate each others' strangeness, try to accommodate themselves to each other. Anyone who has ever loved another person deeply for more than a few weeks has learned several fine Venusian arts: how to lose a round or two graciously, how to see another person generously and forgivingly, how to let go of unimportant needs, quirks, and arguments. Love between flawed, finite human beings cannot endure without those gentle compromises. But there is a dark, numbing side to all that letting-go, beautifully embodied in those horrible, deaf words, "Yes, dear." When Mars progresses into contact with Venus, there arises a volcanic heightening of your need for a more visceral, "present" kind of contact with the people who really matter in your life. It is, emphatically, time to stir the pot. When the aspect involved is a hard one, be careful not to stir it with nuclear warheads—and be careful, while you are at it, of self-righteousness and judgement: always the dark side of Martial energy. Under easier aspects, focus on real renewal and the exploration of serious issues, and don't settle for simply blowing off steam. Why is passion typically easier to sustain early in a relationship than later on? Most people agree that it has something to do with the freshness and sense of discovery of new love, and the corrupting impact upon them of the accumulation of tensions and frustrations that arise further down the road. When Mars comes to Venus, the time has come to attack that slow rot in your standing relationships. The tool for uncovering the new layers of freshness and for releasing those tensions is not a gentle one. It's Mars, the War God, bringer of "discussions." Use the tool; the time is right.

PROGRESSED MARS/NATAL JUPITER

Here's a little mental discipline just to get you in the mood for your progressed Mars aspect to natal Jupiter: imagine that you are Alexander the Great contemplating Asia Minor. Or Sitting Bull realizing that Custer is about to march blindly into that valley at Little Big Horn. The point is, you've got an extraordinary opportunity here. You've got to seize it, though. "Faint heart never won fair maid," and all that. Do you have the temerity you need to claim what you want? Do you have the boldness? **Do you believe in yourself that much?** There is a distinct pattern around this configuration of brief "windows of opportunity." The door opens, then the door closes. Tightly. You went through it, or you didn't. The progressed event itself may be in effect for a long time—two or three years is typical—but it is characterized by a pattern of these now-you-see-them, now-you-don't, openings. Hesitate, and you are lost. Under hard aspects, you may have to pay a finger to gain an arm: a good deal, obviously...but if you stop to think very long about it, the chance evaporates. Under easy aspects in particular, watch out for another dark side of Mars/Jupiter interactions: you might be tempted to shoot yourself in the foot with over-extension and grandiosity. So how can you distinguish the green lights from the red lights? The key lies in simply knowing what you really want. The chance to star in a film, for example, may sound glorious in principle, but is it something that is truly relevant to your soul? The gods, in short, are playing with your **desires** now, trying to teach you how effectively to claim exactly what you truly want, and to ignore what you have been merely **trained** to want. Furthermore, they want that distinction so deeply ingrained in you that it operates as a reflex, not as a considered decision.

PROGRESSED MARS/NATAL SATURN

Your evolving courage (progressed Mars) has arrived at the foot of the cloud-covered mountain (Saturn). **When clients come to me with this configuration, I always imagine that they know exactly what they need to do next, but that they are praying I will tell them it's something else.** That Saturn-mountain always represents something very difficult to accomplish, something around which we typically have both rational and irrational fear. In natal astrology, it's often useful to frame Saturn's place in the birthchart as symbolic of the "Great Work" of one's life, with its natal house, sign, and significant aspects specifying the exact nature of the challenge. Thinking about your Saturn that way sets the stage for a richer understanding of this progressed event because whatever that Great Work might be, the time has come for decisive, damn-the-torpedoes steps toward accomplishing it. Think of it like going to war in winter, especially if the aspect is a hard one. Doing this right is going to rattle you. It's going to destroy your balance and your equilibrium for a while. Your eyes are going to be narrower, your face more wizened, and your speech more laconic. Fortune-tellers generally dread this combination of planets above all others, and they can tell you tales of horror based on it. Many of them are true, but the liberating principle is that climbing the mountain is far easier than facing the consequences of not climbing it. Down that cowardly road lies loss, sorrow, and misfortune. And the higher road, while exhausting and maybe even frightening at times, also promises renewed self-respect, a quiet, formidable pride, and the dignity that comes from stacking up some real accomplishments.

PROGRESSED MARS/NATAL URANUS

Volatility is the uncontested key word here. Put the Martial sparkplug near the Uranian fireworks factory and, in the twinkling of an eye, anything can happen. There's both a cart and a horse here, and unlike the proverb, there is actually a serious question about which one should come first. The "horse" is that you have arrived at a **junction in your evolutionary journey where you need to defend the authenticity of your soul**. The time has come to break some rules, to extend aggressively your right to be yourself. You'll probably have to bring the battle for that existential honesty right under the noses of some people to whom you've in fact given far too much power in the past, be they parents, peers, partners, or employers. Get it right, and they won't be pleased. Get it wrong, and you won't be. And there probably isn't a lot of middle ground. Trouble is, under this combination you'll probably be more than "hot" enough to win. Which brings us to the "cart." And that's **restraint**, and a long view of where your best interests actually lie. Whether the aspect is easy or hard, you may find yourself drawn to the "nuclear warfare theory of urban renewal" right now: in a nutshell, a tendency to use too much force. The easy aspects favor bolder moves; and as always with them, you can simply trust luck a little more. But the bottom line is a wise appraisal of what you really want, apart from all the social programming you've received from parents, friends, and the TV, followed by the daring initiation of an ultimately grounded and reasonable plan for getting it.

PROGRESSED MARS/NATAL NEPTUNE

Illusions and mirages abound when Mars progresses into an aspect with Neptune, and "easy" aspects just make it easier to fall for them. Be especially hesitant about irreversible commitments now. "Things are not as they seem"—and your fervent aspirations of today may seem surreal and irrelevant tomorrow, like the dreams of childhood. Choices characterized by that classic Mars fingerprint—ardent desire—are particularly suspect. Sexual attractions leap to mind, of course. But we can "ardently desire" many things that later prove vaporous: glitzy career changes, extravagant cars or other possessions, even connections with sundry self-appointed gurus, spiritual guides, channels, and "Next Big Thing" shrinks. If you can avoid squandering the contact of Mars and Neptune in any of the ways outlined above, then you're definitely in the top half of the class, spiritually speaking. More importantly, you are ready for a very real and very sacred initiation, but one that is not for the easily unhinged. The archetype that best synthesizes these two planets is that of the **Spiritual Warrior**. The point here is that certain stages in the unfolding of your psychic and spiritual sensitivities are simply frightening, and the "warrior" in you must find the courage to meet them head-on. These developments disorient you; fill you with impressions and energies that undo your accustomed sense of reality. They could be called "psychedelic," although no narrow reference to the use of drugs or sacred plants is implied. You've reached such a liminal point in your evolutionary journey. This higher state of conscious is what you **actually** "ardently desire" at this moment; any other object of desire is a sublimation, and therefore an illusion. You may get it, but it won't feed you.

PROGRESSED MARS/NATAL PLUTO

A four year old imperiously demands ice cream. Mom admonishes, "Say please." Defiant, the kid says, "No!" And mom says, "OK, no ice cream for you." As child abuse goes, this is low-voltage stuff. Most of us would agree that mom did the right thing. But the kid doesn't feel that way! That child feels not only abused, but also out-gunned and out-maneuvered. And his rage is futile. If he expresses it, he senses the drift of the political wind: no ice cream tomorrow either. **So he swallows the fury, the shame, the powerlessness, and the futility**. And, ironically, becomes a little bit more adult. Quite intentionally, the example here is trivial...and the point is that by the time we reach adulthood, we've all had to "stuff" a lot of fury and passion. Repressed sexual desires are part of it too—and we're not talking narrowly about somebody who's "uptight" sexually. We are talking about the universal fact that our glorious pagan animal lusts are forces we don't necessarily choose to express every time they make themselves felt! Smart, obviously—but repressing them still hurts. And Pluto, the Lord of the Underworld, is the place where we keep all that heat locked away. When Mars progresses to Pluto, the gates of that particular hell are blown off their hinges. The heat rises. Get it right, and it's a healing event. It's nothing less than a chance to **dump some of the pain and hurt you've been carrying since you were a kid**—or even from previous lifetimes, if reincarnational imagery works for you. How? The first point to grasp is that this process is only barely cognitive. It doesn't have much to do with understanding or insight, at least not alone. It's far more raw than that. The key lies in the direct expression of that stored-up fire: vigorous physical activity, strong emotions, unabashed tears, the banging of drums, perspiration, berserker-energy. Under hard aspects, there is a real danger of building up too much resistance, followed by the "dam breaking." These aspects definitely have a dangerous dimension; they require your vigilance and cooperation. You've got to express the energies of those pent-up screams, hungers and wails intentionally. Otherwise, especially with the easy aspects, you're vulnerable to impulsive, and ultimately self-destructive, actions—or with the hard ones, accidents.

PROGRESSED MARS/NATAL MIDHEAVEN

In terms of career, a bottom line when progressed Mars contacts your Midheaven is that **if you don't rise, you are going to fall**. The War God has little affinity for the middle ground; it is simply in the nature of this planetary archetype that it favors dividing us into winners and losers, victors and the vanquished, hunters and prey. In the unfolding of your evolutionary journey, you've now reached a point where you need to be taken more seriously by your "tribe." Generally, this drive manifests in terms of career or professional concerns, although we must always be sensitive to the fact the Midheaven means a lot more than your job. The Midheaven is also connected with any public role you play, even if it's unpaid. In one or more of those categories, you are now "ripe" for the satisfaction of offering more of yourself, more of your wisdom and skill, to the larger community. To remain in your present circumstances would eventually feel empty, even degrading. The hitch is that you have to **fight for your right to offer that greater gift**. It requires assertiveness on your part, and therefore courage and self-confidence. You may very well have rivals or competitors. If the aspect is a hard one, then you may be "pressured" out of your present situation— think of the train hitting the toothpaste tube. Under easy aspects, the improvements in your public role are more easily available and claiming them won't be as difficult—but the downside is that it will be dangerously easy to remain in your present situation. All you'll have to do is lower your standards, give up a little dignity, and resign yourself to accepting the lordship of a petty tyrant or two. If that's what you want...

PROGRESSED MARS/NATAL ASCENDANT

The Ascendant is the mask you wear in the world. It's your style, your social calling card. It's the person you seem to be as seen by individuals who don't really know you very well—the check-out people in the grocery store, your friends' friends whom you've casually met once or twice, and probably half your beloved relatives. When Mars progresses into contact with this sensitive point, the time has come to add a little more chili powder to your outward recipe. Think of it this way: **you're getting boring!** That's probably not objectively true, but it's a useful "meditation" for you right now. Your soul is hungry to stir things up a bit, to put a little more pizzazz into your life. Imagine it this way: you meet an attractive stranger at a party. After the hostess has introduced you and wandered off, the stranger says, "Well, tell me about yourself. What have you done lately that excites you?" Scenario A: You say, "Ummm...nothing much. I saw *Titanic* again the other night...?" Scenario B: "Funny you should ask. I'm just back from Katmandu, where I sort of fell in with Mick Jagger, of all people." You've got to admit, Scenario B has a certain panache— and so should you right now! Under easy aspects, basically this is a **call to adventure**. Under hard ones, there's that, plus a tendency toward a certain emotional volatility, along the lines of, "why, for two cents I'd..." So nip those nukes in the bud by spicing up your life.

When you're old and gray, would you rather regret what you'd done or what you hadn't done? Discuss.

THE PROGRESSED MIDHEAVEN: YOUR EVOLVING "COSMIC JOB DESCRIPTION"

PROGRESSED MIDHEAVEN/NATAL SUN

What is the connection between what you do for a living and who you really are? And how much of your real self is expressed through your "life-style?" Whatever your answer, this aspect tells us that the link between your essence and the hat you wear in the world needs to get stronger. To put it crudely, **you are ready to get paid for being yourself!** That's what happens when your evolving place in the community—the progressed Midheaven—comes into contact with the most basic astrological symbol of Identity: the Sun. Your nature and your role in the world need to integrate, to become more reflective of each other. They need to incorporate each other's strengths and perspectives, form a fertile marriage together. If the aspect between them is hard one, then developments in your professional life (or your role in the community) have begun to create a sharp tension with who you really are. These pangs are **a crisis of self-expression**: you are trapped by the mechanical wind-up duties of your outward scene. Something's got to give, and we hope it's not your soul! If the aspect is an easy one, then the crisis is quieter and emotionally less pressing, although the issues remain exactly the same. You've evolved in your outer role to a point where it would be relatively simple to make some encouraging, empowering changes. Time to make that "big move" professionally, time to claim what you want, time to claim your right to be recognized—and recompensed—for who you are. There is no need to feel as if you could train a monkey to do your job! You are ready to put more of yourself into your community. Don't let the chance go by. You, and a lot of other people, have so much to gain.

PROGRESSED MIDHEAVEN/NATAL MOON

The Moon is the wise mother within us all; she nourishes us, senses our needs, knows our tastes and desires. She is beyond reason and law; her only concern is our wellbeing, and she knows that our health and happiness are fed as much by irrational drives as by rational ones. It would be difficult to think of a symbol further removed in spirit from the worldly, outward tone of the Midheaven! Career development is often very logical, disciplined business in which our emotional needs must take second place. Furthermore, our status in the community is subject to cruel vagaries that show no sign of caring a wit for our feelings. And yet now we see your Midheaven progressing into contact with the Moon! What can this mean? Basically, it tells you that **you are currently paying too high an emotional price for your social status or your professional position**. The time has come to integrate the transrational needs of your Moon into your career strategy. What might this look like? For one person, it could be a decision **not** to go after that big promotion. For another, it could be the seemingly irrational choice to quit a lucrative job for a less remunerative one, simply because the second job **felt** better. Under hard aspects, these choices can be more wrenching than under the easy aspects, of course. Still, the issues are identical: you are asked to take your soul into deeper account when navigating the career choices that lie ahead for you. One more note: the Moon is deeply connected with family and home-oriented issues. The "irrational" choice you may be asked to make now might very well benefit those hearth-centered needs, or allow a greater harmony between your outer life and the lives and needs of your nearest and dearest.

PROGRESSED MIDHEAVEN/NATAL MERCURY

You have something to say to the tribe, and you need to be heard. It will feel empowering and right for you to claim that voice, and it will also benefit the people around you—even ones whom you don't know personally. With your Midheaven progressing into an aspect with your natal Mercury, there is an integration happening between your outer role and your thoughts, philosophies, and ideas **Your public voice, in short, has ripened**. You may find yourself drawn to do some writing, even if it's just a letter to the editor. Media in general will become more relevant to your life during this period: maybe you'll be interviewed. Perhaps you'll publish something, or appear on TV or radio. Maybe you'll find yourself speaking in public. Under easy aspects, the whole process will feel quite natural, almost automatic. Under hard ones, it will put you through some emotional changes: you may have "issues" around your self-confidence in the self-expression department, or perhaps around your level of education. What you feel compelled to say may make you some enemies you'd rather not have. But your integrity demands that you express yourself now. This is not a drive that originates in your ego, by the way. It originates in the larger world. It is the very real **need out there** that pulls your voice out of you. Surrender to that process; forces greater than yourself are involved, and they will help you.

PROGRESSED MIDHEAVEN/NATAL VENUS

Not everyone is driven by ambition and the career-game, but we all have a role to play in the community. If we don't feel that we are making some kind of contribution to the process of culture and **getting noticed for it**, there's an emptiness inside us. It's as if we are taking without giving, and that's just not a comfortable situation for most of us. This gift we give to the community doesn't have to be "big;" it doesn't have to involve fame. But it's got to be an expression of something about ourselves which we value. Your role in those regards is poised for a change; you are ready to give a little more, and to do it little differently than you have done it before. Succeed, and the results will be quite rewarding emotionally, and there's good chance they'll improve your financial picture too. The only hitch is that, on your own, you couldn't in a million years ever figure out to make this next step. **You need some help**. You are just not playing with a full deck; half your cards are missing. But there is at least one other person nearby in the same predicament. You need to get your cards together. Your own skills need to be complemented with another set of skills, alien and mysterious to you. Your vision, your values, your talents, your connections—none of them alone are sufficient. So reach out! Form partnerships and alliances now. Under hard aspects, you may have harder time marrying all these differing assets and coming up with a workable plan. Negotiate! You may simply not **like** the other person or people as much as you would under easy aspects. But the critical point is that a "marriage" in some sense of the word is about to happen, and it will have a profound effect upon the shape of your public, visible future.

PROGRESSED MIDHEAVEN/NATAL MARS

People locked in power struggles, clawing their way to the top: the spectacle can be enough to make you turn in despair from the world. There is a drunken madness connected with fame and power, a drunken madness that seems to select for people willing to pay an insane spiritual price simply to stand at the top of the pitiful heap—until the next one like themselves comes along and cuts them down. Politics as usual, in other words—in Washington, in the corporate world, in any profession, even in the "spiritual community." Mars, symbol of human aggressiveness, clearly has a great affinity for the Midheaven! And with your progressed Midheaven contacting Mars, is it time for you to abandon all human charity, all kindness and perspective, and "get yours?" Well, yes, sort of... Think of it this way: **is there anything in this world for which it's worth putting yourself on the line?** Do you have any beliefs worth defending? Something is brewing in your life now that involves your standing up for a cherished value or person. There may be a purely altruistic issue involved: you may, for example, get into some kind of environmental battle or some other ethically-charged public issue. You might be called upon to blow the whistle on a person who is doing some terrible harm. On the other hand, your desires here might not be purely lofty, and that's fine too, so long as you are not descending into cruelty. **It is perfectly legitimate to compete with others and to seek an improvement in one's own circumstances**. This aspect is much connected with entrepreneurial enthusiasms. If, for example, you are a painter, it might be time to pursue placing your work in galleries aggressively. Under easy aspects, be bold and take risks. Under hard ones, be a little more conservative...keep your escape routes open! Otherwise, there's not much difference between them. Either way, Mars will always make you quake a bit...just make sure you're quaking for a good cause!

PROGRESSED MIDHEAVEN/NATAL JUPITER

When the Midheaven progresses into contact with Jupiter, especially under an easy aspect, all the fortune-tellers wish you were a publicly traded company: they'd love to buy shares in you. "Power, honor, glory, and riches" is the general tenor of the prediction, as if you were about to turn to solid gold. Such magnificent prophecies, of course, tend to fall a little flat in practice. Still, there is something worth hearing in them, and not just for their substantial feel-good quotient. Opportunity is definitely knocking now...or opportunities, plural. Here's the key: all that glitters is not gold! That cliché represents probably a hundred thousand years of human experience with the "lucky" planet. Now let's add a complicating observation: gold does glitter. Confused? Well, confusion is a luxury you can't afford right now, especially under the easier Midheaven/Jupiter aspects. You need to make some **decisive, ambitious steps in your career** or in your outward, public life. To make them successfully, all you've really got to know is what you actually, truly want. It's as simple as that. I'll always remember a very poignant session I did with a woman who "had everything." She told me, "I have a wonderful life...for someone else." There's the trap. Jupiter offers real breakthroughs and deeper satisfactions in your work and social life; it also offers empty glitz and inflated illusions—be especially carefully regarding the latter under the hard aspects, by the way. In some significant outward way, you have been **settling for too little**. Time to claim a little more from life: ask for that promotion—and be prepared to look for another job elsewhere if you are refused! Back up your request, in other words, with a real commitment to your own dignity and self-worth. The great god Jupiter loves an attitude like that and will reward you for it. And remember: this aspect isn't only about career. You might move to a better neighborhood, buy yourself a new car, even take a major vacation. Anything you do that **people who don't know you** can see is under the domain of the Midheaven—and set for some improvement now!

PROGRESSED MIDHEAVEN/NATAL SATURN

Saturn may have a bad reputation among gloom-and-doom astrologers, but don't be deceived: when your progressed Midheaven contacts Saturn, satisfying, positive developments can happen in your career. In fact, they **will** happen...if you work for them. That, of course, is the key: really hard work. Sorry. There's no other way. Under Saturn, you have no luck at all—not good, not bad, just zero. What you put in, you get out...to the penny. More deeply, this aspect signals that you have **outgrown** your present professional circumstances. They are not "seemly" for a person of your level of maturity—and by "maturity," we don't narrowly mean your chronological age, although that may be relevant. More centrally, you simply have more to give than your present situation allows you to offer. It's as if Horowitz had to play the spoons. And the only way out of that dilemma is step by step, up the mountain. Under hard aspects, you may think the gloomier astrologers are doing pretty well with their baleful predictions, but look deeper: you are being squeezed out of an old set of circumstances that weren't really tolerable anymore anyway! Under easy aspects, be particularly careful of complacency. You need a change, but on the surface the situation isn't so drastic. A psychotherapist, for example, might have a successful, established practice. When the Midheaven progresses into a sextile with her Saturn, she needs to move her work in a new direction. Maybe she needs some further education. Maybe she needs to move to another city closer to the cutting edge. Those pressures are internal, but if she fails to heed them, she'll begin to feel first boredom, then full-blown burn-out. Effort is the only answer now, and it is an excellent, satisfying one.

PROGRESSED MIDHEAVEN/NATAL URANUS

Probably there is nowhere else in our experience where we are under more pressure to behave conventionally than in our public, outward lives. There, we are all representatives of various "tribal types" and can be easily categorized from afar by people whom we've never even met. And don't be deceived: this doesn't exclude those of us who are marching to "different drummers!" You don't need to be "normal" to be under the tribal thumb; you can embody that stultifying conventionality as a body-piercing punk on a skateboard or as a certifiably paradigm-shifting, quantum-leaping, organic-vegetable-eating New Age media guru! A little compassion for the human condition is appropriate here: we are, after social creatures. We inherit culture. We are enhanced by it, but also distorted by it. And when your Midheaven progresses into contact with Uranus, the time has come to break free of that training. You are ready to **individuate** in terms of your outward, public self. Get it right, and you'll be in serious trouble. Yes, you read that right. Whenever we make a strong response to a pulse of Uranian energy, **we annoy everyone in our lives to whom we have given the power to judge us**. That is really the key. In your lifestyle, and probably in your profession, you are ready to turn a sharp corner, to break free of the conventionalizing pressures that have shaped you and steadied you all your life. This is heady stuff, especially under the hard aspects: pay at least a little bit of attention to the idea that you might overreact or be drawn to unnecessary extremes—but don't pay so much attention to those cautions that you miss the real need for elbow room that's pulling at you now. God knows, the people around you will be reminding you of "caution" enough without your concentrating on it! And one last hint: the single most insidious tool of enslavement that culture wields is the implication that if you take this Uranian path, you won't be "cool" anymore. Not everyone will use that exact word, but when you feel the shaping impact of that withdrawal of respect, know that you are facing the moment of truth: the Uranian initiation.

Progressed Midheaven/Natal Neptune

On the face of it, there could hardly be two astrological symbols more alien to each other than the Midheaven and Neptune. On the one hand, we have our social personality: our job, our reputation, our place in the world—and all our silly status issues. On the other hand, we have our mystical, transcendent sensitivities, and our sense of the transitoriness of all worldly glory. The fortune-tellers, accordingly, tend to paint a dim view of the interactions of the progressed Midheaven with Neptune. Some of them predict a period of drifting and lassitude in one's outward life—that you will simply "not give a damn" about professional matters for a while. (Indeed, that's a particular risk with the soft aspects.) Others prophesy you'll make a gargantuan Blunder: you'll fall prey to some grand illusion in your profession or lifestyle—which is, in fact, more common as a hard-aspect catastrophe. A third branch of fortune-tellers, a little more optimistic but also a bit flaky, suggest that you will certainly become some kind of Great Spiritual Teacher during this period...and in my experience, thinking that way is the single fastest road to becoming a poster-person for the "grand illusion" school of thought! So what is really happening now? In a word, **you need a vision**. In your outward life, in your professional life, you are clueless now. Things might be working well enough in the material sense, but you are uninspired and you have no notion of what to do next! That humbling perspective is the critical insight. You need to withdraw from the battle for a while, "go to the moutain-top," and think...or pray. Ask the gods for a vision. Consult oracles—but don't be too fast to implement any great ideas. Take the whole Neptunian period as a fallow time, a gathering of inspiration, and an exercise in simple faith. And one more tip: treat every "fantastic financial opportunity" as an invitation to contract a dreadful virus.

PROGRESSED MIDHEAVEN/NATAL PLUTO

When your Midheaven progresses into contact with your natal Pluto, it is a call to one of two possible positive eventualities: either the claiming of some significant worldly power, or psychotherapy. That's the bumper sticker version, but it gets us off on the right foot. Seen through the Plutonian lens, the human race is a squabbling, competitive and often treacherous breed. Who rules the world? **People who like power!** And how would you characterize the mental health of people who are so motivated by the love of power that they hold it dearer than sanity, family, peace, and harmony? A rhetorical question for most of us. And the answer explains the lion's share of the history of the world, at least from a cynical perspective. But, like most one dimensional views, that cynicism misleads us. The world is full of decent, loving people who are committed to making a difference in the human story. Some are devoted teachers. Others are activists of varying stripes, even ones with whom we disagree. Environmentalists trying to keep us from killing ourselves. Artists devoted to their work. With your Midheaven progressing into contact with Pluto, you asked to join that blessed band, either permanently or just for the duration of the aspect. Maybe you'll sign right up—you'll certainly have plenty of opportunities when this synchronistic wave breaks on your beach. But maybe that idea scares you so profoundly that you can't even feel it...and that brings us to our second Plutonian eventuality: "psychotherapy." We put it in quotation marks because the word is not intended narrowly; it means "soul-healing." And we don't always need to pay a professional to help us with that process, although if you find the right one, it can be a great support. The point is that whatever has shamed you, whatever has robbed you of your sense of your own power in the tribe and of the legitimacy of your own voice, whatever has taken the lion in you and turned it into a passive mouse, is under developmental pressure now. If it's there in sufficient virulence to block your doing something big in your life now, the Lord of the Underworld wants you to look at it, heal it, and then get on with the important work of helping us save our collective buns.

PROGRESSED MIDHEAVEN/NATAL MIDHEAVEN

If we are focusing primarily on major, Ptolemaic aspects, then the chronology here is simple: all of us are born under a Midheaven/Midheaven conjunction. We hit the sextile around age sixty, and the square at ninety. If we hit the trine, that means we really ate some serious granola because we are about one hundred twenty years old. Obviously, the sextile in late midlife is the most common event here, and we'll concentrate on it. It coincides closely with a major Biopsychic Script milestone that we discussed earlier in the book: the second Saturn Return. That's essentially our initiation into Elderhood, and this Midheaven aspect spices that transition with an enhanced drive to take some responsibility for the soul of the tribe. The true Elder is precious and we all know that truth in our guts and feel instinctively drawn to such a person. All the blither about how we're supposed to "respect our elders" is really mostly the whining of the failed ones—people who have merely gotten old, which isn't of itself much of a spiritual accomplishment. Faced with a real Elder, most of us are disarmed. Such a person triggers an archetypal response in us, and we **naturally desire counsel and advice**. That's the feeling of the sextile, with its implications of something flowing easily, and of a certain urgent excitement and stimulation. The "young" Elder, newly fledged, begins now to feel a sense of respect directed toward him or her by younger people, and more to the point, a certain attitude of **expectancy** on their parts. And he or she must begin, gracefully and only when asked, to share the fruits of years of experience in the world. On the darker end of the spectrum, among the failed elders, we now begin to witness that sad, ancient spectacle: endless unsolicited advice, diatribes against modern culture, and a compulsion to regurgitate the undigested memories of an unexamined lifetime.

PROGRESSED MIDHEAVEN/NATAL ASCENDANT

The geometry of the birthchart dictates that we are all born with the progressed Midheaven gradually closing in on the natal Ascendant. That's about all we can say for sure, since the exact angle between the Midheaven and Ascendant varies from chart to chart and is only rarely a neat ninety degrees. At some point we'll experience a sextile between the two, then possibly (and in no certain order) a conjunction and a square. Folks born in very high latitudes might even experience the progressed conjunction *before* they get to the sextile. In any case, there is a coming together here of two factors: your outer role in the world and your personal touch. In terms of career, the time has come to *invest what you do with more of your own style and personality*, and such steps will very likely be rewarded with improvements in your professional satisfaction, your reputation, and probably in your finances as well. Of course, as usual, success comes more readily under the sextile or the conjunction than it does under the square. Still, even the square is a call to action: it's just that now there is more emphasis on the inner pressures and **sheer necessity** of making the move. In either situation, the key lies in investing more of your personality—your values, tastes, and opinions—in the shape and mood of your outer role in the world.

PROGRESSED ASCENDANT: YOUR EVOLVING STYLE

PROGRESSED ASCENDANT/NATAL SUN

Put on your crummiest bluejeans and a cheap tee-shirt, and see how coolly you're treated when you walk into a fancy store. Dress up, and suddenly those salespeople are transformed into charm school graduates. Most of us figure that one out by the time we've entered our third decade in this world, if not sooner. Afterwards, some of us pointedly wear one style or the other, taking a kind of self-righteous delight in the reactions we get. Others among us enjoy moving between the two costumes, and observing how something as trivial as clothing can completely transform the attitudes and behaviors of those around us. **Style presses people's buttons,** no doubt about it. And style is the domain of the progressed Ascendant, although it's bigger than bluejeans. The Sun, on the other hand, is far deeper; it's close to the core of what you are. Currently, with your progressed Ascendant contacting your natal Sun, the time has come for your style to evolve. **The signals you are sending to the social world have become misleading and counter-productive,** at least in terms of the evolutionary purposes of your spirit. If it's a hard aspect, then you probably do feel socially uncomfortable—sort of goofy—lately. Under easy aspects, the problem is more subtle and less pressing. Either way, you are simply not connecting with the right experiences, or with the right people in the right ways. And the problem, serious as it is, can fairly be called **superficial**—which is to say, it is only on the surface. So the surface must change! Try to become aware of habits of speech, gestures, and, yes, styles of clothing, that are no longer reflective of what you value or what you want to project. Any chance to observe yourself now on video or audio tape is precious, although it may be a bit wrenching (hard aspects) or revealing (easy ones) as well. The hard work of inward changing is already done; all that's happening now is that your style needs to catch up.

PROGRESSED ASCENDANT/NATAL MOON

Maybe you have one of those friends who's become so "psychologically-correct" through years of therapy that you carefully screen every peep you utter to make sure it doesn't reveal a shred of co-dependency or personal disempowerment, not a scrap of patriarchal sexism, not a single "should" or "ought"—nothing that could be leapt upon, discussed, and corrected. In a situation such as that one, in the name of "being in touch with feelings," a lot of real human spontaneity and expressiveness—a lot of true Moon energy—has been repressed. Sleep with someone in a spirit of love and ease for five or ten years, and you begin to get a feeling for that person's Moon... something you could never do with that militant friend. That's how intimate a place the astrological Moon is; we hide its innermost parts until we feel lots of comfortable, instinctual trust for the other person. The Moon is where you keep your fantasies, your whimsies, and all your feelings that make no sense. Revealing it is risky business. You can get hurt. On the other hand, if the Moon remains completely protected, you feel utterly lonely. With your progressed Ascendant contacting your Moon, the time has come to **integrate more of the softness and realness of your innermost self into your outward style**. Bottom line, you are becoming emotionally isolated, and that's the main reason you are feeling moody lately—and those moods are simply stormier and more unexpected under hard aspects than they are under easier ones. No matter what the aspect, it's helpful and healing now to try to be a little more **whimsical**. Make more "**I feel**" statements. Warm your heart with anything that brings out tenderness in you—adopt a kitten, have a baby, visit dear old soul-friends. Cry. Laugh. Reveal. Create.

PROGRESSED ASCENDANT/NATAL MERCURY

Good ideas and command of the right words to express them are two different realities. How many times have you seen empty eloquence, or even simple loudmouthed verbal pushiness, eclipse the better ideas of a person who just didn't have as much panache with the spoken word? If your progressed Ascendant is contacting your natal Mercury through a hard aspect, there is tremendous developmental pressure on you now in terms of getting your thoughts out into expression: you are feeling "silenced" and, hopefully, you are ready to do something about that! If the contact is through an easy aspect, then it feels much more like flowing evolution: you are finding the real power and tone of your natural voice. In either case, you will learn as you speak, of course—the "I never knew I knew that until I said it" phenomenon is thick with you now. The real emphasis here, whether the aspect is easy or hard, is not upon **learning** so much as upon **expressing what you already know**. If you have the slightest inclination to write, honor it now—and probably the universe will practically be begging for you to do just that! People will be asking you to put something down on paper for them; appealing writing classes may appear; letters, be they to friends or to editors, will be bursting inside you. You may find yourself with a new computer—or an inviting new pen, or desk, or office, or e-mail program! Books probably play an inspiring, directing role in your experience now too; it's as if the gods and goddesses themselves are directing you through the printed word. Mercury times also often bring mind-expanding, liberating chances for travel and "education"—the latter meaning not only school in the formal sense, but also workshops, enriching conversations, and private efforts simply to learn.

PROGRESSED ASCENDANT/NATAL VENUS

Sometimes we meet people with whom we think real friendship or even a romantic bond could potentially develop, but nothing happens. Literally nothing. Nobody calls anybody; we never see each other again. Life is full of those missed connections, and a little simple math about the numbers of hours in a day suggests that we're better off: who could possibly have time for all those people? With your progressed Ascendant triggering your Venus, make the time now! Astrology is very sensitive to the timing of our meetings with our soulmates—the people who are critical catalysts for our evolutionary journeys—and this aspect is one of the most powerful indicators of those kinds of encounters in the whole system. The hook is that **you must take the initiative**: that's the nature of the Ascendant. The ball is in your court. Under hard aspects, the circumstances are more daunting, and many barriers exist between you and the people with whom you must connect: distance, other relationships, existing responsibilities and attitudes. Everything flows more easily if the aspects are harmonious —but then, as always with the "good" aspects, letting the chance slip through your fingers is also that much easier. Part of the synchronistic wave that's breaking on your shores now is that your "evolving style" is embracing more "Venusian" qualities—which, in a nutshell, means that you are becoming more attractive. This may very well have physical expressions, but the word "attractive" means a lot more in reality than it means in glamour magazines. You'll find yourself feeling warmer and friendlier, more comfortable socially, more interested in other people. All of that is simply the way your Body-Mind-Spirit system is saying to your soulmates, "Hey! I'm over here! Come have a look!"

PROGRESSED ASCENDANT/NATAL MARS

Sometimes in life it just comes down to fight or die. If you're not fierce, if you refuse to defend yourself and your rightful boundaries, you'll be wounded. Or used, exploited, and otherwise hung out to dry. What about justice and fairness? What about gentleness? Forgiveness? Transcendence? They have their seasons, but the War God has a season too, and with your Ascendant progressing into an aspect with Mars, **a season of conflict is upon you now**. So be decisive. In the evolutionary journey of your soul, you are facing a critical juncture. A nemesis stands between you and the full richness of experience that potentially lies ahead for you. That nemesis may take human form, but in reality the demon is fear itself. The time has come to do battle with the inner mouse! **The aim, simply, is to win**. That is a deeper statement than it might appear to be. If your nature is already passionate and intense, be wary of going too far, of getting drunk on rage and doing more damage than is necessary. If you are a milder creature, make sure you rattle the saber loudly enough to ensure that you get what you need. Again: the aim is simply to win, no more, no less. Under hard aspects, the battle will come to you; you can't avoid it, except perhaps by capitulating utterly. Under easy ones, you may actually need to **precipitate the issues**: an old "truce" has outlived its usefulness. Since the Ascendant is connected with your outward style, you have evolved now to a place where you need to **look** more formidable as well as **be** more formidable— a quality which paradoxically can reduce the potential unpleasantness of this aspect markedly for the simple reason that someone who looks dangerous is less likely to be attacked than is someone who seems to be easy pickings. So be direct, and ask for what you want with steadiness in your eyes. One more hint: an excellent tactic here is to make sure that you are in strong physical condition. It's harder to growl and bare your teeth plausibly when you are feeling flabby and slow.

PROGRESSED ASCENDANT/NATAL JUPITER

Two people, equally competent, apply for the same job. The first one is very careful not to over-represent her skills or her qualifications; she guards against seeming presumptuous or arrogant and she is especially careful not to come across as pushy. The second person, while courteous and appropriate, expresses more confidence in her ability to handle the job than she actually feels. She also "interviews the interviewer," asking probing questions about the down side of the position and implying that while she is interested, she is far from desperate. Who gets the job? Person number two, nine times out of ten. **Confidence in yourself breeds confidence in others toward you**. As the song says, "nobody knows you when you're down and out"—or even when you look as if you might be. With your progressed Ascendant interacting with your natal Jupiter, you need to add a little more bigness, self-confidence, and even a spice of "Hollywood" to your external behavior. Let people know that you are capable of extraordinary things. Put a little "healthy grandiosity" in your style. A fortune-teller would prophecy "good luck" here, especially if the aspect involved is an easy one. That happy prediction can be absolutely true, but to trigger that "luck" in your life, you need to incorporate a little more flair into the mask you wear in the world. **You've got to look like someone to whom lucky things might happen!** So spend a little money, juice up your style—and your lifestyle. Live a little larger. Be careful though—always, the dark side of Jupiter is simple over-extension. It's not so much a question of your being "too pushy;" more like your asking for the wrong things. Asking for glitz instead of substance, for appearance instead of reality. Is that a greater danger under the hard aspects? Not in my experience. Under the hard aspects it's just a little harder to get whatever you are chasing than under the easy ones—whether or not you need it!

PROGRESSED ASCENDANT/NATAL SATURN

Vast industries are driven by our collective phobia about the aging process. But for the majority of us, one glance and most people can guess our ages with reasonable accuracy no matter how much we've spent on disguising our years. Fearing the maturational process is futile; it happens anyway. And, even though this idea doesn't get much press coverage, there are some really pleasant dimensions of getting older. It's good to be taken more seriously, for one thing. With your progressed Ascendant aspecting your natal Saturn, **the time has come to integrate your years, as gracefully as possible, into your outward appearance**. People who do a good job of navigating this territory often find themselves going through their closets and getting rid of their more "trendy" clothing. That's not such a big deal in and of itself, but it is emblematic of this process. You are ready to broadcast to the world, not your age, but rather your level of maturity. **You are making a bid to be taken more seriously!** And you need to do that: your destiny now lies through a door that only opens to you if you seem more substantial, competent, and responsible—more Saturnian—than your current habits and styles dictate. This is not an unflattering characterization of your past; only an impressive foretaste of what you are becoming. Under hard aspects, you will probably find that to cross this bridge, you must pay a social price in terms of people who'll not be able to cross it with you, or support you in the process. You may, if you need them, get some sharp reminders of where you are in the aging cycle—somebody with whom you thought you were flirting calls you "sir" or "ma'am," for example. Under easy aspects, the process is naturally a more flowing one, and might not even be very noticeable until you look in the mirror one day. In either case, as is so typical with Saturn, you may face a mountain to be climbed in your life, and the climb itself is the magic that moves you forward into this deeper, wiser state.

PROGRESSED ASCENDANT/NATAL URANUS

Your lifestyle is about to take a sharp turn off the beaten path, onto the Road Less Travelled. Then, when you discover how crowded that Road is with nervously trendy people patting themselves on the back under the banner of **that** particular cliché, you'll take another turn, spin twice, spit over your left shoulder, and turn into someone truly unprecedented. **Claiming your right to be yourself**: that is the soul of the planet Uranus. It is about freedom—as Jeff Green put it so eloquently, the "freedom from the known." And the "known" here is defined as everything conventional people view as "obvious common sense," all their little formulas for how to be a sane, successful, "normal" person. You have simply reached a point in the journey of your spirit at which you need to gather some experiences which lie outside the pale of the typical human trajectory. You need "a walk on the wild side," in other words. Too many people have their hooks in you, steering you with their approval and disapproval, their smiles and their snorts. Under hard aspects in particular, claiming the liberty of your soul is quite costly: those people will make you pay the price of freedom, to the last penny. It's still a bargain. Under easy aspects, the process is "luckier;" simply said, you can get away with more. So do that! With the progressed Ascendant contacting Uranus even your appearance will reflect this feeling of breaking free from social constraint: Mr. Normal sprouts an earring; Mr. Hip buys a three-piece suit. Those two images are important! One of the easiest errors to make in understanding Uranus is to imagine that it is always about becoming more "alternative." The real wisdom lies in grasping **who it is you've been trying to impress**, and claiming that power back.

PROGRESSED ASCENDANT/NATAL NEPTUNE

When the Ascendant progresses into an aspect with natal Neptune, two very different symbols dance together. The Ascendant is concerned with your outward appearance; your style; the mask you wear in the world's eye. Those considerations could not have less meaning for Neptune, which is focussed always on the Eternal Moment, upon the soul, and not upon "mere appearances." There is a great potential for lassitude in this interaction. Neptune can fill you with a sense that "nothing matters" or that "this too shall pass." Whatever the aspect, there is a real danger of drifting into situations which at best are meaningless and at worst involve some serious moral compromise— and in many ways that kind of trouble is **more** available under easy aspects, not less available. So what needs to be done? How can this energy be directed positively and consciously? Here's the key: the Ascendant is always about some distinct, decisive **choice** you make in the world. And with Neptune and the Ascendant interacting, **the time has come to take some obvious spiritual action**. So join a church. Take a yoga or meditation class. Go on a Vision Quest. Enter Jungian analysis. Make a serious commitment to studying evolutionary astrology. The critical point here is that **this action must be visible**. It must **externalize your inward spirituality**, and feed your journey through the gathering of relevant experiences, teachings, and human relationships. Fight the lassitude and dreaminess! This is a magical time, if you only stay awake!

PROGRESSED ASCENDANT/NATAL PLUTO

Ninety-nine percent of all social interaction is superficial stuff with a big emphasis on mutual entertainment, face-saving, and conflict avoidance. And anyone who's got a big "attitude" about that superficiality would certainly make a dreadful dinner companion. Still, there are times when all that wit and charm, all that skillful dodging of life's darkness, begins to cloy. There are times when strong, naked emotions need to be exchanged with certain special people in our lives, times when important words need to be said. You are definitely in such a time. This is always a touchy transition, moving from ego-supporting social chatter into sometimes ego-shattering realness. It must be done with a deft hand. With your progressed Ascendant aspecting your natal Pluto, the time has come to deepen your grasp of those strategies. The key here is not only the generation of insights; it lies more in the **effective expression of insights**. You are being asked to integrate your Plutonian depths into your social personality. Be careful, especially under hard aspects, of using too much force, too abruptly. You might blurt out truths with the best of intentions, but with catastrophic results gone badly awry. Under easy aspects, the dangers lie in the opposite direction—serious truths might be told so smoothly that they go in your listener's right ear and out the left. "I told you that!" means very little if the other person says, "I never heard you say it." Lying to yourself is easier under the gentle aspects too. Regardless of the aspect, the situations and issues regarding which you need a more straightforward style of expression tend to become pressing now. Choosing the "I don't want to talk about it" route becomes harder as this synchronistic wave breaks in your life. Denial becomes untenable and transparent, and shallow politeness unbearable. So seize the moment: say what you see.

PROGRESSED ASCENDANT/NATAL MIDHEAVEN

Most of us have some kind of work in the world, and a really good rule of thumb is that person we are on the job and the person we are on Saturday night with our dear friends are different creatures. That's natural enough; the people we contact through our work don't necessarily **want** to know who we are as an individuals. When the guy comes to fix your refrigerator, you don't care about his favorite TV shows or the state of his sex life. Your psychotherapist's political opinions probably don't come up in your sessions together. Most of the time it's best for our "professional" self to be an edited, streamlined, stripped down version of who we really are. But not when the progressed Ascendant is hooked into the Midheaven; then there is a need to **create more of a connection between our work and our personality**. Under an easy aspect, there is often a real opportunity to do just that, and great benefits available to us if we succeed. Here, for example, we might find a person presented with an opportunity to become a buyer for a retail store. Suddenly her own personal tastes and judgements leave their mark on the inventory, which begins to sell better, and she's given a raise...unless she slept through the opportunity. Under the hard aspects, you might experience a painful clash between what your real nature has become and the role you are expected to play publicly or professionally. Something has got to give, and it would be better if it were the job!

PROGRESSED ASCENDANT/NATAL ASCENDANT

Naturally, the scope of possibility for aspects between these two points is limited. We are all born under the conjunction, by definition. After that, it just depends on how fast the Ascendant is moving and how long we live. In terms of major aspects, most of us will experience the sextile; many of us, the square; a few, the trine. In any case, we are looking at two closely-related factors and prying their meanings apart is the trick. The natal Ascendant represents the way you naturally present yourself to the people around you. Call it your style or your vibrations. The progressed Ascendant is the same, except we stick the word "evolving" in front of style or vibrations. Your outer presentation changes with time. In any aspect between the progressed and natal Ascendants, the key lies in keeping them in tune with each other. Under the sextile or the rarer trine, it's relatively easy. The feeling is of "coming into yourself." You generally feel more confident socially and personally at this stage of your life than ever before. If you can avoid the trap of becoming too glib or slick, it's a wonderful development— one of the paydays in the maturational process. Under the square, there is tension between what you've become and **who you imagine others think you are**...the latter often being more connected to the natal Ascendant. At such a time, you need the mirrors that trusted people hold before you, and the courage to look into them—and the grace to learn and grow, despite your advancing "maturity!"

PART FIVE

SYNTHESIS

CHAPTER ELEVEN

PUTTING IT ALL TOGETHER

Peeking ahead? Then go back! Without the first ten chapters behind you, the territory we are about to enter is a moonless crocodile swamp on a foggy Halloween night. You'll get lost for sure, and wind up backstroking through the quicksand. We are about to start speaking the **language** of predictive astrology—and to speak, one needs words. That's been the purpose of the first four sections of the book: vocabulary lessons. Now we are ready to start forming sentences, putting all that we have learned about predictive astrology into an orderly system.

Think back: When was the last time your life was really simple? If you are like most of us, you're going to have to do a lot of thinking. Even in "idyllic" childhood, every day brings new challenges and uncertainties. By the time we reach adulthood, we are torn by a thousand compulsive, contradictory whims, pressured by clashing responsibilities, tempted by cynicism, beguiled by God or sex or literature or money, and generally spread as thin as the butter on a refugee's breadcrust. That observation leads us to a bedrock perspective on all astrological predictions:

☆ The complex reality of life as we actually
experience it makes it clear that simple,
unambiguous astrological predictions must
almost invariably be wrong.

"Next year looks wonderful for you! I see nothing but happiness."
If someone makes that kind of prediction for you, enjoy it—but don't
believe it. Similarly if someone gazes into your birthchart and gasps—
be alert, but never despair. Again, think back: When was the last
time something so unambiguously terrible happened to you that
you couldn't turn it at least partly into strength and wisdom and
compassion? And when was the last time you had a perfect year, free
of any kind of stress or conflict? Life just isn't like that, and if astrology
is going to serve as an accurate metaphor for life, then it can't paint
such simple-minded pictures either.

YOUR ACE IN THE HOLE

Neptune the Teacher. Saturn the Trickster. One fired by a quick passage
of Mercury over the Ascendant, the other by a transit of Venus a
week later. The progressed Sun bearing down on a square to natal
Uranus. Progressed Moon changing from Aries to Taurus in the third
house. Progressions of Mercury, Venus, Mars. Transits of everything.
The biopsychic script. The root prediction. Strong responses, weak
responses. Developments at the level of meaning. Developments at the
emotional or psychological level. Possible courses of action. How does
the reading of progressed Mercury in *The Changing Sky* differ from the
interpretations spelled out by Dane Rudhyar, Liz Greene, Karen
Hamaker-Zondag, Maritha Pottenger, Demetra George, Robert Hand,
Jeff Green, Donna Cunningham, or some other astrological writer?

It's enough to give you a headache.

Don't reach for the aspirin. Predictive astrology is tricky, but not
nearly so tricky as the previous paragraph—or previous chapters—
might suggest. You have an ace in the hole. Strip out all the necessary
but confusing technical details we have absorbed about transits
and progressions, and that ace leaps out: **the really important
predictive factors move so slowly that most of the time they are
between trigger points and can be safely ignored.** What this means in
practice is that, at any given time, your interpretive work centers on
three or four major configurations. Learn to pick them out, and you're
halfway to mastering predictive astrology.

☆ A few major astrological turning points dominate each decade of an individual's life. By initially limiting his or her attention to those critical transitions, the predictive astrologer gains perspective and clarity.

Most of what follows in this chapter is aimed at helping you to think strategically as you approach predictive astrology. Each situation is different, but there are many guidelines and rules of thumb that assist you in establishing your interpretive priorities.

Before we get down to details, there is some good news. You have an ace in the hole, as we have seen. But that's not all. You also have...

THE ACE UP YOUR SLEEVE

Too many astrologers fail to play this second ace, and the price they pay for their failure is that their interpretations are dry and abstract. The ace you have up your sleeve is your own humanity. Let the symbols touch you. Don't just understand them. You have to **feel** them, too. How? It's not hard. Don't let the unfamiliar language fool you: behind that veil of words lies the infinitely mysterious world of ordinary, everyday experience. When you are talking about the progressions of Venus, remember how you felt the last time you abandoned a cherished old romantic ideal and allowed yourself the space to love someone in a newer, deeper, richer way. **That's** the real Venus.

The best astrological library you will ever have is in your head—and in your heart. Stacked on its shelves are your memories, your experiences, your joys and your heartbreaks. The only trouble with the library is that all the books are written in the wrong language: English. To play the ace you have up your sleeve, you have to translate them into the language of astrology. Why bother? Because in translating those experiences, you clarify them, expressing them in the most precise emotional language humanity has ever devised.

Intuition? Is that what we are talking about? Yes—provided you don't let that word stand for something otherworldly. The carpenter knows **intuitively** whether that nail will hold the weight placed on it. The psychotherapist has a **feeling** that father issues are going to dominate her work with this particular client. What is the source of those intuitions? Is it merely experience? Is it some mystical psychic function? Is it some combination of the two? Whatever it is, that "something" is the ace you have up your sleeve in predictive astrology. Do the intellectual work—there is no way around that. Learn about Teachers and Tricksters. Absorb all that follows about interpretive strategies. Then **listen to your heart**—and talk about what it is telling you.

STRATEGIC OVERVIEW

In astrological interpretation, there are many schools of thought, and many bright, sensitive people occupy each wavelength of the spectrum. Like you and your uncle and everyone else, I personally can see the world only through my own eyes. I want this book to work; I want it to be a practical guide to predictive astrology. To accomplish that, I am recording a set of strategies and techniques that I have found consistently effective and reliable in my own practice. If you're a beginner, I suggest you adhere to them quite closely at first. They might not be perfect for you—but they will save you a lot of flopping around like a fish out of water, which is what I looked like when I was figuring this stuff out for myself.

Even if you are a more experienced astrologer with clear ideas of your own, I think you can still learn from the rest of this chapter. And I could probably learn a few things from you.

Let me lay my cards on the table: I am biased toward order; the approach developed below is orderly and methodical. (But I do know some **very** chaotic astrologers who seem to get fine results.) I am biased toward coding times of crisis and stress as **the** critical periods of personal growth. (But I have seen people undergo remarkable changes without benefit of adrenaline.) I am biased toward believing that the purpose of life has something to do with growth and change. (But I am aware of many people with viewpoints contrary to my own in this regard who seem to be content.) I am biased toward believing that to a very great extent we create the reality we experience with our own attitudes and expectations. (But I have seen extremes of fortune and misfortune strike people for no apparent reason.)

FOUR NETS

Astrological symbolism is like a vast haunted forest full of brambles, dark pine savannas, and boiling watercourses. Getting lost is easy. I do know some trails to follow, and the locations of some mysterious glades and grottoes. I have also in my explorations encountered more than one red-eyed grizzly bear. Follow me and I'll teach you what I have learned. Then follow yourself and maybe you can discover great territories I have never seen, and perhaps never will see.

The dark woods of astrological symbolism: Who lives there? Who are the inhabitants? Let's assume that the forest creatures come in many sizes and that we want to capture representatives of each class. We set nets of differing weights and meshes, and then we wait. Our first net is a mighty one, woven of thick rope. Along comes a mouse. He leaps through the net as if it weren't there at all. But later we do catch a grizzly bear. Our second net is lighter. The bear rips it like damp tissue paper, but along comes a fox. We catch him, too. Our third net is lighter and finer still. Soon we have captured that mouse and a number of birds. Finally, we set the finest net of all—and discover that the forest is alive with gnats and mosquitos.

Try the same approach with the predictive astrological symbols. Pass a succession of four nets—we will detail them below—through the chart. Your heavy net won't catch much, but what it does catch are existential grizzly bears. These are the really elemental "turning point" transits and progressions that come along only a few dozen times in the course of a lifetime. Once you have absorbed the contents of the first net (if any!), then pass the second net through the chart. You won't pick up mosquitoes, but you don't want to be bothered with mosquitoes now anyway. What the second net catches are Teachers and Tricksters to be sure, but not the true grizzly bears—we've already caught them! Just the foxes.

Now don't be too quick with the third net. Consider what you caught in the first two passes. Let it sink in. Beginning astrologers might want to forget the third and fourth nets for a while and concentrate on digesting the contents of the first and second. In those two nets you have all the basic material you ever need in order to grasp the **outlines** of a period in your life. Don't overwhelm yourself. No need to generate more symbolism until you have unraveled the message of the symbolism you already have. Above all, don't fall into the common quagmire of thinking that the contents of the third net will help you understand the contents of the first two. It never works like that, which brings us to another basic principle:

> ☆ The first net gives meaning to the second, the
> second gives meaning to the third; the third to the
> fourth; always in that order.

Now you're ready to set your third net—mice and birds. We are still catching Teachers and Tricksters, but only minor ones. The idea is not that certain planets are **inherently** more influential than others; what we are driving at is that each planet can clobber extremely sensitive trigger points and thereby create sweeping changes—or it can brush against relatively unimportant regions of the birthchart and pass in comparative anonymity. It is still Teacher and Trickster work, but moving down the continuum of significance toward what we might call "fine tuning."

Finally, with the contents of the third net woven into the broad thematic material we pulled from the first two nets, we complete our survey of the astrological forest by setting our fourth net. Don't assume that what we catch here can be easily ignored. Ever try ignoring mosquitos? The fourth net yields nothing of thematic value, nothing that helps us grasp the great patterns of resistance and opportunity that shape men's and women's souls. What it gives us are the triggers: as we learned earlier, the fast-moving astrological influences serve to **precipitate into actual events** all the deeper material we discovered in the other nets.

No survey of an astrological situation is complete without passing all four nets through the birthchart. **Some surveys, however, are clearer and more effective if left incomplete.** If the radio weather report is too long, sometimes your mind drifts away and you end up still not knowing if it is going to rain tomorrow. Astrological weather reports are exactly the same. Set all four nets only if you really feel the need to be informed of every nuance and every detail. Otherwise, set fewer nets, and **never** make the mistake of setting the fourth net without having set the first three. That's like worrying about the temperature in Thule, Greenland—and then getting stuck in the rain without an umbrella in your hometown.

Let's look at each of the four predictive nets in detail. For purposes of clarity and easy reference, I am simply going to list the transiting or progressed configurations associated with each net, along with references to relevant chapters earlier in the book. To use the lists, first use what you learned in the previous chapters to identify the transits and progressions that are currently affecting trigger points in your birthchart. Then compare those configurations to the lists below, determining which of your current astrological events fall into each of the categories.

□ □ □

Net One

1. The progressed Sun changing sign or house (chapter eight).
2. The progressed Moon passing through the first house (chapter nine).
3. Any progressed planet or angle (except the Moon) conjunct, square, or opposed to the natal Ascendant, Midheaven, Sun, or Moon (chapters eight and ten).
4. Transiting Saturn, Uranus, Neptune, or Pluto conjunct, square, or opposed to the natal Ascendant, Midheaven, Sun, or Moon (chapter four).
5. Any Saturn return (chapter six).
6. The Uranian opposition (chapter six).
7. The "Great Convergence" (chapter six).
8. The progressed Sun conjunct, square, or opposed to any natal planet or any angle (chapters eight and ten).

Net Two

1. The progressed Moon in any sign or house (chapter nine).
2. The progressed Sun trine or sextile any natal planet or angle (chapters eight and ten).
3. Any progressed planet or angle (except the Moon) conjunct, square, or opposed to any sensitive point other than the Sun, Moon, Ascendant, or Midheaven (chapters eight and ten).
4. Any progressed planet or angle (except the Moon) changing sign or house (chapter eight).
5. Transiting Saturn, Uranus, Neptune, or Pluto conjunct, square, or opposed to any sensitive point other than the Sun, Moon, Ascendant, or Midheaven (chapter four).
6. Transiting Jupiter conjunct, square, or opposed to the natal Sun, Moon, Ascendant or Midheaven (chapter four).
7. Transiting Uranus, Neptune, or Pluto changing houses (chapter five).

Net Three

1. Transiting Saturn, Uranus, Neptune, or Pluto trine or sextile any sensitive point (chapter four).
2. Any progressed planet or angle (except the Moon) trine or sextile any sensitive point (chapters eight and ten).
3. Any aspects made by transiting Jupiter not covered above (chapter four).

4.   All "biopsychic script" material other than Saturn returns, the
     Uranian opposition, and the Great Convergence (chapter six).
5.   Transiting Jupiter or Saturn changing houses (chapter five).
6.   Any aspect to any sensitive point made by the progressed
     Moon (chapter nine).

NET FOUR

1.   All transits of the Sun, Moon, Mercury, Venus, or Mars through
     any aspect to any sensitive point (chapter four).
2.   Any aspects made by the progressed Moon to natal planets
     (chapter nine).

And there they are, the four nets that serve the astrologer's fundamental purpose: to maintain order and perspective on the flow of
insights the symbols create, keeping him floating on the tide, helping
her ride the flood rather than drowning in it. Let's answer a couple of
theoretical questions, then flesh out what we have seen so far with
some concrete guidelines and procedures.

THE SCOPE OF TIME

Imagine that you knew every word in *Webster's Unabridged*, but not a
thing about grammar or syntax. Language would still seem utterly
mysterious to you. That's about where you are now in your work with
predictive astrology. If you feel overwhelmed, relax. You're probably
doing better than you think. The four nets will help you get organized.
So will the guidelines that are given below.
  Astrology's complexity presents a challenge. Let's define one more
problem as clearly as we can, then have a look at the overall solution.
  The problem, in a nutshell, is that there are an awful lot of trigger
points around the chart. Along with the ascendant and the Midheaven,
there are ten astrological planets, counting the Sun and Moon. Each one
makes aspects to its seven major-aspect trigger points, spreading a web
of trines, sextiles, squares, and oppositions around the chart. That
means that each birthchart contains eighty-four invisible trigger points,
plus the obvious conjunctions with those twelve critical zones. That
yields a total of **ninety-six** buzzers to be pressed by transiting or
progressing planets.
  Bear with me for some more numbers. The transiting Sun makes a
circuit of the birthchart in exactly one year—and in that period contacts
each one of those ninety-six trigger points. That is an average of one hit
every four days. The Moon makes the same circuit each month—and in

a typical lifetime, it touches each of those ninety-six trigger points about nine hundred times. Throw in Mercury, Venus, and Mars, and you begin to get the picture. **The fast-triggering planets never rest**. At least one of them is virtually always sitting on a sensitive zone, creating the day-to-day events through which the meanings of the slower transits and progressions become clear to us. If we were to list all the aspects made by the triggering planets over a period of a few weeks, that list would fill several pages.

So that's the problem. How about the solution?

How long a period do we want to study? A day? A month? A year? Ten years? Our choice dictates the number of nets we are able to pass through the birthchart—and that gives us some control over just how complex we will allow the predictive situation to become. If we're analyzing a period of a couple of years—a true Teachers and Tricksters time frame—then we must sacrifice the fourth net. Why? Because in a period of that length, the fast planets form literally hundreds of aspects, and that's too many for our minds to process.

Similarly, sometimes we want to stand back and get the big picture. What are the major chapters of this entire **lifetime**? That is strictly first-net material. In such an analysis, not only the fourth, but also the second and third nets must be sacrificed.

At the other end of the spectrum, we find the ultraprecise fine tuning afforded by using all four nets at once. This is certainly legitimate astrology, but when we undertake such analysis, we must limit our attention to short periods of time—rarely more than a week or two. Even at that, we must widen the mesh of our fourth net. Forget the transits of the Moon. They are so multitudinous that we never use them unless we are limiting ourselves to an analysis of a single day. Also, we might very well choose to consider only conjunctions, squares, and oppositions formed by the other triggering planets, dropping the softer, less dramatic trines and sextiles for clarity's sake. Again, our task is to arrange our approach to the symbols strategically, always aware of how readily they might overwhelm us.

In my own astrological practice, I work with a very large number of people. As a result, I generally meet with an individual every year or two, doing an interpretation that carries through until our next meeting. A discussion of fourth-net issues is therefore out of the question. Often, I make no mention of third-net material either. My policy has always been to go as deeply as I can into a few **critical** transits and progressions rather than trying to cover a greater number of them more superficially. This is simply my personal style. Other astrologers work with fewer clients, meeting with them regularly and delving deeply into the fourth net, much in the manner of regular psychotherapy. In my own personal life or with my wife or my close friends, creatures caught in the third and fourth nets never slip away without a lengthy interview. If the Moon whispers, in other words, we might stay up into the wee hours talking about it. Like myself, you will develop your own style, based partly on your natural inclinations and partly on a realistic assessment of the number of astrological events you can weave together into a coherent whole without blowing any of your psychic fuses.

Whatever choice you ultimately make, there is a pair of immutable astrological principles which looms over your decision:

☆ As you clarify the timing of minor events,
your scope narrows and your sense of the big
picture fades.

☆ As you gain clarity regarding the big picture, you
correspondingly lose precision in timing the actual
events through which the big picture manifests in
daily experience.

These principles are not purely astrological; they have to do with the fact that astrology cannot exist in a vacuum. Without a human mind to behold the symbols, there is not much point talking about astrological patterns. And as soon as a mind starts looking at anything, it imposes upon that object the limitations of its own intelligence and perspective. Early in this century, physicist Werner Heisenberg proved that you can know an electron's position **or** you can know its mass and energy—but the more you know one, the less you know about the other. A parallel "uncertainty principle" seems to exist in astrology. You can know what is going on today and you can know what is going on this decade, but as your knowledge of one increases, your understanding of the other must inevitably decrease. Assess your goals carefully, then take your choice.

IMPACT THRESHOLDS

Let's say you want to catch a fox—but not just any fox. You want a big one. Little ones don't interest you. Get out net number two, as usual. But now take a closer look. It has a feature you hadn't noticed before: it is slightly adjustable. You can make the mesh a little wider or a little narrower, depending on what you want to catch. How? By adjusting the orbs of the aspects. As we learned in *The Inner Sky*, there is nothing rigid about aspectual orbs. Two planets 6 or 7 degrees away from a perfect square aspect exist in a relationship of **friction**—but should that aspect close up more tightly, then the level of friction between them increases geometrically. When do we declare that the friction has reached a level of intensity at which we "officially" notice it? What, in other words, is our **impact threshold**? That is a purely arbitrary question. You have to decide for yourself. If you want to catch only big foxes, then set that impact threshold high: consider only aspects within two degrees of exactitude. If you want to catch little foxes too, then spread the orbs wide—7 or 8 degrees, if you like.

Personally, I prefer narrow orbs in all predictive work, especially with Teachers and Tricksters. As always, my primary aim is to reduce the chart's message to its essentials. Narrow orbs contribute to that clarity, although they cost us some subtlety. Wider orbs work well enough with the triggering planets. A good rule of thumb is that the more slowly a transiting or progressing planet is moving, the higher should be your impact threshold, which is to say, the narrower the orb.

Here are the orbs I use in my own work. Try them for starters, then branch out on your own.

Progressed Sun	2.5°
All other progressed factors (except the Moon)	1.5°
Progressed Moon	5.0°
Transiting Jupiter	5.0°
Transiting Saturn	3.5°
Transiting Uranus	3.0°
Transiting Neptune and Pluto	2.0°
All other transits	6.0°

Remember that there is nothing rigid about any of these orbs. Never stick to them slavishly. Remember, too, that if progressed Mercury is 2 degrees away from a perfect square to your Sun, you are probably already feeling it. If, on the other hand, that same progressed Mercury is a couple of degrees away from a sextile to your relatively obscure Neptune, other astrological issues are probably making themselves felt much more dramatically. Let that aspect close up another degree or so, then try to hear its message. For those more subtle influences, your impact threshold is naturally higher.

DETECTING PATTERNS AND THEMES

Once, you had to learn to see patterns in the world. Now, if you want to become proficient at predictive astrology, you must learn to see patterns in the symbolism. How did you first learn the world's patterns? By **watching**! And that is exactly how you need to learn to see astrology's patterns, too: you need to watch them for a while. Experience, practice, attention—those are the methods and there is no substitute for them. But I can offer you some guidelines that might speed the process.

GUIDELINE NUMBER ONE: Pass net number one through the chart. Stop. Relax. Before going any farther, think carefully about what you have discovered.

Even with your eyes closed, you know that anything net number one manages to snag is likely to be a grizzly bear. Imagine that you have had a backache all week, the IRS is nitpicking you, your mate has been in a lousy frame of mind for a few days, your car is broken down in the driveway—and yesterday you discovered that you were going to unexpectedly inherit ten million dollars! All in all, a pretty good week, right? That inheritance is a grizzly bear, something out of net number one. The other stuff is net-three or net-four material—definitely influential, but in this case overwhelmed by the bear. Our first guideline is a critical one: it prevents us from losing the big picture.

Sometimes net number one won't catch anything. You have two choices in that case, and both of them are effective strategies. The first is simply to go on to net number two, and see what you catch there. The second strategy—and the one I favor—is to stretch the first net a little farther into the past and a little farther into the future. Sooner or later, you run into a grizzly bear or two. Those encounters are always truly pivotal turning points in life. Most of the lesser events that follow or precede such momentous times can best be interpreted in terms of aftermath or prelude—we are recovering, regrouping, and solidifying, or we are preparing, perhaps only half-consciously, for a new beginning.

The simplest case—at least from the interpretive point of view—is when you find yourself staring into the eyes of one big grizzly bear. That event—the progressed Sun entering Sagittarius, for example—shapes your feelings about everything you find in the other nets. Understand it as thoroughly as you can, and try to see how every other transit or progression for a couple of years on either side of the central event draws some of its meaning from that solar progression.

How? Perhaps by supporting it—the progressed Moon, for example, might enter the ninth house, putting your heart (Moon) in the Sagittarian-flavored "House of Long Journeys Over Water." Maybe transiting Saturn (self-discipline) conjuncts Venus in your sixth house (responsibilities) at the same time. Unlike the progressed Moon, this event puts tension on the Sagittarian solar progression. Your evolving identity may be moving into a more free-spirited phase—but simultaneously, the pressures of ethics and responsibilities (Saturn) in your close relationships (Venus) are increasing. Two contradictory themes have emerged. Neither can be ignored. But net number one must always take precedence. Knowing that the Sun has entered Sagittarius flavors our reading of the Saturn transit, giving us perspective we might never have attained had we attempted to view that event in a vacuum: those relationship responsibilities must be honored, but also redefined and adapted to the needs of the evolving self. That, in this particular astrological situation, is the true meaning of the Saturn-Venus contact.

Often, you find more than one grizzly bear in your net. Then two or three different major turning points are coinciding—always a colorful time. Understand each one individually, then use your head: How do they fit together? Is one of them occurring a little sooner than the other? Do they support each other? If so, how? Are there contradictions between them? What kind? Is there any common ground? Can you imagine a way in which one might have a balancing effect upon the other? In the rare situation in which one bear is telling you to turn left while the other wants you to turn right, and there is no apparent hope of reconciliation, apply a rule of thumb: Give precedence to the slower-moving configuration. It's the larger of the two bears. However, try to view that last option with the same eagerness you might apply to the question of amputating a broken leg—it might be a legitimate strategy, but it's also a last resort. The real art in astrology lies in **synthesis**, not amputation. Often, it is in absorbing **both** sides of an existential paradox that the full power of astrology emerges.

Never violate guideline number one. Trust it to aim you at the heart of the matter, pulling you safely past the trap of mistaking passing fogbanks for mountain ranges.

GUIDELINE NUMBER TWO: After passing net number one through the birthchart, do the same with net number two, carefully integrating what you find there into the first net patterns you have already analyzed.

Would you rather be cornered by an angry grizzly bear or by a rabid fox? Personally, I would be quick to climb a tree no matter which creature was after me. It's the same with net number two—number one holds all the bears, but number two can leave you hanging from the high branches almost as easily. Ignore the second net only when you want nothing but the **broadest outlines of a lengthy period** in your life. Otherwise, a grasp of net number two is essential to our understanding of any predictive situation.

The material we discover in the second net supports, balances, and clarifies the major first net themes, but only if we have already thoroughly understood them. If we have not yet grasped the big picture, then second-net transits and progressions only muddle us even further. As you approach second-net issues, never ask yourself simply, "What does this mean?" Ask instead, **"In the light of the patterns I have already uncovered, what is the meaning of this secondary configuration?"**

Second-net transits and progressions do have meaning in their own right—it's just that we learn much more when we see them in their larger context. If someone's progressed Moon, for example, is passing through her seventh house, we can be pretty sure her heart (progressed Moon) is currently absorbed in relationship issues (seventh house). Events there (house symbolism) are dominating her emotional life right now. If her progressed Moon is also in Aries, we can add that the psychological lesson (sign symbolism) she currently needs to learn in her relationship life revolves around the rightful use of assertiveness and honest confrontation (Aries Endpoint)—and that if she fails to grasp the lesson, we can expect a lot of pointless emotional detonations (Aries Shadow). All this is a straightforward analysis of a single predictive factor as if it were operating in a vacuum. The interpretation is very likely accurate, and would probably help the woman come to grips with her situation. But let's watch how the symbolism comes alive when we apply the logic of guideline number two...

Pass net number one through the same birthchart. Any bears? Yes—the woman in our example is twenty-nine years old and she is in the midst of her first Saturn return. She's making the break from adolescence into midlife, trying to crystallize through some visible rite of passage her newfound maturity (Saturn). Maybe she feels lonely, maybe not, but we do know for sure that inwardly, this is a solitary time. She has to experience herself moving under her own power, guided by her own vision, perhaps cooperating with others, but never allowing herself to play the role of anyone's child. Under the pressures of the Saturn return, she is acutely aware of her age, the brevity of life, and the need to get on with it. Underlying everything is the risk of collapsing into resignation—the Trickster's version of this astrological event.

Now interpret her Arian seventh-house lunar progression in the light of her Saturn return, remembering our basic principle that second net material draws part of its meaning from whatever first net developments are occurring simultaneously. It sounds harder than it is. Try it—the woman in our example is experiencing a major biopsychic event, a solitary Saturn time in which she attempts to leave behind all that binds her to her youthful past. What effect do you think such developments might have upon her ongoing relationships (seventh house)? How, in other words, does the Saturn event bear upon the lunar one? Forget astrology. Play the ace you have up your sleeve: your humanity. Perhaps she is asserting her independence (Aries) within a marriage, claiming her right to pursue her own self-discovery. Divorce? Not necessarily. Her marriage may very well be improved after the fireworks have all been ignited. Perhaps her husband is unintentionally trying to hold her back in her adolescent personality, feeling threatened by her new seriousness and strength, and resisting her efforts to free herself from worn-out behaviors. In this case, he represents her Arian seventh house challenge. If she rises to that challenge, her marriage is updated. It stays alive. Running away accomplishes nothing. Neither does blaming her husband for her powerlessness. The same goes for slamming doors and muttering. All Trickster work. The Teacher within her wants her to crystallize her Saturn by thrusting her newly discovered individuality, solitude, and self-determination into the awareness of her intimate partners. Her second-net lunar progression becomes the vehicle through which she expresses her first-net Saturn return—and by grasping the first net, we deepen our understanding of the second.

Now forget the Saturn return. What if that same Arian lunar progression occurs as the progressed Sun is entering the **fifth** house? Again we have a grizzly bear, but one with a different coat. The woman in question has come to a major existential turning point. For a very long time, her Sun has been in the fourth house, where her evolving identity (progressed Sun) was often hidden in her own psychic depths (fourth house)—and perhaps also buried away in the affairs of home and family (fourth house again). Now she is ready to emerge into the fifth house territory of playfulness, sociability, and creative self-expression. What does her mate think of that? Very likely, no matter how supportive he wants to be, something within him is shaken by the change in her behavior. The patterns into which their marriage (and her other deep friendships) have settled must change—and such change rarely occurs without stress. Her life mates do not understand her anymore. It's not their fault, and it's not her fault either. "Fault," in this case, is an Aries Shadow word, a term to be avoided. The problem is essentially one of communication. She must **relate assertively** to her husband and friends, **informing** them of her newfound playfulness and creativity, letting them know that where she once required privacy and stability (fourth house), she is now eager for adventure and emotional intensity (fifth house) in her interactions with them. Above all, she must hang in there, giving both herself and her loved ones time to make the adjustment—the progressed Moon may remain in Aries and the seventh house for as long as three years.

In both examples, the emotional focus (progressed Moon) lies in learning to take a more Arian approach to seventh house circumstances. That is what this second net event contributes to our understanding in its own right. Beyond that, the two examples are quite distinct. In the first, the woman asserts her Saturnine need for respect into the relationship sphere; in the second, she asserts her playfulness and creativity. In either case, certain fundamentals remain constant—she must rewire her intimate network to allow herself space for growth—but beyond that core, the flavor of the two interpretations varies widely. It is in the **interplay** of the first and second nets that the human reality of the situation emerges and the astrological symbols begin to hint at their true power.

GUIDELINE NUMBER THREE: Make a firm decision regarding the scope of time within which you are operating.

Our astrological "uncertainty principle" comes into play at this point. If we set the third net, we will certainly catch some mice and birds—but in trying to hold on to them, we are inevitably going to have less time to study the bears and foxes we caught in our first two nets. If we add the fourth net, the problem is compounded exponentially. As our attention to astrological subtleties increases, our sense of the big picture invariably fades. Be as clear as you can about this: you can have a precise analysis of the day-by-day events of a short period—at the price of some loss of clarity regarding larger evolutionary issues—or you can have the grand scheme laid out clear as a blueprint, provided you are willing to sacrifice the web of minor details of which life is actually composed. Which decision is right? Both, equally. It depends on where your interests lie, and at guideline number three, a decision must be made and firmly upheld.

If you choose to maximize your comprehension of the big picture, forget about nets three and four. The mice, birds, and mosquitoes you have snared there will only confuse you. You have already captured everything you need in order to analyze the major life themes of a three-to-five-year period. They are waiting for you in the first and second nets. Go over what you discovered there with a magnifying glass, trying to pick out every nuance of meaning, every interplay, every contradiction, every alliance—and then skip ahead to guideline number four.

If you choose the close-focus approach, you will empty the third net, and perhaps the fourth—but not yet. Even if you are interested only in the events of one afternoon, you can **never** under any circumstances disregard entirely the grizzly bears and the foxes. Remember the source of our "uncertainty principle"—it was not purely astrological; it arose from the interaction of **human consciousness** with the **astrological symbols**. Like our eyes, our intelligence must choose between the long focus or the short one. We need to work realistically within the framework of our mental limitations.

The trick, if you're doing close-focus work, is to keep the location of the grizzlies and the foxes in the back of your mind. Let them fade, but don't lose sight of them completely. Whatever your aim, the first two guidelines remain the first two guidelines. **Always** pass the first net through the chart, then the second one. Absorb what you find there. Let it register, but don't **dwell** on it. You might, for example, remember a first-net event—a Saturn return—as you consider in detail a brief transit of Jupiter through a conjunction with a tenth house Mercury. In that third-net event, a time of opportunity (transiting Jupiter) is arising in connection with the individual's communication skills (natal Mercury) and expressing itself in the context of career or social status (tenth house). The event is relatively minor in nature, unfolding over a period of two or three weeks. But it jogs something in your memory. That critical Saturn return! Public identity and self-respect are big issues there—and this small-potatoes transit of Jupiter plugs right into those larger questions. Whatever is going on under the influence of Jupiter, the individual is certainly **ripe** for it—the first-net Saturn event guarantees that. Do we then launch into a long discussion of the Saturn return? No—not if we are doing close-focus work. We simply **emphasize** that Jupiter event in our interpretation—and correspondingly deemphasize other third-net transits whose relationships to the background of grizzlies and foxes is more tenuous.

What are the cut-off points for each net? Avoid rigidity, but some good rules of thumb run like this:

For **decades or longer**: Consider only the first net.

For **three-to-four-year periods**: Add the second net.

For **one year**: Add the three or four most striking third-net events.

For **six months**: Full third net; begin fading nets one and two.

For **one month**: Continue fading nets one and two; bring in all fourth-net conjunctions, squares, and oppositions (except those involving the transiting Moon).

For **one week**: Full fourth net, including the transits of the Moon through the houses but excluding all other transiting lunar events.

For **one day**: Full fourth net.

GUIDELINE NUMBER FOUR: Think. Feel. Talk. Speculate. Play. Make jokes. Abandon sophistication. Get intense. Tell stories— and above all enjoy yourself.

Symbol reading is an art, and nearly a lost one. That seemingly half-magical ability is what separates astrologers from students of astrology. One glance at the hieroglyphics and immediately a smile crosses the experienced astrologer's face. Thoughts pour out, connecting, reconnecting, as his mind or her mind soars into the intimate structure of some stranger's inner life. Concentration is intense. Intellect is cooking. Engagement with the interpretive process is total—but one striking perception leaps out above all the others: that the astrologer is having a ball.

Good astrologers invariably seem to be enjoying themselves when they work. That's not just a spurious observation. Quite the contrary— that observation is the essence of guideline number four. Astrology is as serious as life itself, but effective interpretation and a spirit of playful abandonment are inseparable concepts. To say that symbol reading is fun is certainly true. More to the point is the assertion that symbol reading must be fun or it **doesn't work**. Like a child, the astrologer must **play**. He or she must cultivate **spontaneity**—that way the wisdom of the deeper self is engaged in the interpretive process.

How do you do it? Let the images come. If, as you look at the frustrating Saturn transit, a picture arises in your mind of a donkey pursuing a carrot dangling out on the end of a stick, then **talk about that image**. Tell it like a story. Get into it. Get excited about it. Don't worry about looking naive or unsophisticated. **Feel it**. If no images arise spontaneously, try to make one up. Invent something. Or go read Greek mythology or Aesop's fables or the Bible or *Wind in the Willows* or whatever. Fill your mind with pictures—and use them. Why? Because the combination of childlike enthusiasm and archetypal imagery is the doorway to the unconscious mind. Only the unconscious can truly unlock a symbol, because this is the only part of us smart enough to juggle all these balls at once.

Teachers, Tricksters, four nets, countless triggers, the root prediction—how can you keep all that material straight and still manage to **play**? It's a good question. But here's a parallel: Pressure on your toes, the swing of your arms, the unevenness of the ground—how can you **walk** and still manage to enjoy the scenery? The answer, in both cases is the same: experience. Astrology, like walking, is something you must **learn**. Each process—walking and interpreting astrological symbols—undeniably has intellectual components, and if we are fuzzy about them, we'll stumble. But neither process can be fully described by calling it "intellectual. "

Start learning predictive astrology the same way you started walking—by figuring it out. Look at the concentration and joy etched into the face of that two-year-old as she takes her first real stroll around the block. You'll probably look the same as you first study the journeys of the Teachers and Tricksters around your own birthchart. Pure intellect, straining its own limits—just like the kid. But you'll improve, too.

This is a methodical book you've been reading. It's full of new vocabulary, highlighted concepts, prefabricated interpretive strategies, and practical guidelines. Mind stuff. I wrote it like that because I know there is no way around the first step in learning astrology, and that is to absorb intellectually the meaning of all the basic symbols. No matter how playful or intuitive you are, if you don't know what Taurus means, you're not going to have much to say when someone sets a birthchart down in front of you.

It is not easy, learning astrology. In a better world, it will be taught in universities and taken as seriously as psychology or physics. (We're working toward that goal right now with the effort to found The Kepler College of Astrological Arts and Sciences in Seattle, Washington, in fact.) Ultimately astrology is just as complex as either of those disciplines—or, better said, like psychology and physics, a study of astrology eventually disappears into vaster questions about the nature and meaning of life itself. Still, despite astrology's complexity, anyone can read *The Inner Sky* and this book, and taking them together, begin to harness some of the helpfulness of this ancient art-science. Even a little bit of astrological knowledge can serve a useful purpose—especially if you **enjoy** that knowledge, and thereby use it to spring the lock on the treasure house of your own unconscious mind. Once again, the pleasure that comes from working with the astrological symbols is not a spurious side effect. To the contrary, in astrology, joy is a **method**. To earn an astrological degree in that enlightened university, you would have to burn the midnight oil memorizing other people's ideas, just like in any other field—but you would also have to pass courses like "Spontaneous Story Telling 101" and "Recovering Innocence." If there are any skeptics in my reading audience, they are going to love that last line, but I stand by it: The rigidly controlled, unremittingly adult, highly sophisticated personality simply cannot get close enough to the simplicity and spontaneity of the unconscious ever to be a very effective astrologer. That, at least, is how it appears to me.

As you describe the transits and progressions your nets capture, listen to yourself. Make connections. Free-associate. Don't be quiet about it, either. Speak up! Share the process with a friend. You will probably find that if you can relax and play, your knowledge of the symbols **spoken out loud** is deeper than you might have imagined. Try to put what you see into words—and make them playful words. Talk about a transit or progression from net number one—a grizzly bear. Go into detail about it. Does it remind you of a tale from the *Arabian Nights*? Then talk about that, too. Next, pass the second net through the chart. What have you caught? Three foxes, each one squabbling with the other two. Talk about each one. Talk about their disagreement. Wait a minute—is there something about that second fox that reminds you of one of the characters in that *Arabian Nights* tale you just told? Bullseye: you've made a connection. Now you have a **name** for that second fox that links him irrevocably to the grizzly bear. In astrology as in literature, that kind of **metaphorical consistency** makes for sharp focus and a high level of emotional engagement. Astrology is not life—like any other art, it is only life's shadow, only a myth. So make it an artful one! Make it a myth like one of the old ones, shocking, stark, electric, evocative of truths beyond the realm of words. How? Start by absorbing predictive astrology's technicalities. Next, learn to trust the symbols. Then remember to **feel** what you are talking about. Finally, follow guideline number four—and **play**!

CHAPTER TWELVE

ARTIST, EVANGELIST, MADMAN

There are only a handful of astrological symbols, but when it comes to making up birthcharts, the cosmos is infinitely inventive. Apart from the relatively rare instance of two infants born at the same moment in the same city, each person's chart is uniquely his or her own, as unrepeatable as a perfect aria. Similarly, each moment of time has its unique astrological weather, shaped by the endlessly varying dance of the transiting planets. On top of that, progressions provide every birthchart with its own "inner weather," unfolding independently from outer influences. Each astrological case, in other words, is a special case, and to a very great extent, every astrological interpretation is a creative act. Guidelines can be given and patterns discovered, but if the full power of the symbolism is released, every scenario is as unprecedented as a face or a fingerprint.

For you who are reading, the main impact of all this uniqueness and complexity is that, if you choose really to **use** astrology, sooner or later you must leave the beaten path and proceed on your own. You can learn certain stock interpretations from this book, just as I have learned from others. Those interpretations have stood the test of time and of honest appraisal. But ultimately you must go beyond any piecemeal, prefabricated interpretation. You must enter *terra incognita*, and creatively unravel an unprecedented interplay of transits and progressions as they pass through an unprecedented birthchart. With the four nets we described in the previous chapter and a general understanding of astrological symbolism, success at that task is yours for the effort of claiming it. But sooner or later, you have to close the book and trust yourself!

The rest of this chapter is devoted to presenting a sample predictive interpretation. Little that you encounter below is likely to be directly applicable to anyone except the individual in question. My aim is only to show you transits and progressions in action and to give you some practical experience with the four nets.

VINCENT VAN GOGH

Figure 1 shows the birthchart of the famous nineteenth-century painter Vincent Van Gogh, whose passionate, impoverished life stands as a tragic archetype of unrecognized artistic genius. Born in Zundert, Holland, on March 30, 1853, at about 11:00 A.M. local mean time, Van Gogh presents an explosive birthchart, promising a colorful, dramatic life—and warning of wild imbalances and excesses.

As always, our first step is to study the birthchart itself. As we learned in chapter two, the natal chart is the **root prediction**. No transit or progression is likely to create events that are not already foreshadowed there.

Space requirements necessitate that our preliminary tour of Van Gogh's birthchart be a brief one. Fortunately, although his chart is problematic in many ways, it is also fairly straightforward astrologically. Both Sun and Moon are in fire signs—Aries and Sagittarius, respectively. That combination suggests enormous intensity of character, vitality, determination—and the risks of emotional thermonuclear war. The man has vast reservoirs of sheer willpower. The question is, Can he **channel** them into some great work? His psychological need for that "great work" is clearly shown by the house placements of the Sun and Moon. With each one in a work-oriented house, the stabilization of Van Gogh's fiery spirit is dependent upon establishing himself in some meaningful public role (Sun in the tenth house) through which he can express his emotional need to be valued for his usefulness to other people through his skills and talents (Moon in the sixth house).

A glance at the aspect grid reveals a striking fact: The artist's tenth house Arian Sun—clearly the kingpin of the birthchart—is **completely unaspected**. Like a downed high tension line, it jumps and crackles out of control and out of context—unless through some mammoth act

NAME: VINCENT VAN GOGH
DATE: MARCH 30, 1853
PLACE: ZUNDERT, NETHERLANDS

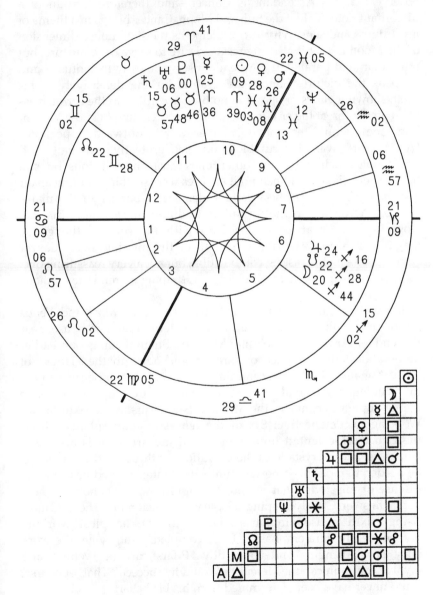

FIGURE 1

of will, Van Gogh manages to harness that blind energy to some steadying tenth house task.

Completing our quick survey of the artist's primal triad, we observe that his Ascendant is Cancer—and therefore introduces a discordant note. Unlike the Sun and Moon, Cancer brings in a theme of inwardness and sensitivity. It complements the sixth house dimension of the Moon in that it also suggests a desire to serve or to nurture, but other than that parallel, the Ascendant serves mostly to confuse—and deepen—the picture. Cancer the Crab is lurking defensively in his shell, showing claws or showing nothing according to the seriousness of whatever threat the environment produces. Getting to know Vincent Van Gogh would not have been easy. His outward appearance (Ascendant) was inscrutable and self-protective—distant and unreadable much of the time, other times warm and solicitous, but still hard to get a fix on. And behind it all, fires were seething, adding an air of urgency and probably a certain element of danger to the man's "vibes." According to the formula introduced in *The Inner Sky*, Van Gogh was the warrior (Aries Sun) with the soul of the gypsy (Sagittarian Moon) wearing the mask of the invisible man (Cancer Ascendant)—an interesting combination, but not a very reassuring one. Let's take a deeper look at the chart now, keeping in mind the methods we learned earlier.

If we study the chart more closely, we see that Mars and Venus lie conjunct in Pisces in the tenth house. Later in the same house, near the end of Aries, we also find Mercury. Strengthening our earlier observations, the presence of three more bodies in the "House of Career" again indicates the centrality of a clear, stable public identity in maintaining his mental equilibrium. Further developing the same theme, Jupiter is conjunct the Moon in Sagittarius in the sixth house. Work again. **Perspective: Six of the ten astrological planets lie in the two work-oriented houses of the birthchart.** That is a striking emphasis, and it crystallizes the evolutionary thrust of the man's life: he needed to mold his otherwise unfocused intensity and passion into a **sense of mission**. What mission? Each of the planets holds a piece of that answer. Clearly, helping people was a great motive here (Cancer rising; sixth house emphasis). He would be happiest working independently (Fire emphasis). To be completely satisfying, the work must be challenging and competitive (Mars), artistic (Venus), and involve communication (Mercury). Would he succeed? That, of course, could never have been determined from his birthchart.

Three planets lie in Van Gogh's eleventh house, all in Taurus—Pluto,

Uranus, and Saturn. Simply having that much **energy** in a house makes it important, regardless of what planets we find there. Goal setting, strategies, establishing clear priorities—these are critical evolutionary themes for Van Gogh. To support that kind of clearheadedness about his own future, the artist needed to form meaningful **alliances** with people on similar tracks, which is again basic eleventh house stuff. Could he do it? Again, that is uncertain. If he succeeded then we would see the positive influence of those three eleventh house planets growing increasingly apparent in his character and circumstances over the years. He would become deeper psychologically and more aware of a sense of larger mission in his life (Pluto); he would grow in innovativeness and independence (Uranus); and he would gain self-discipline and competence (Saturn). If he failed to absorb the lessons of his eleventh house stellium, then their influence would still grow, but not in a helpful way. Pluto would turn to a poisonous sense of life's emptiness and ultimate futility, and perhaps the flowering of true psychopathology; Uranus would burst into foolish rebelliousness and plain eccentricity; and Saturn would decay into loneliness and despair. As astrologers, all we know for sure is that as his life unfolded, a strong response to those three planets would become more and more critical to his well-being. He had to learn that for someone like himself, happiness depended upon honest psychological self-scrutiny followed by submission to some great task (Pluto), hard work (Saturn), and the courage to follow his own stars wherever they might lead (Uranus).

Neptune is the only remaining planet. It lies in its own sign, Pisces, and in the ninth house. What does it mean? No one living today has any experience with Neptune in Pisces. As I write, with that planet's 164-year orbital period, all those born with this placement are gone. Certainly, with Neptune in Pisces, Van Gogh had a remarkably vivid imagination. This is the generation of the Impressionist movement in painting, men and women who painted not objective reality, but the subjective process of **consciousness observing reality**. What about Neptune's house placement? The ninth house refers to our overall picture of reality, the lens through which we peer at life. Van Gogh saw through the eyes of Neptune—idealistically, compassionately, and with unrelenting **subjectivity**. High principles arise here—but so do quixotic compulsions and romantic unrealism.

A few paragraphs can hardly do justice to a birthchart, but at least now we can grasp the outlines of the sky over Holland on that March morning. By touring Van Gogh's birthchart, absorbing the root prediction, we have prepared ourselves for the challenge of predictive astrological work. With his fiery nature and his compulsion to leave a mark on the world, any transit or progression that suggests a long period of quiet work in the local post office is immediately suspect—the root prediction alone legislates against that. Similarly, with his disconcerting mixture of brusqueness and sensitivity, of inscrutability and lack of personal restraint, any astrologer calling for "a relaxing period of unruffled popularity" is likely to be in error. Why? Because that astrologer has violated the cardinal rule of predictive astrology—he has ignored the message of the birthchart, and thereby lost perspective on the man's transits and progressions.

So, here he is: Vincent Van Gogh, the warrior, with the gypsy's soul, wearing the mask of the invisible man. Let's see what happens when life's Teachers and Tricksters begin stimulating various dimensions of his birthchart into active development.

As we learned in chapter eight, the progressed Sun is the most powerful of all predictive factors. Although it covered only 37 degrees in Van Gogh's brief lifetime, its motion established the skeleton of his developmental pattern. A quick glance at his birthchart reveals the Sun's course—and the course of his life. At birth, the Sun was in 9° Aries 39'. A series of conjunctions with trigger points stretched before it. First, after passing through an arc of 16 degrees, the progressed Sun would contact Mercury. Approximately four years later it would enter Taurus and the eleventh house almost simultaneously—they nearly coincide in Van Gogh's chart. When would this transition occur? To know precisely, we must calculate, but roughly speaking each degree of the progressed Sun's motion corresponds to one year of life. In other words, at about age twenty the Sun would leave Aries and the tenth house, and Van Gogh would definitely enter a new phase of living. Almost immediately, the progressed Sun would contact Pluto, which lies at the beginning of Taurus. About six years later, a solar conjunction would form with Uranus, and then, at about age thirty-seven, with Saturn. This corresponded quite precisely with the end of the artist's life, so there is no need to look further. His death could certainly not have been **predicted** astrologically, but since it did occur at that time, that is where our analysis ends.

What about other first-net factors? Are they not important, too? Most definitely, as we see below. But the progressed Sun is life's kingpin, and much of our broad perspective on Vincent Van Gogh's biography arises from its short, but dramatic arc through his birthchart.

Let's begin with the progressed Sun's first major conjunction: its contact with Mercury. This occurred at age sixteen. Van Gogh was still young, and his freedom of response to astrological factors was not so great as it would be in later years. Still, a solar progression is **always** critical, even in childhood. Certainly something significant was brewing. What? Start by reviewing the root prediction. Mercury lies in Aries and the tenth house. A **potential** was there, awaiting a trigger. That potential has to do with learning and with change (Mercury) expressed stressfully or forcefully (Aries) in the public arena (tenth house). With the progressed Sun aiming its beam of self-awareness at that dimension of the young artist's consciousness, we would certainly expect significant changes in his public status (tenth house), a period of intensive learning (Mercury), and a peak in his stress levels (Aries). A modern astrologer would counsel the boy to trust his intelligence (Mercury), and to recognize that even though he was still young, he had an opportunity now to learn skills that would support his life-long career development—and that if he didn't learn them now, the opportunity would not return .

What actually happened? In modern times, such a factor operating in a sixteen-year-old's birthchart would likely refer to schoolwork, or perhaps to selecting a course of study to be pursued in preparation for later career developments. In the nineteenth century, adolescence was shorter. Van Gogh's parents decided that he had had enough schooling and that it was time he began to earn a living. They contacted his Uncle Cent, who was a partner in the successful art firm of Goupil and Company in the Hague. It was arranged that young Vincent would be taken on in the business, where his interest in art would be given a practical outlet. He moved from the family home and began learning the business side of the art world. He was enthusiastic and conscientious, and generally made a success of the move.

Jupiter lies in late Sagittarius in Van Gogh's sixth house—and as the progressed Sun conjuncted natal Mercury, it also trined natal Jupiter. That is a second-net event, but since this trine coincides with the first-net conjunction, we need to include it in our interpretation. Thus, at this point in Van Gogh's early life, two major solar events coincided. Along with the Mercurial developments, the artist's evolving identity (progressed Sun) was temporarily enhanced and supported (trine) by opportunity (Jupiter) in the work department (sixth house). The chance to work in the most successful art publishing firm in Europe fell into his lap as a result of being related to a man who could open that door for him. Jupiter delivered the sixth house **luck** promised in the root prediction—and Van Gogh seized it.

No astrological factor operates in a vacuum. Another first-net event was occurring at the same time as these solar events. Progressed Mars was conjuncting Van Gogh's Sun. His evolving courage (progressed Mars) was fusing with his tenth house Arian identity. Assertiveness in the working arena is the aim here, although it would be unrealistic to ignore the subjective dimension of the event—this was a highly **scary** (Mars) time for the young man. Reality demanded that he "go for it" in the professional department, but did he have the courage? The evolutionary astrologer would be full of encouragement here, telling the boy that an opportunity was here to be seized, but that it would take determination (Mars) to make a success of it—and that if he did succeed, that determination would do more than get him a job. It would be the sparkplug igniting his destiny pattern.

Clinching the knot, we find another first-net event: Van Gogh's progressed Midheaven was also conjuncting the natal Sun. His evolving relationship to society (progressed Midheaven) had reached a critical turning point. His social role (progressed Midheaven) was ready to reflect his essence (natal Sun). Clearly, it was time for him to take the initiative in the professional dimension of life.

Van Gogh, with his natural enthusiasm, took to work at Goupil's with great determination and apparent happiness. Doubtless, with his strong tenth house, he felt intuitively that personal well-being and professional success were intimately linked for him. Presumably, he was happy to leave childhood behind and to get on with his life. He learned rapidly, with his natal Mercury stimulated by the solar progression. After four years in the Hague, his hard work was rewarded: he was promoted and transferred to Goupil's London branch.

Van Gogh arrived in London in May 1873—and his progressed Sun arrived at the cusp of his eleventh house at the same time. He closed the first "volume" of his life and began the second, in a new country. A few months later, the Sun progressed out of Aries and entered Taurus. Again, a lifeshaping turning point was reached, this time from a motivational (signs!) viewpoint. In a year, yet another milestone was contacted—the progressed Sun formed a perfect conjunction with Pluto in the fall of 1874. Remember that all transits and progressions have "orbs"—the solar Pluto conjunction was certainly in effect when Van Gogh arrived in London. Once there, it built up momentum—and remained in effect for a couple of years after its peak. Astrologically, the artist's move to London came at a momentous time. With such a powerful array of solar events arriving simultaneously, we must see it as nothing less than a new beginning.

How do we unravel such a combination of factors? No "canned" interpretations are likely to be very precise in a situation like this one. The meaning of the Sun's progression into the eleventh house is shaped in part by its progression into Taurus, and both must interact with a strong Plutonian theme. Interpreting each event separately is an effective tactic—provided we remember to put them all together again before we open our mouths! Otherwise, we lose sight of the **uniqueness** and **particularity** of the configuration.

The progressed Sun changing sign or house is a complex event, and we must always consider it from two distinct perspectives. First, it refers to an **immediate change**. Basic elements in one's psychology or circumstances shift into new patterns, and the change is invariably signaled by events that later prove to have been **symbolic of the new period the individual is entering**. The second perspective is grander— a **new phase** of life is beginning, and that phase will take decades to develop completely. In our second perspective, we realize that even though symbolic events are important, the true meaning of the Sun's passage through a new sign or house can never reach any kind of mature expression right from the outset. Like most lessons in life, the meaning of the new solar situation takes a while to learn.

Van Gogh was ending a tenth house phase of life and beginning an eleventh house cycle. Up to his arrival in London, his evolving identity had been content to express itself through socially defined and socially acceptable outlets (tenth house territory). Now, with the Sun entering the eleventh house, that identity would begin to express more of its own **personal** goals and needs (eleventh house territory). The seeds of the end of his conventional career at Goupil's were planted now, although he continued to work for the firm for three more years. Also, with his Sun progressing into the traditional House of Friends, the focal point of his awareness broadened to include an identification with larger groups of people or perhaps with social movements. Career, in the narrow sense, lost some of its power to shape his behavior.

The progressed Sun changing signs added to the turning-point quality of this period in Van Gogh's life. He was born with the Sun in Aries, and no matter how long he lived, he would retain a fundamentally Arian identity. The Sun's progression into Taurus did not change that—but it did add a Taurean set of motivations to his Arian behavior. The urge for stability increased in him, as did a hunger for calm. He fell in love with his landlady's daughter, and apparently wanted to marry her—but when he got up the courage to declare his affections (remember that Cancer ascendant!), he was rebuffed, and became depressed. His newfound Taurean need for a stable home environment was denied.

Perhaps the most significant of Van Gogh's Taurean solar developments was his budding appreciation of the beauty of nature, an awareness that was not to blossom fully for another decade. As we learned in *The Inner Sky*, a love of nature is Taurean bedrock. The artist's newfound Taurean aesthetic sensibility was not to develop fully until many years later, when he entered his mature creative period, but we see the roots of it right here, when he was only twenty.

What about the progressed Sun's contact with Pluto? At its best, this is a planet of altruistic visions, the urge to "do something big." At its worst, Pluto fills awareness with a spirit of futility and emptiness. As Van Gogh settled into life in London, his evolving identity collided with life's ultimate Plutonian questions—and we know that he would either collapse into despair or stretch into some larger, more socially conscious motivational framework. Art critic and biographer Ian Dunlop describes this period of the artist's life in these terms: ". . . his thoughts became more and more obsessed with questions of religion and man's purpose on earth. He began to feel that the life of an art dealer was not particularly edifying, nor particularly purposeful. [He] went through the motions of his job, but with little enthusiasm." The darker side of Pluto was working on Vincent Van Gogh, pushing him toward a crossroads where he would choose between despair or the search for some larger philosophical picture—and the intensity of that period was magnified by the fact that his progressed Sun had just changed both sign and house. His old life—and therefore his old picture of the world—was falling apart. Something had to give.

Increasingly, religion occupied Van Gogh's mind. He became withdrawn and "spent most of his time in a small room...reading the Bible with another gloomy young man..." The Plutonian pressures were building, although the progressed Sun was now passing the peak of its conjunction with the dark planet. Finally, with the Sun about a degree and a half beyond Pluto, Van Gogh was dismissed from his job with Goupil after impulsively leaving the gallery during its busiest season. The date was April 1, 1876—two days after his twenty-third birthday. Other astrological pressures were evident at that time. Transiting Pluto was sextiling his Ascendant from the eleventh house, stimulating (sextile) an urge to set some loftier goal for himself (eleventh house). Simultaneously, transiting Neptune was conjunct his natal Pluto, having a similar effect, perhaps adding a note of unreality and psychological "acting out." Transiting Uranus (impulsiveness) was squaring (friction) his natal Saturn (reality testing). These are **second-** and **third-**net factors. As we extend our focus to the **fourth** net, we see why April first was the day the card castle came crashing down. Transiting Sun was conjunct the natal Sun—and all Van Gogh's innate Arian explosiveness was heightened. Then the trigger: Transiting Mercury arrived at his Midheaven. Normally, this is not a major event, often involving nothing more than a little talk with the boss. In this case, so much mental energy had accumulated that the "little talk with the boss" became a turning point in the young artist's life.

Let's review this critical Plutonian period in the light of the root prediction. Van Gogh was a highly idealistic man (Moon-Jupiter conjunction in Sagittarius) with a profound sense of destiny (four planets in the tenth house; two in the sixth). He showed, however, a tendency to go off "half-cocked" in a needlessly passionate, undirected way (unaspected Arian Sun; heavy fire emphasis). Considering all those factors, we surmise that his best bet for sustaining mental equilibrium lay in finding a stable, meaningful career. Van Gogh was the kind of man for whom maintaining structure was essential: otherwise, his innate explosiveness could damage him.

And what happened from 1873 to 1876? His progressed Sun changed house, changed sign, and conjuncted Pluto. All his old structures failed simultaneously. At the motivational level, he left Aries and entered Taurus. At the circumstantial level, he forsook the comforting strictures of the tenth house and entered the disconcerting freedom of the eleventh, changing countries in the bargain. And on top of it all, the Plutonian force pressed all his searching, hungry philosophical buttons and raised specters out of his unconscious mind. It was here, in his mid-twenties, that Van Gogh began to become unhinged—but also to activate his awesome creative potential.

Instinctively, the artist understood that to recover his equilibrium, he needed to find a role in the community—but now that role must be of a **Plutonian** nature. With his naturally idealistic nature heightened and driven by the dark whip of Pluto, he became increasingly obsessed with religion and resolved to become a preacher or a missionary. Shortly after being dismissed from Goupil, with Uranus trining his work-lucky Jupiter, Van Gogh was taken on as a kind of curate by a Methodist minister in a London suburb. His progressed Ascendant, meanwhile, was moving into a critical zone: it was entering the second house, suggesting a deep crisis in self-confidence, and also squaring Uranus—a factor that suggests that Van Gogh's evolving outward style (progressed Ascendant) was now clashing (square) with his true individuality (natal Uranus). The combination of self-doubt and the heightened extremism and impulsiveness of a hard Uranian-Ascendant progression led to an unstable, uncertain period. Under pressure from his family (Uranus!) and complicated by his own insecurity, Van Gogh caved in, leaving Britain and the church and accepting a job in a Dutch bookstore—again arranged by his Uncle Cent. The artist's heart was not in the work. He spent his time doodling and staring into space. After three months, he left.

The urge to be a missionary continued to consume him. With his family's assistance, Van Gogh spent the next couple of years studying to enter seminary. Unfortunately, his heart was not in academic studies either. His tutor observed that it was difficult to be angry with someone who was so "consumed with a desire to help the unfortunate." But altruism did not help Van Gogh to conjugate Latin verbs, and he began to cast about for alternatives.

Two critical first-net astrological events were brewing at this time. The first was that transiting Saturn was bearing down on Van Gogh's Sun. From mid-1878 to mid-1879, reality (Saturn) collided (conjunction) with his ambitious identity (natal Sun in Aries and the tenth house). This configuration always suggests a confrontation with hard facts, a time when nothing short of clear thinking, fair compromise, and a commitment to work can ensure happiness and continued growth— and for Vincent Van Gogh, the arena of that battle was his career. Underlying that positive potential lurked Saturn the Trickster attempting to overwhelm Van Gogh with lies about bitterness and impossibility. Clearly, an evolutionary astrologer would counsel him that now was the time for him to **do something**, to take some serious, concrete step—and above all, not to wallow in sorrow or feelings of defeat.

The second major event unfolding at this time was yet another first-net solar progression, just beginning to develop. Van Gogh's progressed Sun, in mid-1878, was about 2 1/2 degrees away from **conjuncting his natal Uranus**. The peak of that highly dramatic aspect was still two or three years away, but already we can begin to see the exaggerated impulsiveness, misanthropy, alienation—and genius— so characteristic of the Uranian emphasis. Foreseeing this critical development, the astrologer would counsel Van Gogh against succumbing to his innate rashness, helping him realize that his evolving identity (progressed Sun) was about to encounter the spark of his unique individuality (natal Uranus), but that currently, under the Saturn period he needed to prepare by disciplining himself, mastering the combination of hard work and patience that would prepare him for the larger developments just now gathering momentum in his psyche.

Saturn peaked first. Realistically abandoning his impossible dream of being admitted to seminary, the artist resolved to enroll in a three-month course in a Belgian school of evangelism. His mother observed at this time, "I am always so afraid that wherever Vincent may be or whatever he may do, he will spoil everything by his eccentricity, his queer ideas and view on life." Her Uranian analysis proved accurate; Van Gogh was not popular with his teachers, and he failed to pass the course. Bitter disappointment took over. Why? Because of failure? No—because Van Gogh refused to accept the reality of study and self-discipline, and with Saturn transiting through a conjunction with his Sun, that was a fateful mistake.

The Committee of Evangelization agreed to reconsider their judgment in a few months. Meanwhile they agreed that the artist could hold Bible classes in a harsh, ripped-up, slag heap of a Belgian mining district called the Borinage—at his own expense. Van Gogh labored in that classic Saturnine landscape for six months, all the while experiencing Saturn's conjunction with his Sun. The progressed Sun, too, was slowly approaching his Uranus—and the pencil drawings he did during this period begin to show some of his later power, although there is little to suggest that Van Gogh himself took them very seriously. At any rate, in July 1879, with Saturn nearing the end of its long transit of his Sun, the committee again passed a negative judgment and Van Gogh's mission as an evangelist was over—and once again the much needed support of a meaningful role in the community (natal tenth house Sun!) collapsed beneath him.

The progressed Sun's approach toward the conjunction with Uranus now begins to dominate the artist's consciousness. In any strong response to this planet, individuality rises above the pressures of conformity. One's inner nature asserts itself, and for a while, that person faces the terror of standing truly alone, without the support of culturally prescribed patterns of living. For anyone, it is a frightening, stressful time. For a man like Vincent Van Gogh, who **needed** cultural support to balance his tendency toward quixotic imprudence, such a Uranian emphasis was perilous. Had he consulted a modern astrologer at this time, he would have heard much about slowly, quietly straining to hear that deep inner voice—and even more about the impetuous foolhardiness that sometimes masquerades for true individuality, leading people over the brink into the clutches of Uranus the Trickster.

Stripped of all social support, Van Gogh wandered aimlessly back to the Borinage. He wrote at this time, "Involuntarily, I have become... a kind of impossible and suspect personage in the family... I think the best and most reasonable thing for me to do is to go away and keep at a convenient distance, so that I can cease to exist for you all." Classic Uranian words. Family failed. The church failed. Depression overwhelmed him—and in that state of abandonment, the true note of his real **Uranian individuality** sounded through the fog. He wrote, in 1880, "I said to myself, in spite of everything, I shall rise again: will take up my pencil, which I have foreseken in my discouragement, and I will go on with my drawing. From that moment everything has seemed transformed for me."

In October 1880, with the progressed Sun in a nearly perfect conjunction with Uranus, and with opportunity-weaving Jupiter transiting over his natal Sun, Van Gogh moved from the Borinage to Brussels to meet other artists and obtain instruction. His true destiny had begun to break through the sediment of cultural and familial expectation—right on schedule.

Still, the progressed Sun would remain within the orbs of its conjunction with Uranus for a couple more years. More steps and more realizations—and more perils—lay ahead of Vincent Van Gogh. Also, another first-net event was brewing: a Saturn return. In the inexorable rhythm of the biopsychic script, the time had come for the artist to make the transition from youth into maturity. Again, Van Gogh's energy and enthusiasm were colliding with reality.

In the summer of 1881, he returned home to Zundert, intending to make peace with his family. He continued to work hard at his drawing, although he had chronic difficulty in getting the proportions right. His efforts were relentless, and improvement occurred. So far, so good. The Saturn return, as we learned in chapter five, is a time when through self-disciplined effort, we make real our vision of our adult future. Van Gogh was off to a fine start. Then, in late summer, his young widowed cousin arrived for a visit. He fell in love with her. She was quite oblivious to his infatuation (his Cancer Ascendant again) and when he finally approached her, she was shocked, replying, "No, never, never!" With his natural impulsiveness emphasized and further unbalanced by the Uranian solar progression, the artist refused to take no for an answer. He pursued the woman doggedly, writing her countless love letters after she returned home. At one point, he actually journeyed to Amsterdam to see her, but got no farther than her parents—she had fled upstairs to her bedroom and refused to come down. The situation was awkward for Van Gogh's own parents, owing to the family connections. They implored their son to accept his cousin's rejection, but Van Gogh **refused to accept reality**, thereby setting himself up for the overwhelming bitterness and frustration of a partially failed Saturn return.

As his frustration mounted, tension between the artist and his father increased. Finally, on Christmas Day, 1881, just before his twenty-ninth birthday and still early in his Saturn return, Van Gogh refused to go to church, and his father's rage detonated—he threw his son out of the family home. Van Gogh wandered to the Hague, describing feelings "as if one were lying bound hand and foot at the bottom of a deep, dark well, utterly helpless."

During this period he met a woman, a prostitute named Sien, who was ill, impoverished, pregnant, and responsible for the care of her sick daughter. Van Gogh's Cancer Ascendant compassion overwhelmed him. He took the woman in, and in a short while, declared his intentions of marrying her—a clearly Uranian action in that it violated all the current cultural norms of behavior. They met with his progressed Moon in the sixth house—stimulating his deep urge to help other people—but soon his Moon had entered the seventh house (House of Marriage), and their relationship began to develop seriously. Van Gogh's association with Sien—always troubled—was the nearest he ever came to experiencing a fulfilling bond with a woman.

Near the end of his Saturn return, the **reality** of that relationship crashed through the idealistic myth Van Gogh's increasingly unbalanced mind had created. In June 1882 after three weeks of fever, he entered a hospital where he learned that he had contracted "what they call the 'clap,' but only a mild case." He remained with Sien, without any apparent recriminations, for several more months, finishing out his Saturn return with her. Finally in September 1883, he became disillusioned and left, moving to a bleak moorland in the north of Holland where many painters were gathering.

His Saturn return over, Vincent Van Gogh now moved into midlife. He had passed one of the most pivotal turning points in the biopsychic script. What had he learned? Like most Saturn experiences, it had been a difficult time but a productive one. On the negative side, he had fallen in love with an unreachable woman—his cousin—and in the ensuing drama, had been virtually disowned by his family. Unable to accept the necessary **solitude** of the Saturn return, he had rebounded into a relationship with a prostitute that left him drained and diseased. **All this misery arose from one distinctly Saturnine source: the artist's inability to separate his wishes, fears, and dreams from reality.**

Positively, by the end of his Saturn return, Vincent Van Gogh was utterly, unflinchingly committed to pursuing his destiny as an artist.

Everything else had fallen away. The progressed Sun's contact with Uranus gave him the vision, and Saturn supplied the effort and self-discipline.

Success or failure? You decide. Like most human developments, Van Gogh's Saturn return and his Uranian progression contained elements of each. Scarred, but determined, he moved ahead into his middle years.

During the years 1883 through 1886, several powerful progressions were brewing in Vincent Van Gogh's birthchart. Mars had progressed into a square with his Ascendant. His evolving assertiveness and his evolving anger were applying tremendous friction (square) to his naturally inward and reticent mask (Cancer Ascendant). His efforts to support himself as an artist in north Holland had failed, in part because of his misanthropic inability to make contact with other artists, patrons, and dealers. His need to assert himself professionally (progressed Mars was in the tenth house) clashed with his withdrawn Cancerian nature. He returned home in the Christmas season of 1883, attempting feebly to patch up relations with his family, doing so partly out of financial desperation. Despite their warm acceptance of him, Van Gogh was nasty and irritable during this period, quick to take offense. The progressed Martial square activated the deeper Arian shadow material in the man—and energy he should have applied to learning to include legitimate strategies of assertiveness (Mars) in his behavior (Ascendant) was squandered on pointless argumentativeness directed at safe targets. The Trickster won.

Two other progressions developed more harmoniously. Van Gogh's progressed Sun was now applying to a sextile to his ninth house Piscean Neptune, while his progressed Venus was crossing Uranus. Each of these developments had a mammoth impact on Van Gogh's evolution as an artist.

Locked into that Piscean Neptune were the seeds of the Impressionist movement in painting, the urge to **paint consciousness** rather than to paint reality. Under the progressed solar sextile, the middle years of the 1880s saw the true potential of the Neptunian vision integrated into Van Gogh's evolving identity. Although his reclusive patterns of living had actually afforded him little personal contact with the philosophies of Impressionism, he wrote, "I should be desperate if my figures were correct... real artists... do not paint things as they are, traced in a dry analytical way, but as they... feel them." Gradually, his vision as an artist was taking form.

Simultaneously, Van Gogh's progressed Venus came to Uranus, just as the Sun had done four years earlier. With the solar progression, the emphasis had been upon the absorption of the man's true individuality (Uranus) into his self-image (progressed Sun)—he had begun to think of himself as an artist. Now, with Venus crossing Uranus, the focus was less on his identity as a whole and more upon his evolving artistic sensibilities themselves. They too were ready to absorb his Uranian individuality. Allied with the solar sextile to Neptune, the period of Van Gogh's mature artistic genius was initiated. In early 1885, he completed what is often considered to be his first true masterpiece, a painting entitled *The Potato Eaters*. Art critic and biographer Ian Dunlop describes the work in these words: "It may be the masterpiece of the Dutch period that some have claimed it to be, but... it is Vincent incarnate, an ugly, ill-mannered painting, dark, gloomy, awkward, passionate and full of feeling." Despite the uncharitable tone of these words, they illuminate the critical astrological point: Van Gogh had at last begun to express **himself** through his art. His evolution as an artist (progressed Venus) had at last fused (conjunction) with his visionary individuality (natal Uranus). He was ready to begin his real work. Everything else had been mere preamble.

Progressions of Venus over Uranus also have relationship connotations, often suggesting breakups, deep changes, and unusual events. Van Gogh lived out all of these possibilities. It was with Venus approaching the conjunction that he and Sien finally went their separate ways. In 1884, he had a bizarre (Uranian!) courtship with an older woman, which culminated in her attempting suicide with strychnine. And finally, on March 27, 1885, his father died of a heart attack—which abruptly ended another stormy relationship for Van Gogh. The latter two events were flavored emotionally by the presence of Van Gogh's progressed Moon in the eighth house—the traditional "House of Death." At his father's demise, **transiting** Uranus was also opposing **natal** Venus, creating a kind of astrological double whammy. As usual, the triggering transits of the inner planets worked within the framework of the great Uranian-Venusian potential to actually mark the day of the father's heart attack. In his birthchart, Van Gogh has a conjunction of Venus and Mars in late Pisces. When his father passed away, **transiting** Venus and Mars formed a conjunction on that same point—another double whammy.

As the solar progression to the sextile of Neptune tightened up, Van Gogh found himself studying art, first in Antwerp, then in Paris, where for the first time, he had direct contact with the work of other Impressionists. During this period, he became fascinated with color.

Dunlop says this of Van Gogh's two years in Paris: "He arrived a painter of dark pictures, he left a painter of color and light." In the "City of Light," he also took up piano lessons, feeling that color and music were linked. A friend observed that "during the lessons Van Gogh was continually comparing the notes of the piano with Prussian blue and dark green and dark ochre... the good man [his teacher] thought that he had to do with a madman." The lessons were not continued, but the obsession with music and light and color gives some indication of how deeply Van Gogh was touched by the soft, etheric energies of Neptune.

Neptune's darker side touched him, too. Already apparently a bit unhinged mentally, Van Gogh was seemingly destabilized by the "mystical" planet at the same time that it was filling him with inspiration and vision. To his contemporaries, he seemed a little "cracked," to use the word of one of his fellow art school pupils. Despite his oddness, one very important relationship did begin during this time—he met artist Paul Gauguin and the two men became friends.

Sexually, we know little about his activity at this time other than a snippet from a letter he wrote to his sister: "I still go on having the most impossible, and not very seemly, love affairs, from which I emerge as a rule damaged and shamed and little else." Neptune again. By the time Van Gogh left Paris, Neptune the Trickster had also left one more scar on his spirit: he began his legendary excessive drinking. In a letter to Gauguin, he described himself as "nearly an alcoholic."

It was in this inspired, but unbalanced, state that Vincent Van Gogh boarded the train for the city of Arles in the south of France to begin what many view as the most magnificent outpouring of artistic genius that any man or woman has ever squeezed into twenty-nine months.

To say he began a descent into hell is also accurate.

What was occurring astrologically as Van Gogh crossed the line into active genius? As we see below, the artist's journey to Arles was marked by a number of highly charged transits and progressions, but towering above all of them was the motion of the progressed Sun. As he boarded the train in Paris, the Sun had progressed to 13° Taurus 44'—still within a degree and a half of sextiling his Neptune, but, far more significantly, **just over 2 degrees away from conjuncting his natal Saturn.** It was this all-powerful first-net event that was to dominate the texture of the artist's attitudes and circumstances for the remainder of his life.

Saturn! The bogeyman of traditional astrologers—and certainly a challenging planet, even if our astrological attitudes are thoroughly modern. As his Sun bore down on Saturn, Van Gogh's evolving identity (progressed Sun) needed to fuse (conjunction) with solidly Taurean reality testing (natal Saturn in Taurus). He needed to develop realism and self-discipline as never before. To sink his teeth into some **great work**—that thought, so clearly indicated in the root prediction itself, now moved onto center stage. With his progressed Sun absorbing the spirit of the ringed planet, Van Gogh had clearly come to a tight squeeze in his developmental pathway. To get on with his life, he had to be fully willing to accept reality and to work strategically and effectively within its limitations, dealing practically with issues like money, health, relationships, and time. If he failed, then the experience would be a devastating one, as his evolving identity (progressed Sun) collided (conjunction) with reality (Saturn), and any phony, romantic, self-aggrandizing games he had been playing with himself blew up in his face.

We know from past experience with his birthchart that Vincent Van Gogh invariably responded explosively to the motions of his progressed Sun. When it conjuncted Mercury, he left home and began an intensive time of learning and traveling—Mercury territory. When it simultaneously changed house and sign and conjuncted Pluto, he not only literally moved to a new country but also began his metamorphosis from a seemingly happy, popular, but unimaginative young professional into a gloomy, misanthropic religious fanatic. As the progressed Sun contacted Uranus, he rebelled against religion, family, and society, and realized his true identity as an artist—Uranian territory. With the progressed Sun stimulating his Neptune through the sextile aspect, he began to paint pictures of color and light, images reflecting the Neptunian process of consciousness as it observes reality. And now, with the Sun bearing down on Saturn, would he learn the ringed planet's lesson, or would it destroy him?

Astrologically, of course, there is no way to answer such a question. Only history can reveal the way Van Gogh or anyone plays the almighty wild card of willpower. We do, however, see patterns in his responses up to this point. **In each solar progression, Van Gogh made a healthy choice for his development as an artist, and a self-destructive one for his development in every other way.** Would that pattern hold? Again, that is a question for historians, not astrologers. We do know that given the artist's brash, unrealistic temperament, the Saturn progression would challenge his self-image right down to its roots. As never before, he had to change to adapt to reality. All the evolutionary astrologer could do would be to counsel him about honesty, self-discipline, and the need for realistic assessments of circumstance and, likely, all the fortune-teller could do would be to further torture his spirit with fearful prophecies.

Van Gogh boarded the train for Arles a changed man. During his two years in Paris, his identity as an artist had been further refined. Several astrological events had contributed to this clarification. We have already discussed the overwhelming significance of the progressed Sun sextiling Neptune. Another first-net event—Uranus transiting through an opposition to his natal Sun—had further helped him to separate his true identity from the wishes and expectations of others. He had not been popular in Paris, not a "member of the club," but he had separated from the herd and begun to see the world illuminated by the gleam of his own inner eye. The twin Uranian towers—genius and alienation—stood tall in him. Saturn had been transiting through his first house throughout the period as well, and was now leaving that sensitive zone. Supported by the self-discipline and relative humility of that important building transit, Van Gogh had used his time in Paris well, studying new techniques, learning, constructing the foundation of a new expression of personality.

In the spring of 1887, Van Gogh's progressed Moon left his ninth house and came to his Midheaven—an important second-net event. During the ninth house lunar progression which dominated his Parisian period, he had been engaged in stretching, expanding, and learning, which are classic ninth house activities. The Moon was also in Pisces throughout that phase of his life, strengthening and supporting the imaginative Neptunian energies—and tempting him increasingly into a life of dissolution. With the Moon's arrival at the cusp of his "House of Career," Van Gogh knew intuitively that his period of education had ended and it was time for him to emerge into the public (tenth house). He lingered in Paris for a few months, but when the Moon progressed out of lackadaisical Pisces into fiery Aries, he packed his bags. True to Luna's mood-shifting nature, his attitude suddenly changed. Six weeks later, Paris was behind him and he was living in Arles, bursting into a new Arian beginning.

Third- and fourth-net events help clarify the turning point quality of that day in February 1888. Most significantly, Venus had now progressed to a point within the orbs of a sextile to Van Gogh's Piscean Neptune. What could this mean? Earlier in the artist's life, Venus had followed the progressed Sun across his Uranus—in the first instance, his self-image (progressed Sun) absorbed the Uranian individuality; in the second, his artistic identity (progressed Venus) did the same.

Similar logic applies to the progression of first the Sun, then Venus, through the sextile to Neptune. In Paris, Van Gogh had come to **think of himself** (progressed Sun) in Neptunian terms, transfixed by color, sound, and light. Now, as he entered the most inspired period of his short life, **his artistic identity** (progressed Venus) was itself ready to absorb the Neptunian vision. This is a third-net event, but also a good example of how we sometimes need to adapt our general interpretive guidelines to fit specific individuals. For an artist, **any** progressed Venus event takes on heightened importance, since so much of that person's destiny is affected by aesthetic developments.

Triggering the tensions and potentials built up by all these transits and progressions, we also observe a trio of fourth-net events—always insignificant in and of themselves—actually pushing Vincent Van Gogh to the train station on that winter morning in Paris. The transiting Sun was in the ninth house, traditionally the "House of Long Journeys." Transiting Mercury was conjuncting his Midheaven. Mars had moved to the cusp of his expressive fifth house after being buried in the more withdrawn confines of the fourth house for many weeks. Simultaneously, the red planet was triggering his changeful Arian Mercury through an opposition aspect. Had the higher nets been relatively empty of potential, little of consequence would have come of any of these minor transits. As it was, they were as "inconsequential" as the book of matches in the dynamite factory.

Try to keep your perspective: Don't let these details swamp you to the point that you forget the kingpin first-net event of the period— **Van Gogh's progressed Sun was bearing down on Saturn**. That uncompromisingly stark influence, felt vividly already, was tightening its hold on the artist's mind with every breath he took.

Immediately upon arriving in Arles, Van Gogh launched himself into a Saturnine frenzy of productivity that was to continue unabated until his death twenty-nine months later. Ian Dunlop describes the period like this: "Vincent instinctively realized that he had found himself, that all the years of study were beginning to pay their reward, that he no longer needed props like his perspective frame, nor preparatory drawings done in charcoal on his canvas. He had only... to set himself down before his subject and paint..." Van Gogh himself described his burst of artistic enthusiasm more prosaically. "I am hard at it," he wrote, "like a Marseillais eating bouillabaisse." Progressed Sun the Teacher, in this regard at least, was thoroughly internalizing the lesson of Saturn: Quit worrying and doubting and procrastinating and **just do it**! Few finer examples of the stark glory of a strong Saturn could be found than Vincent Van Gogh's relentless, impassioned dedication to his art during this period, and even more so, later on when everything seemed to be collapsing around him.

Darker seeds were evident, too. The stress of the solar-Saturn contact combined with the intensity of the lunar progression through Aries to produce a dangerous level of psychic tension in the man. Where would it be released? Certainly, much was sublimated into painting, but there were other, more Neptunian outlets for that pent-up explosiveness. In a letter to his brother, Van Gogh described the enormous mental strain involved in executing a complete oil painting, usually outdoors in the heat, bugs, and wind, each day. He ended, ominously, with these words: "After that, the only thing to bring ease and distraction is to stun oneself with a lot of drinking or heavy smoking." He also often visited the local brothel, although physical deterioration was apparently leading to at least some degree of sexual impotence by this time.

After several months of solitude, on October 23, 1888, Van Gogh's good friend from the Paris days, artist Paul Gauguin, moved to Arles. Van Gogh was extremely enthused about his arrival. Transiting Sun was just entering his playful fifth house, and transiting Venus (friend-ship) was trining its own natal position. Van Gogh worshipped Gauguin, and viewed him as his superior. "I always think my artistic conceptions extremely ordinary when compared to yours," he wrote. For his own part, Gauguin, never one to hide his light under a bushel, played on Van Gogh's feelings of inferiority. Now, remember that Van Gogh was a tenth house Arian with a Sagittarian Moon—a fiery man. Playing second fiddle to anyone did not come naturally to him, although his Sixth House Moon did open him up to a bit of hero wor-ship. With his Sun in Aries, he was naturally, instinctively competitive. Remember also that his Sun was **unaspected**—that competitiveness was difficult for him to understand, control, or perhaps even to acknowledge, which made the situation all the more volcanic. Add a touchy first-net event: transiting Uranus (explosiveness) was beginning to apply friction (square aspect) to Van Gogh's withdrawn **mask** (Cancer Ascendant). And then add an important trigger: Van Gogh's progressed Moon, on the day Gauguin arrived in Arles, was in a virtually perfect conjunction with his natal Sun—his evolving emotions (progressed Moon) fused (conjunction) with his innate, unowned competitiveness (unaspected Arian Sun). Van Gogh's fiery heart was as unstable as a vial of nitroglycerine in the hands of a Neanderthal.

At first the competitiveness between the two men turned to creative productivity. Working mostly outside and always on different subjects, they managed to stay out of each other's hair. Tension was brewing though. Gauguin learned that one of his works had been sold for five hundred francs—certainly a blow to the impoverished Van Gogh's pride. Also, Gauguin was often in the whorehouse and especially in the light of Van Gogh's apparently advancing sexual impotence, this too was a blow. Winter was approaching. Painting outdoors was becoming impossible. Gauguin and Van Gogh were increasingly pressed into claustrophobic intimacy. At one point, in a cafe, Van Gogh threw a glass of absinthe in his friend's face. Once at least, Gauguin prepared to leave Arles. But something bound the two men together. With his progressed Sun nearing Saturn, a modern astrologer would have counseled Van Gogh to be wary of dependency at this time. Saturn times are not necessarily lonely, but they do require **self-sufficiency**. Yet Van Gogh held on to Gauguin like a man clinging to a cliff by his fingernails. Once, when Van Gogh confronted his friend about his intentions, Gauguin replied that he was planning to leave Arles—and Van Gogh tore a sentence from the newspaper that read, "The murderer has fled." That's how thick it had gotten between them.

The ax fell two days before Christmas. Transiting Uranus was dead square Van Gogh's Ascendant, ripping away at his misleading Cancerian mask. Uranus was also opposed to his Mercury, adding an element of giddy extremism to his mental processes (Mercury). The progressed Moon in fiery Aries was still within about 2 degrees of his Sun, still heightening and emotionalizing the artist's rage and competitiveness. A Jupiter return was occurring—normally a cause for celebration, but always tempting us to overplay our hand. The progressed Sun had squeezed to within a degree and a half of Van Gogh's Saturn, and his progressed Venus was **precisely** sextile his Neptune, triggering the peak release of that inspired—but irrational— energy. Touching off the fuse was a classic fourth-net event: violent, impulsive Mars, the ruler of Van Gogh's Sun sign, was within 1 degree of squaring his Saturn, spotlighting the Solar conjunction with the same point. What little self-control (Saturn) he had was being chafed (square) by a passing flush of temper (transiting Mars).

What happened? With tension high between the men, Gauguin went out for an evening stroll on December 23. Van Gogh followed him, but Gauguin gave him a hard look and he returned to their house. Seething with psychic pressure, Van Gogh took a razor blade in his right hand, held his earlobe in the left, and slashed himself. Legend says he severed the entire ear. More likely just the earlobe was cut. Either way he was bleeding profusely. Wrapping the detached earlobe in newspaper and donning a large beret to obscure the damage, Van Gogh made for the whorehouse where he expected to find Gauguin. Not finding him there, he handed the package to a prostitute named Rachel and made his way back home.

All hell broke loose. The police were called. They found Van Gogh comatose. He was taken to the hospital. Gauguin himself did not return until the next morning, and after summoning Van Gogh's brother, he left for Paris. Van Gogh remained hospitalized for a couple of weeks, and on January 7, 1889, he was allowed to return home. A healed ear and a healed heart, however, are not the same things. Vincent Van Gogh, never the most stable of men, had crossed the line we draw to distinguish ourselves from those whom we call mad. Theories abound on the cause of his self-destructive insanity. Some attribute it to epilepsy. Others to alcoholism, complicated by the poisonous nature of the low-grade absinthe he loved so well. Some call it schizophrenia. Some suggest his deterioration was linked to the venereal disease he had contracted from Sien years earlier. Astrological explanations are not meant to compete with any of these ideas. They stand on their own as **symbols of the evolutionary, spiritual, and psychological issues** he was facing at the time. Could he live in the real world? That was the solar-Saturn question that increasingly pressed upon him.

Three more "mental breakdowns"—whatever their nature— followed in the month of February. Uranus (instability) was still opposing Van Gogh's Mercury (thinking processes) and squaring his Ascendant (outward appearance). The progressed Sun continued to inch up on Saturn. The Moon still blazed away in Aries, where it released its irrational fires in the tenth house—the most public of all terrains. And then another trigger arrived: transiting Mars entered Aries and bore down on Van Gogh's beleaguered natal Sun. Trouble (Mars in Aries) with his social position (tenth house) collided (conjunction) with his identity (natal Sun). The conservative local residents of Arles were getting a bit spooked by the behavior of their new neighbor. Kids taunted him. His landlord pressured him to leave. In late February, a petition was circulated demanding his internment. With Uranus squaring his Ascendant, the pressure of society (Uranus) attempted to cave in his social personality (Ascendant). On February 27, 1889, Van Gogh was taken, without protest, to the hospital.

After some weeks of uncertainty in which more attacks occurred, Van Gogh voluntarily left Arles and committed himself to the insane asylum at Saint-Rémy. To a minister who had befriended him he said, "I am not fit to govern myself or my affairs"—and later put forth the wild idea of joining the French Foreign Legion, such was his mix of lucidity and madness. On the date of his entry into the mental hospital—May 8, 1889—the **transiting** Sun conjuncted Saturn, echoing the far more profound advance of the **progressed** Sun toward the same point. Now just a shade over a degree separated the two.

Life in the asylum at Saint-Rémy had a steadying effect on the artist. He began to work again, often venturing out during the summer to paint local cypresses. But still his attacks continued, diagnosed as "intermittent epilepsy." He told his sister that he was afraid to venture out into wide open spaces for fear of the feelings of solitude (Saturn!) that seized him there. Although he did 150 paintings during his year at Saint-Rémy, he began to feel stultified and feared "losing his energy" (Saturn again).

Often, during the time when the Moon is progressing through a house, a burst of activity is noticed right at the beginning of the period, and again, near the end. This, of course, is especially likely if the final degrees of the house contain a trigger point or two. The Moon had entered Van Gogh's tenth house toward the end of his stay in Paris. Now, about three years later, that emotional chapter (progressed Moon) was finally drawing to a close. We would expect some culmination of public recognition or activity (tenth house), especially as Luna approached the artist's sensitive Mercury in late Aries. True, his internment in the asylum would certainly have a limiting effect on the scope of public developments, but it would probably not stifle them entirely.

In January 1890 an article acclaiming Van Gogh as an unrecognized major artist appeared in the prestigious art journal *Mercure de France*—right as the progressed Moon conjuncted his natal tenth house Mercury. A few months before, he had been asked to present some of his work at an exhibition to be held in Brussels later in 1890. Now, as the exhibition opened, the article drew attention to his paintings, not all of it favorable—in fact, one member of the committee reacted so violently and insultingly to Van Gogh's work that another artist, Toulouse Lautrec, challenged him to a duel. Nothing came of it, but that was the kind of Arian tenth house notoriety that began to surround Van Gogh. At the exhibition, one of his paintings sold for four hundred francs. In the spring, ten more of his paintings were displayed at another prestigious exhibition, and again, they received a great deal of attention. Unfortunately, with the progressed Sun now just a fraction of a degree from conjuncting Saturn, Van Gogh suffered another attack, the worst one ever. He lay in a state of "torpor" throughout March and most of April 1890. When he recovered, he was resolved to leave Saint-Rémy, and in mid-May he packed his bags and left for the north.

At the advice of fellow artist Camille Pissaro, Van Gogh moved to the town of Auvers to the northwest of Paris, placing himself under the care of a Dr. Gachet, a specialist in nervous diseases who was himself something of an artist and "knew how to cope with difficult characters." Transiting Jupiter was sextiling the Sun, and the move seemed auspicious. At first, Van Gogh was suspicious of Dr. Gachet, who gave him "the impression of being rather eccentric." Soon, however, trust developed between the two men. On June fourth, Van Gogh wrote "We are great friends already."

Auvers suited Van Gogh. A small town, it bordered on a river in a land of hills and rolling fields of wheat. Fueled by the final weeks of his Arian Moon progression and operating under the peaking aspect of his progressed Sun crossing Saturn, the artist set to work with unparalleled determination. His mental energy—and mental agitation—were further increased by the onset of yet another second-net event: progressed Mars was approaching a conjunction with his natal Mercury. Evolving assertiveness (progressed Mars) fused (conjunction) with his mental attitude (natal Mercury), promising intensity of drive, but threatening more rashness and violence. Van Gogh lived in Auvers for just seventy days. During that time, he executed **seventy** oil paintings, and over **thirty** drawings and watercolors—a prodigious output, much of it of shocking beauty. The work took its toll on him physically and mentally. Describing the effort in an unmailed letter to his brother on July 23, the artist wrote, "I am risking my life for it and my reason has half foundered because of it."

Shortly before he wrote those words, the progressed Sun had finally arrived at the exact conjunction with Saturn. For Van Gogh, the challenge to adapt his picture of himself (progressed Sun) to the demands of reality (Saturn) had reached a crescendo. How would he respond? Van Gogh picked a foolish, pointless quarrel with Dr. Gachet over the framing of another artist's work, distancing himself from an important source of support. More seriously, his brother, upon whom Van Gogh was dependent financially, was experiencing money trouble—a development that, to the vulnerable, exhausted artist must have felt like Saturn's noose tightening around his neck.

In early July, Van Gogh's progressed Moon left Aries and entered Taurus, immediately triggering a conjunction with his Pluto. Recall that years earlier when the progressed **Sun** had contacted the same point, Van Gogh had entered his gloomy, desperate period of religious fanaticism. Now, with the progressed **Moon** moving through the same terrain, we might expect a microcosm of the same emotional territory to reemerge, although in a far milder and more transitory form. Also, after the fever pitch of an Arian Moon progression, Luna's entry into calmer Taurus can easily be experienced as a "let down," perhaps even a depressing one. An evolutionary astrologer would have counseled Van Gogh to **slow down**, to attend to his body, to "stop and smell the roses," and generally to recognize that the emotional Arian battle was now over. All that stood between him and some much needed relaxation was his battle-ready emotional attitude—a mood that was no longer necessary or appropriate.

On the last Sunday of July 1890, Mars, by progression, was less than 1 degree from conjuncting Van Gogh's Mercury. The progressed Sun stood a mere 8 minutes of arc beyond the precise conjunction with Saturn. Touchy, explosive Uranus was transiting through a nearly perfect square to his Ascendant. And triggering everything, the progressed Moon was **exactly**—to the minute—conjunct natal Pluto. Van Gogh's heart (progressed Moon) could have been filled with a grand, expansive view of life's purpose and a grounded investigation of his own psychological motivations (Pluto the Teacher)—those, and a perfect confidence in his ability to weather the current storm. But Pluto the Trickster can easily speak to man when he is tired and nearly broken, and his tales are of life's ultimate futility, meaninglessness, and impossibility.

Vincent Van Gogh, with his heart full of Pluto's darkness, walked out into the twilight that July evening and shot himself in the chest with a borrowed revolver. The bullet entered his body just below the heart. Concealing the blood of the wound in his coat, he staggered back to the inn where he was staying. When he failed to show up for dinner, the innkeeper became concerned and went to Van Gogh's room to investigate. Immediately Dr. Gachet was summoned, along with the police. Lying calmly in his bed, Van Gogh was smoking a pipe.

The artist's brother, Theo, was contacted in his Paris office the following morning—Van Gogh had refused to reveal his home address—and he arrived in Auvers later that day. Van Gogh's first words to him were "missed again"—the black humor of Pluto. The two men conversed, and Van Gogh seemed lucid and not in any great physical pain. Later, he said to Theo, "The sorrow will last forever." His urge to live had been quenched. In the middle of the night he lost consciousness, and at about one in the morning, in his brother's arms, Vincent Van Gogh died.

He was arrogant. He was foolish. He wasted his own life. The cup is half empty.

He left a legacy of beauty that will thrill humanity until the Sun scorches life from the earth. The cup is half full.

No words can contain the mystery of one individual's passage among us. The purpose of astrology is not to write epitaphs. It is a tool of the living, a lens of clear seeing and an ally in the endless battle against the Trickster within us all. Astrologically, nothing else matters. Van Gogh's wisdom went beyond this world when he died, and astrology cannot recover it. Only his art remains, and traces of his story, like runes in a lost language, to be deciphered, cautiously, in the light of the Moon and the Sun and the stars.

CHAPTER THIRTEEN

WEATHER WORKING

Amsterdam is a cold, wet city. The westerlies blow damp and hard across the barrenness of the North Sea and whistle through the misty streets. For someone accustomed to the temperate climate of North Carolina, Holland in late autumn is a hard place to be. Ten minutes after getting off the train, I had a cold. In a month, I suspect I would have had pneumonia.

The year was 1973. I was twenty-four, on the road, and hovering between dreams of glory and the soggy homesickness of an apprentice vagabond. I rode into Amsterdam station with my backpack, my Eurailpass, and no plans. It was, despite the weather, one of the luckiest blunders of my life. A few months earlier the city had opened its new Van Gogh Museum. I remember the place as clearly as yesterday: a vast, airy building with many ascending levels, each one surrounding an empty core of free space, just a shaft of nothingness left wide open. Each level was dense with art, and at the foot of the central space, there was a cage of brilliantly colored parrots. I climbed from level to level, dumbstruck, watching the artist's life unfold through his paintings and drawings, watching madness and genius consume him, all the while pierced and jangled by the mad squawking of the caged birds. The effect was unnerving, but so is Van Gogh's art.

After seeing the sheer magnitude of the collection in Amsterdam, it's difficult to imagine that there would be any paintings left over for other museums. But Van Gogh's work seems to be everywhere. Every major art museum I have ever visited seems to have at least an example or two of his work. One of the hazards of life in the twentieth century is that we become numb to numbers. To learn that Van Gogh did a hundred and fifty paintings while confined to the mental asylum or that he did seventy paintings during the final ten weeks of his life might not sink in—but walking past those canvases, row upon row, each one executed with vision and craft, and an overwhelming intensity makes those numbers real. We begin to grasp some sense of the man's accomplishment. Add the fact that he died at age thirty-seven, sick, poor, and mad, and the story takes on almost heroic proportions. If it were fiction, we would dismiss it as unrealistic.

Van Gogh may seem like a flawed superman—and with our human predilection for making gods in death out of those whom we make exiles in life we can easily find ourselves distorting the realities of his biography to the point where it actually begins to seem romantic and enviable.

But this is a man who cut off his own earlobe! This is a man who once drank turpentine! This is a man who brought pain to anyone who ever got close to him!

Darkness and light. Madness and vision. Suffering and joy. This is not just Vincent Van Gogh's story; it is your story and mine and everyone else's. Each script is different, but in some ineffable way, each character is the same. Humanity: crazy, violent, and selfish. Inspired, loving, and transcendent. Above all: mysterious.

And it is into that fathomless well of human mystery that astrology lowers a lantern. What does it reveal? Only shadows. Only deeper darknesses.

What **is** this craft we practice? Disperse the smoke-screen of so-called "occultism" that has always surrounded astrology. Forget the protests of scientists who declare unreal anything that slips through their nets of measurement. Shake off the chill fog of fatalism, of cynicism. Let go of knowledge and understanding. Rip away everything but the rawness of life itself: moment-to-moment consciousness. Seconds. Milliseconds. The microstructure of perception: feeling, action, reaction. **That** is astrology's territory. **That** is what we seek to map in our birthcharts, our transits and our progressions. Like the stark beam of a laser playing on the night-blackened face of an ancient canyon, astrology explains nothing. It only illuminates the veins and fissures in the impenetrable wall. It gives clear seeing. Clear understanding we must supply ourselves.

And truly clear understanding is a quixotic dream. Ultimately, the clearest understanding you can hope for is still nothing more than a **picture in your head**. Albert Einstein once likened the universe to a pocket watch we can never open. We see the hands turning. We construct theories about how the watch operates. But we can never know! Teachers and Tricksters are like that: only theories. Only constructions. Only one way of accounting for the ticking of the watch.

Astrology's purpose is to help you see. Beyond that, you are on your own. Like the lantern in the well or the laser in the dark canyon, astrology **illuminates** life—but it can never live it for you. When Mercury, for example, progresses to a conjunction with your natal Uranus, we know that your evolving intelligence is about to have the rug pulled out from underneath it. In what way? To a great extent, that depends on what you have done up to now. What have the Teachers taught you? How have you been fooled by the Tricksters? Exactly what that Mercury-Uranus contact means depends partly on what kind of future you have already created for yourself—in the **past**. And astrologically, there is no way we can know that. Astrologically, all we can really grasp are the **outlines** of the issue you are facing. Society—Mom, Dad, your friends, the television set—has assured you that some particular "truth" is a stable foundation upon which to build a mental picture of reality. And now, in the natural evolution of your ideas (progressed Mercury) that "truth" has been checkmated. That perspective no longer works. In your innermost self—your "heart of hearts" (natal Uranus)—you have always dimly suspected the deeper truth. But when the lie collapses, it will bring the house down with it. No matter! You are **ready** to build a new model anyway. You need one. Up until now, the old view didn't do you any harm, but if you continue to hold on to it in this wiser, more mature stage of life, you limit yourself.

What is the nature of the Mercury breakthrough? The astrologer can even help clarify that question. What sign and house are involved? What else is going on simultaneously in other transits or progressions? What is the general thrust of the root prediction—the birthchart—itself? All this material adds three-dimensionality to the picture, clarifying, amplifying, and sharpening the essential themes of the period. But does it say what the period means to you personally? No. That is up to you. And how do you discover its meaning? Only by living it.

To live the lessons of the Teachers takes more than a knowledge of transits and progressions; it takes courage. It requires enough humility to let life correct our misperceptions—and enough fortitude to defend the truths we have seen even when everyone thinks those truths are symptoms of our wrongheadedness. We must be both mountains and willow trees, flexible, strong when we need strength—and willing to bend and flow and bow down our heads when life demands that. Alertness must never leave us, yet we must seize the chance for rest when it comes—and then sleep with one eye open. The seasons of our moods and the seasons of circumstance must be in perfect, efficient alignment. We must penetrate every illusion, however comforting. We must freeze like a green-eyed cat when the mouse of opportunity strolls by. We must wait, still as a stone, for the right moment—then, like the cat, every cell of our body must rocket forward as if that mouse were the last scrap of hope in this arm of the galaxy.

Endless alertness. Perfect centeredness. Confidence—and humility. Flawless action—and unfailing sensitivity. A sense of life's seriousness—and a sense of the cosmic joke. That's what it takes to follow the way of the planetary Teachers. And the alternative? The Tricksters await you, rubbing their hands together in anticipation.

Who can succeed? Who can live like that? Not me. Not anyone I ever met. Maybe a Christ or a Buddha could do it, but for most of us, living like that is only an inspiring fantasy. Some days we get up on the wrong side of the bed, and we will likely continue to do so.

What can we do?

Start by remembering Vincent Van Gogh.

Like ourselves, Van Gogh led an ambivalent life. With his fiery nature, he was an extremist. With his upper hemisphere emphasis, his inner life was simply more **visible** than most. Those two factors serve to add vividness to his story and to sharpen its contrasts. His life is instructive astrologically not because he was so different from the rest of us, but primarily because his nature demanded that he **act out** nearly every whim that arose from his depths. Beyond that quirk, he was one of us—half angel, half devil, an unpredictable blend of wisdom and idiocy.

Was his life a success? Only a hopeless romantic could endorse that idea. This was a man who damaged everything he touched, and wound up lonely and pitiable with his own bullet buried in his chest.

Was Van Gogh a failure? An hour in that museum in Amsterdam dispels that viewpoint too—unless you are someone who thinks life can be explained between the covers of a psychology book.

To understand Vincent Van Gogh—and ourselves—we need subtler categories than failure and success. The universe the astrological Teachers describe for us is beyond us. Perfection like that is an impossibility, inspiring perhaps, but always out of reach. The Tricksters' universe, too, is a phony one. An abstraction. No one really lives there either. Nobody is that unremittingly stupid, lazy, and evil. The Tricksters' picture of our lives is only an overblown warning, just handwriting on the wall.

Astrology is not life; it is a **metaphor** for life. A symbol. Life is that moment-to-moment consciousness firing in the synapses of your soul or your brain or whatever you choose to name it. Being a symbol, astrology **represents** reality, and in representation there is always distortion. No way to avoid that. Only life itself could stand as a perfect symbol of life—and the overwhelming complexity of **that** symbol is what leads us to astrology in the first place. We **want** some simplification, and are willing to pay the price of a little distortion for it. The trick is to understand the **nature** of the distortion in each symbol system. Then we can correct for it—or at least know where to expect surprises.

Astrology is not the only useful symbol system that partly distorts what it seeks to represent. They all do it to some extent. Take traditional pre-quantum science—another popular symbol system. It works, as a metaphor, but it twists experience into logical patterns, and leads us to undervalue the irrational—or the "unmeasurable," as we put it earlier. And sooner or later, that distortion catches up with a person. The "irrational" nips him where he least expects it.

What is astrology's distortion? How does it bias our perceptions away from the reality of life? The answer is simple, but understanding it is essential to the right use of the symbolism: astrology "believes in" perfection. In any situation, the astrological symbols dare to speak of the **ideal**. They challenge us to reach for the impossible, to make perfect use of every moment. In that ideal world, each perfect moment establishes a basis for the next perfect moment, like a chain of flawlessly executed cut emeralds evolving through a succession of idealized geometrical forms.

What if someone gets lazy and sneaks in a lump of coal? What, in other words, if we really blow it and succumb hook, line, and sinker to the Trickster? I know I have done that at times. My guess is that you have too. Astrologically, the chain is then broken. Everything collapses. The catch is that you and I, unlike the astrological symbols, are **accustomed** to imperfection. We deal with it every day. We, more than the symbols, have learned to correct it, to pick up the pieces and get on with our lives.

Perhaps imagination is the key. Often we live a very different life there than the one we act out with our bodies. Certainly, when we fall for the Trickster within us, we hurt—and instinctively we **imagine** the course that events would have taken had we been more alert. And maybe in that imagining, we in part correct our mistake. Or perhaps, as we compare that fantasy to the mess we have actually created, we even learn the lesson more deeply. In this world of imperfection, so different from the clearer universe the symbols portray, we have learned to be **survivors**, turning even defeat and embarrassment into wisdom. That capacity for regeneration, rightly used, can transmute Tricksters into Teachers, and send us onward, more powerful than ever.

In working with transits and progressions, never forget the distortion inherent in the symbols themselves. In each instance, they offer a crystal-clear picture of what is **supposed to happen.** Like an aloof, indifferent god, they describe precisely what you are to learn. And they are never wrong—at that level. Our task, as interpreters, is to make the ideal world of the astrological symbols relevant to the universe we actually inhabit. We must make them **work**—that is, we must harness them to the task of promoting human growth. To accomplish that, we need to fan the flames of hope and imagination. We must recognize that there is no mistake so fundamental that it can invalidate our capacity for self-regeneration. Astrology is a product of the human mind, but life... life is beyond us. That mystery contains loopholes—miracles, grace, magic—that no astrologer has yet understood. Forget that wild card, and astrology is a dangerous system—and this is a dangerous book. Why? Because in describing perfection, astrology asks us to go beyond the limits of the possible.

Trust these symbols—carefully. Let them guide you. They are sometimes painfully incisive, but if you are strong and honest, they will never betray you. Whenever you have settled into a comfortable lie, whenever you have agreed to be less than you could be, they will undermine your game. They will inspire you, embarrass you, cajole you, insult you—into growing. At times, they will lift you beyond yourself. You will glimpse the **order** that underlies the seeming chaos of daily experience. Trust them—but never let them stand between you and the naked reality of your life. Learn to listen to the symbols, but learn to silence them too.

Above all, remember this: **The astrological symbols, in and of themselves, are powerless.** They are only symbols. They are only the weather report.

You—magician, life master, time shaper—are the weather.

CANTO 120

I have tried to write Paradise

Do not move
Let the wind speak
That is paradise

Let the Gods forgive what I
have made
Let those I love try to forgive
what I have made.

—EZRA POUND

HOW TO LOOK UP TRANSITS

Working with transits is a delight. It is almost as simple as opening a book. You will need only two tools: a birthchart and an ephemeris.

You open the ephemeris to the day in question, and read out the positions of the transiting planets. That is all there is to it. The book is arranged much like a calendar, month by month. Different formats are available, but a quick look at any one of them usually reveals the setup.

The only limitation you are likely to encounter is that the ephemeris gives the planetary positions once every twenty-four hours. For most purposes, that is plenty of accuracy, especially with the slow planets, whose motion in that period is miniscule. Occasionally, you might want to calculate the exact place of a transiting planet at a particular moment **within** that twenty-four-hour period. That is hair splitting in most cases, but if you are drawn to experiment, you can learn the procedures in the detailed treatment of the subject in the back of *The Inner Sky*.

THE TEACHERS AND TRICKSTERS EPHEMERIS—1999-2010

In the following pages, I have included a shortened version of an ephemeris. It includes only the slow planets: Jupiter, Saturn, Uranus, Neptune, and Pluto. Their positions are given for the **first day** of each month. In most cases, the motion of these "Teachers" and "Tricksters" during the month is slight and you can easily guesstimate where they are at intervening times. Their **sign** positions are given only for January of each year and for the months when they change from one sign to another. Otherwise, for clarity's sake, only the **degree** of the planet within the sign is listed.

This shortened ephemeris is no substitute for a real one. It leaves out the important triggering action of the quick planets, but it will give you an overview without the complexity (or cost) of a normal ephemeris.

Important Note: The planetary positions listed in this shortened ephemeris are not "rounded off" in the normal way. One degree (1°) Aries means the planet lies somewhere between 0 degrees 0 minutes Aries and 0 degrees 59 minutes Aries—in other words, somewhere in the **first degree** of Aries. Similarly, 30° Taurus means a position somewhere between 29 degrees 0 minutes Taurus and 29 degrees 59 minutes Taurus—in the **thirtieth degree** of that sign.

	1	2	3	4	5	6	7	8	9	10	11	12
♃	22°♓	28°	4°♈	12°	19°	25°	1°♉	5°	5°	3°	29°♈	26°
♄	27°♈	28°	30°	4°♉	8°	12°	15°	17°	18°	17°	15°	12°
♅ (1999)	11°♒	13°	15°	16°	17°	17°	17°	16°	14°	14°	13°	14°
♆	2°♒	3°	4°	5°	5°	5°	4°	3°	3°	2°	2°	3°
♇	10°♐	11°	11°	11°	10°	10°	9°	8°	8°	9°	10°	11°

	1	2	3	4	5	6	7	8	9	10	11	12
♃	26°♈	28°	3°♉	10°	17°	24°	1°♊	6°	10°	12°	10°	6°
♄	11°♉	11°	13°	16°	20°	24°	27°	30°	1°♊	1°	29°♉	27°
♅ (2000)	15°♒	17°	19°	20°	21°	21°	21°	20°	19°	18°	17°	18°
♆	4°♒	5°	6°	7°	7°	7°	6°	6°	5°	4°	4°	5°
♇	12°♐	13°	13°	13°	13°	12°	11°	11°	11°	11°	12°	13°

		1	2	3	4	5	6	7	8	9	10	11	12
	♃	3♊	2°	4°	8°	14°	21°	28°	5♋	10°	14°	16°	15°
	♄	25♉	25°	26°	28°	2♊	6°	9°	13°	15°	15°	14°	12°
2001	♅	19♒	21°	22°	24°	25°	25°	25°	24°	23°	22°	21°	22°
	♆	6♒	7°	8°	9°	9°	9°	9°	8°	7°	7°	7°	7°
	♇	14♐	15°	16°	16°	15°	15°	14°	13°	13°	13°	14°	15°

		1	2	3	4	5	6	7	8	9	10	11	12
	♃	11♋	7°	6°	8°	11°	17°	23°	30°	7♌	13°	17°	19°
	♄	10♊	9°	9°	11°	14°	18°	22°	25°	28°	29°	29°	27°
2002	♅	23♒	25°	26°	28°	29°	29°	29°	28°	27°	26°	25°	26°
	♆	8♒	9°	10°	11°	11°	11°	11°	10°	9°	9°	9°	9°
	♇	17♐	18°	18°	18°	18°	17°	16°	16°	15°	16°	17°	18°

		1	2	3	4	5	6	7	8	9	10	11	12
	♃	17♌	14°	10°	9°	10°	13°	18°	25°	2♍	8°	14°	18°
	♄	25♊	23°	23°	24°	27°	30°	4♋	8°	11°	13°	14°	13°
2003	♅	27♒	28°	30°	2♓	3°	3°	3°	2°	1°	30♒	29°	30°
	♆	10♒	11°	12°	13°	14°	14°	13°	12°	12°	11°	11°	11°
	♇	19♐	20°	20°	20°	20°	19°	19°	18°	18°	18°	19°	20°

		1	2	3	4	5	6	7	8	9	10	11	12
	♃	19♍	18°	15°	11°	9°	10°	14°	19°	25°	2♎	8°	14°
	♄	10♋	8°	7°	7°	9°	13°	16°	20°	24°	27°	28°	27°
2004	♅	1♓	2°	4°	5°	7°	7°	7°	6°	5°	4°	3°	4°
	♆	12♒	13°	14°	15°	16°	16°	15°	15°	14°	13°	13°	14°
	♇	21♐	22°	23°	23°	22°	22°	21°	20°	20°	20°	21°	22°

		1	2	3	4	5	6	7	8	9	10	11	12
	♃	18♎	19°	18°	15°	11°	9°	10°	14°	19°	25°	2♏	8°
	♄	25♋	23°	21°	21°	22°	25°	29°	2♌	6°	9°	11°	12°
2005	♅	4♓	6°	7°	9°	10°	11°	11°	10°	9°	8°	7°	7°
	♆	14♒	15°	17°	17°	18°	18°	18°	17°	16°	15°	15°	16°
	♇	23♐	24°	25°	25°	25°	24°	23°	23°	22°	23°	23°	24°

		1	2	3	4	5	6	7	8	9	10	11	12
	♃	14°♏	18°	19°	18°	15°	11°	10°	10°	14°	19°	25°	2°♐
	♄	10°♌	8°	6°	5°	5°	8°	11°	15°	18°	22°	24°	26°
2006	♅	8°♓	10°	11°	13°	14°	15°	15°	15°	13°	12°	11°	11°
	♆	16°♒	18°	19°	20°	20°	20°	20°	19°	18°	18°	18°	18°
	♇	25°♐	26°	27°	27°	27°	26°	26°	25°	25°	25°	25°	26°

		1	2	3	4	5	6	7	8	9	10	11	12
	♃	9°♐	14°	18°	20°	19°	16°	12°	10°	11°	15°	20°	26°
	♄	25°♌	23°	21°	19°	19°	20°	23°	26°	30°	4°♍	7°	9°
2007	♅	12°♓	13°	15°	17°	18°	19°	19°	19°	18°	16°	16°	15°
	♆	19°♒	20°	21°	22°	22°	23°	22°	21°	21°	20°	20°	20°
	♇	28°♐	29°	29°	29°	29°	29°	28°	27°	27°	27°	28°	29°

		1	2	3	4	5	6	7	8	9	10	11	12
	♃	4°♑	10°	16°	21°	23°	22°	19°	15°	13°	14°	17°	23°
	♄	9°♍	7°	5°	3°	2°	3°	5°	8°	12°	16°	19°	21°
2008	♅	16°♓	17°	19°	20°	22°	23°	23°	23°	22°	20°	20°	19°
	♆	21°♒	22°	23°	24°	25°	25°	24°	24°	23°	22°	22°	22°
	♇	30°♐	1°♑	1°	2°	1°	1°	30°♐	29°	29°	29°	30°	1°♑

		1	2	3	4	5	6	7	8	9	10	11	12
	♃	29°♑	7°♒	13°	20°	24°	27°	27°	24°	20°	18°	18°	21°
	♄	22°♍	21°	20°	17°	16°	16°	17°	20°	23°	27°	1°♎	3°
2009	♅	20°♓	21°	22°	24°	26°	27°	27°	27°	26°	25°	24°	23°
	♆	23°♒	24°	25°	26°	27°	27°	27°	26°	25°	25°	24°	24°
	♇	2°♑	3°	3°	4°	4°	3°	2°	2°	1°	1°	2°	3°

		1	2	3	4	5	6	7	8	9	10	11	12
	♃	27°♒	4°♓	10°	18°	24°	30°	3°♈	4°	1°	28°♓	25°	24°
	♄	5°♎	5°	3°	1°	29°♍	28°	29°	1°♎	5°	8°	12°	15°
2010	♅	24°♓	25°	26°	28°	29°	1°♈	1°	1°	30°♓	29°	28°	27°
	♆	25°♒	26°	27°	28°	29°	29°	29°	28°	27°	27°	26°	27°
	♇	4°♑	5°	6°	6°	6°	5°	4°	4°	3°	3°	4°	5°

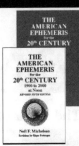
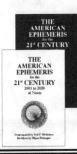

More from Steven Forrest

The Inner Sky: How to Make Wiser Choices for a More Fulfilling Life

Discover your dynamic self. Learn about your deepest motivations. Make positive decisions for optimum impact. Steven Forrest has written lively text that encourages free choice—not fate. The author provides directions for uncovering your hidden potential. Nothing is "carved in stone" when it comes to your personality—you *can* change. Forrest skillfully guides your journey as you seek out and find new areas of inner strength, wisdom, and personal growth. **(B131X-BKCS) $14.95**

The Book of Pluto: The Power to Transform Your Life

Steven Forrest tackles this planet of intensity with his wit, wisdom and compassion. He interprets Pluto through house, sign and aspect (both in natal charts and in current patterns) with great sensitivity, incredible honesty, and in his wonderfully literate style. He covers people's "navigational errors" and wounding scenarios with Pluto. We descend into hell and get a glimpse of heaven in this book. Both darkness and shadow as well as inspiration and saving grace are discussed. **(B155X-BKCS) $15.95**

The Night Speaks: A Meditation on the Astrological Worldview

The Night Speaks, written with Steven Forrest's wonderfully evocative style, has awed and inspired readers. He traces the wonder of astrology and the human/cosmic connection. He discusses some scientific information as to why and how we might explain astrology, but keeps, throughout, a mystical, transcendent feel. When doubting friends ask "Why do you believe in that stuff?" refer them to this book. It explains! **(B149X-BKCS) $12.95**

Credit card orders call toll free:

1-800-888-9983
Monday - Friday 8AM to 5PM Pacific Time
We accept VISA, MasterCard, Discover and AMEX

Send check or money order to:

ACS
5521 Ruffin Road
San Diego, California 92123

Shipping and Handling Fees:
Up to $30 add $5; up to $45 add $6; up to $60 add $7; up to $75 add $8
(Outside US: up to $30 add $7; up to $45 add $10; up to $60 add $13; up to $75 add $16)

International Orders:
Payment in US Dollars only by International Money Order or Credit Card
Prices subject to change without notice.

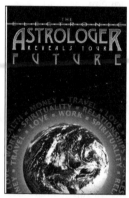

ALSO BY ACS PUBLICATIONS

All About Astrology Series of booklets
The American Atlas, Expanded 5th Ed. (Shanks)
The American Ephemeris Series 2001-2010
The American Ephemeris for the 20th Century [Noon or Midnight] 1900-2000, Rev. 5th Ed.
The American Ephemeris for the 21st Century [Noon or Midnight] 2000-2050, Rev. 2nd Ed.
The American Heliocentric Ephemeris 1901-2000
The American Heliocentric Ephemeris 2001-2050
The American Sidereal Ephemeris 1976-2000, 2nd Ed.
The American Sidereal Ephemeris 2001-2025
Asteroid Goddesses (George & Bloch)
Astro-Alchemy (Negus)
Astrological Insights into Personality (Lundsted)
Astrology for the Light Side of the Brain (Rogers-Gallagher)
Astrology for the Light Side of the Future (Rogers-Gallagher)
Astrology: The Next Step (Pottenger)
Basic Astrology: A Guide for Teachers & Students (Negus)
Basic Astrology: A Workbook for Students (Negus)
The Book of Jupiter (Waram)
The Book of Pluto (Forrest)
The Book of Saturn (Dobyns)
The Book of Uranus (Negus)
The Changing Sky, 2nd Ed. (Forrest)
Cosmic Combinations (Negus)
Easy Astrology Guide (Pottenger)
Easy Tarot Guide (Masino)
Expanding Astrology's Universe (Dobyns)
Finding our Way Through the Dark (George)
Future Signs (Simms)
The International Atlas, Rev. 4th Ed.
Hands That Heal, 2nd Ed. (Bodine)
Healing with the Horoscope (Pottenger)
The Inner Sky (Forrest)
The Michelsen Book of Tables (Michelsen)
Millennium: Fears, Fantasies & Facts
New Insights into Astrology (Press)
The Night Speaks (Forrest)
The Only Way to Learn Astrology, Vols. I-VI (March & McEvers)
    Volume I, 2nd Ed. - Basic Principles
    Volume II - Math & Interpretation Techniques
    Volume III - Horoscope Analysis
    Volume IV- Learn About Tomorrow: Current Patterns
    Volume V - Learn About Relationships: Synastry Techniques
    Volume VI - Learn About Horary and Electional Astrology
Planetary Heredity (M. Gauquelin)
Planets on the Move (Dobyns/Pottenger)
Psychology of the Planets (F. Gauquelin)
Tables of Planetary Phenomena, Rev. 2nd Ed. (Michelsen/Pottenger)
Twelve Wings of the Eagle (Simms)
Unveiling Your Future (Pottenger/Dobyns)
Your Magical Child, 2nd Ed. (Simms)
Your Starway to Love, 2nd Ed. (Pottenger)